Britain and the Threat to Stability in Europe, 1918–45

INCREASING PRESSURE.

Frontispiece: 'Increasing Pressure' by David Low – cartoon appeared in the *Evening Standard*, 18 February 1938 (used with permission of the Centre for the Study of Cartoons and Caricature, University of Kent at Canterbury).

Britain and the Threat to Stability in Europe, 1918–45

Edited by
Peter Catterall with C.J. Morris

Leicester University Press
London and New York

Distributed exclusively in the USA and Canada by St. Martin's Press

Leicester University Press
(a division of Pinter Publishers Ltd)
25 Floral Street, Covent Garden, London, WC2E 9DS

First published in Great Britain in 1993

Distributed exclusively in the USA and Canada by
St. Martin's Press, Inc., Room 400, 175 Fifth Avenue, New York, NY10010, USA

British Library Cataloguing in Publication Data

A CIP catalogue record for this book is available from the British Library

ISBN 0 7185 1483 1

Library of Congress Cataloging-in-Publication Data

Britain and the threat to stability in Europe, 1918–47 / edited by
  Peter Catterall and C.J. Morris
      p.   cm.
    "Papers . . . presented at the fifth annual Summer School of the
Institute of Contemporary British History and the Government
Department of the London School of Economics, held in London in July
1922"—Pref.
    Includes bibliographical references and index.
    ISBN 0–7185–1483–1
    1. Great Britain—Politics and government—1910–1936—Congresses.
2. Great Britain—Politics and government—1936–1945—Congresses.
3. Europe—Politics and government—1918–1945—Congresses.   4. World
War, 1914–1918—Influence—Congresses.   I. Catterall, Peter, 1961– .
II. Morris, C.J. (Catherine Jane), 1965– .
DA578.B75 1993
941.082—dc20   93–14503
                                                                              CIP

Typeset by Florencetype Ltd, Kewstoke, Avon
Printed and bound in Great Britain by Biddles Ltd., Guildford and King's Lynn

To Pat Costall

Contents

List of contributors

Robert Boyce is senior lecturer in the Department of International History, London School of Economics.

Peter Catterall is the director of the Institute of Contemporary British History and visiting lecturer in History at Queen Mary and Westfield College, London.

Alan Dobson is senior lecturer in the Department of Politics, University College, Swansea.

Michael Dockrill is reader in War Studies at King's College, London.

Sir Charles Kimber was the founding secretary of Federal Union.

Carolyn Kitching is a research student in the Department of Humanities at the University of Teeside.

Louise London is a British Academy fellow at Royal Holloway, London.

Enrique Moradiellos is the author of *Neutralidad benevola: El gobierno Britanica y la insurreccion militar Espanola en 1936*.

C.J. Morris is a research student at the Institute of Communication Studies, University of Leeds.

Anne Orde lectures in the history department at the University of Durham.

Anita Prazmowska lectures in the Department of International History, London School of Economics.

John Ray is a retired schoolmaster, the author of a number of historical works and a member of the RAF historical society.

Dick Richardson is senior lecturer in the Department of Humanities at the University of Teeside.

Ralph White is senior research fellow in the Department of Politics and Contemporary History, University of Salford.

Alan Wilkinson is an honorary canon at Portsmouth cathedral and the author of a number of works on recent church history.

Preface

The papers in this volume are drawn from amongst those presented at the fifth annual Summer School of the Institute of Contemporary British History and the Government Department of the London School of Economics, held in London in July 1992. The theme of this conference was 'Britain and Europe: The Search for a Role since 1918'. The various papers presented explored the nature of this relationship, not least in the context of Britain's broader world role and relationships with the USA and its empire, in a series of chronologically organised sessions. This book draws together the papers covering the period 1918–45. The companion volume covering the years 1945–92, is edited by my colleagues Brian Brivati and Harriet Jones and is entitled, *From Reconstruction to Integration: Britain and Europe since 1945*.

The initial conference was held at a time when, with the beginning of the UK Presidency, the question of Britain's relationship with Europe was extremely topical. This question certainly has not become less topical during subsequent events. One of the objects of the Institute of Contemporary British History is to explore current issues such as this in an historical context. It is our hope that these two volumes will indeed succeed in this task.

I should like to take this opportunity to express thanks, on the part of the Institute, to the UK Presidency Unit of the Foreign and Commonwealth Office and to BAT Industries Plc for their generous support for the initial conference. I should also like to thank all the contributors to this volume. Finally, but by no means least, I must thank Kate Morris for helping me with the editorial work and Alec McAulay of Leicester University Press for his support and encouragement.

Peter Catterall
Institute of Contemporary British History
London, March 1993

Introduction

Peter Catterall

Britain's proximity to the Continent did not necessarily dictate an orientation towards Europe and European concerns. At the end of the nineteenth century Britain was the centre of a vast, far-flung empire. As a result British strategy was 'blue water', based on the projection of naval power and oriented to the needs of her empire. Her military commitments – the Omdurman campaign, the North West Frontier and the Boer War – were imperial. Britain's self-image was as an imperial, more than a European power. Though part of European culture, the ties of sentiment and language were to the daughter communities of the Dominions and America, rather than to the distinctive societies across the Channel. It was of an imperial federation that Joseph Chamberlain dreamed when Colonial Secretary from 1895–1903, an aim firmly resisted by Colonial Premiers keen to defend their independence. It was felt that in the long-term only such large territorial blocs would be able to compete with continental powers such as the United States on equal terms. Some however, such as Cecil Rhodes, even aspired to a wider Anglo-Saxon Union, a dream shared by some American commentators.[1] European federation was not on the agenda.

This is not to deny the important trading, investment and other links Britain had with Europe. On the eve of the First World War Britain and Germany were the principal trading partners of each other. Britain also had well-established strategic interests on the Continent. Maintaining the balance of power in Europe had long been a traditional aim of British policy. In the nineteenth century the aim had been to maintain this balance whilst making the minimal commitment to the Continent. The maintenance of the balance of power between potential European enemies was indeed designed to avoid the necessity of such Continental entanglements, leaving Britain free to protect her imperial interests. The object was to contain the risk of invasion, and keep European conflicts off British soil. This aim indeed overrode efforts to forge closer physical links with the Continent in the 1880s. The potential risk of invasion, and fears of cultural contamination,[2] were the main reasons why the first attempt to build a Channel Tunnel was then abandoned.

At the turn of the century Britain's strategic outlook worsened. In 1898 the passage of Germany's first naval law and the Russian acquisition of the Manchurian warm water naval base at Port Arthur appeared to pose strategic threats at opposite ends of the empire. These problems were tackled by the tacit recognition of the improbability of war with the USA and the conclusion of a treaty with Japan in 1902 thereby freeing British warships to meet the German threat in home waters. Subsequent testimony from the architects of the German naval programme makes clear that the intention was to push Britain into an alliance with Germany, as had happened with Japan, in a search for security following the Russo-French alliance of 1894. This was, however, not how it was seen by either British policymakers, or the public, at the time.

The German threat was to lead to an adjustment of Britain's military as well as naval strategy. As a result in 1906, for the first time in peacetime, Britain began to plan for a commitment of troops to the Continent. At the same time as Britain's global capacity was declining, with Britain relinquishing naval supremacy to the Americans in the western hemisphere and to the Japanese in the Far East, she was thus also, of perceived necessity, being drawn into a more active role in the maintenance of the balance of power in Europe.

This did not mean a move to a large standing army on the Continental model. It did mean the formation of a British Expeditionary Force, which was duly despatched to France on the outbreak of the First World War. This was the start of an unprecedentedly large commitment of British troops to Continental battlefields, essentially on the Western Front. Casualties were similarly unprecedented, and remain unmatched, in any subsequent war. Some 745,000 British servicemen died in the First World War, whilst the casualties of the Continental powers were even higher. The psychological and theological impact of this slaughter has been examined in considerable detail.[3] Its effect on thinking about European identity and unity, and on the relationship between Britain and Europe, has however been less closely scrutinised.

At first sight the impact of the Great War in this area appears confused and conflicting. President Wilson's diagnosis that the war had resulted from the clandestine diplomacy and untrammelled aggression of autocratic, territorially based empires led to his declaration in favour of national self-determination. The Europe that emerged from the post-war settlement accordingly contained even more political units.

The most prominent international movement of the pre-war period meanwhile became one of the war's many casualties. The Second International, with its bureau in Brussels, had been a forum for the European socialist movements since its founding in Paris in 1889. Unlike Wilson it had believed, not in the democratic nation-state as the guarantor of peace, but in the international co-operation of the working classes of Europe; a hope that proved a chimera in 1914. The ideal of international socialism, however, did not disappear. There continued to be a number of international political and trade union organisations during the inter-war years.[4] After the Bolshevik Revolution the Left in Europe was, however, itself split.

At the same time, the slaughter of the First World War left many in no doubt of the need for pan-European peace. There had been some attempts to explore means of guaranteeing peace before 1914. The first Hague conference in 1899 had established a Permanent Court of Arbitration, though this remained an ineffective body. Even earlier the notion of a Concert of Europe, formed by the great powers, had, in the aftermath of the Napoleonic period, provided a limited and informal but not unsuccessful means of resolving disputes.[5] The impact of the war by 1916 and, particularly after the Bolshevik Revolution of October 1917, the need to maintain popular support for the war effort by promising a means of ensuring that there was no repetition, led to a search for more effective and permanent ways of policing international disputes.[6] By the time the victorious powers foregathered at Versailles the idea of a League of Nations had been examined in some detail by policymakers in Britain, France and the United States. 'Europe,' proclaimed the South African Premier, Jan Christian Smuts in his *The League of Nations: A Practical Suggestion* dated 16 December 1918 'is being liquidated and the League of Nations must be the heir to this great estate'.[7]

British commitment to this idea of a League of Nations was enthusiastically promoted by statesmen such as Lord Robert Cecil after the First World War. This was not just because of popular support for the League created by the peace-makers, although this clearly existed. The League of Nations Union became the embodiment of the aspiration that the Great War should prove to be 'the War to end Wars', membership peaking at 406,868 in 1931.

The post-war settlement also left Britain with a continuing role in the European security system: British soldiers were not to be withdrawn from the Rhineland until 1930. However, more was also required from the British than simply the performance of occupation duties. After 1919 British involvement was central to the maintenance of European security. The fundamental problem here was the French need for security against Germany. The refusal of the American Senate to ratify the Versailles Treaty and the unavailability, not to mention the unsuitability, of the Russians as an ally, meant that the main potential source of support for the French was therefore the British.

The British were well aware of the potential threat renewed conflict in Europe posed to their security. They were therefore prepared, as in the Locarno Treaty of 1925, to broker an agreement between France and Germany to guarantee Germany's existing western borders. The value of such agreements to the French was, however, somewhat negated by the British unwillingness to use force to guarantee them. European security in the 1920s therefore rested upon the French army, whilst the British sought to further the long-term stability of the Continent by seeking German reconciliation to the post-war settlement. Not having suffered two German invasions inside a lifetime, they did not share French anxieties. Some British statesmen, such as Ramsay MacDonald, indeed felt such French fears were themselves obstacles to Franco-German reconciliation.

The achievement of this reconciliation as the main route to securing lasting European peace had been instanced by Winston Churchill as early as 1911. It was also to be the fundamental aim of the process of European integration after the Second World War. This movement did not, however, originate then. A number of figures in the Europe of the 1920s pointed to the need for greater European unity. This was not just for security reasons. They also argued that Europe needed to draw together as an economic unit, both to compete effectively against the Americans and to demonstrate the superiority of capitalism to the Soviet system.

One of these, Count Coudenhove-Kalergi published his *European Unity* and founded the Pan Europa movement in 1923. On 5 September 1929, in a speech to the League Assembly, the French Prime Minister, Aristide Briand, made a more dramatic call for European integration, drawing on Coudenhove-Kalergi's ideas. This was a scheme to which he turned in his unceasing search for security. Foiled in attempts to secure substantial security arrangements against Germany, he sought instead to restrain it by submerging it into a supranational Europe, economically integrated and politically interdependent.

Although the British approved the idea of Franco-German reconciliation this particular scheme did not commend itself to them. There were some enthusiastic reactions from Conservatives such as Leo Amery, who had already been a member of the Pan Europa movement since 1925. With the blessing of his party leader, Stanley Baldwin, who was himself later to speak approvingly of the ideal of a 'United States of Europe',[8] Amery made a speech welcoming the Briand Plan. He, however, made it clear that Britain could not be a member of any resulting body. This was a view with which Coudenhove-Kalergi concurred, sensing that Britain's transatlantic and imperial ties remained more important. There were concerns (described below in Chapter 2) that the scheme would impact negatively on British trade and offend Dominion governments seeking imperial preference.

The British therefore withheld their blessing from the Briand Plan. Other European states, taking their cue from the British, were similarly lukewarm, a response which effectively sealed its fate. The British throughout the 1920s repeatedly proved unequal to the task of simultaneously reassuring the French, meeting German aspirations and squaring their own interests. This was to prove the case again at the World Disarmament Conference of 1932–4, which is examined below in Chapter 3. Part of the problem was, as Amery commented at the time of the Briand Plan, that 'Britain's heart lies outside Europe.' In the 1930s her strategists nevertheless had to pay increasing attention to the growing threat forming on the Continent. However, this threat had to be confronted within the context of Britain's extensive obligations elsewhere.

With the addition of the former German colonies and Ottoman provinces governed after the First World War under League of Nations mandates, these imperial commitments were even more extensive than they had been at the turn of the century. The resources Britain had to defend them with were, however, even more meagre. The threats that had to be met had, at the same time, become more menacing. Whereas Japan and Italy had both been Britain's allies in the First World War, in the 1930s they were both clearly potential enemies. Discontented with their spoils from the post-war peace settlement they both became revisionist powers; Japan invading Manchuria in 1931 and Italy seizing Abyssinia in 1935. Britain's naval strength was clearly overstretched in the face of the prospect of a three-theatre war against Germany, Italy and Japan.

The realisation that Britain had too few ships had driven Admiral Fisher in the years before the First World War to pursue instead the leap in naval firepower that dreadnoughts offered.[9] In the inter-war period this problem of too few ships was compounded by the naval agreements reached in Washington in 1921–22 and in London in 1930. The Washington agreement established a tonnage ratio for capital ships (warships of over 10,000 tons carrying larger than eight inch guns) of 5:5:3:1.75:1.75 for Britain, the United States, Japan, France and Italy respectively. It also saw the end of the Anglo-Japanese alliance at the behest of the Americans and the imposition of a ten year moratorium on building capital ships, extended further to 1936 at London. Rapid Japanese naval construction at the end of this period meant that by the end of the 1930s their naval strength in the Pacific was equal to that of the British and Americans combined. There was, however, little co-ordination between the British and Americans in meeting this growing threat. At the same time the British had to consider the potential problems the Italians might pose in the Mediterranean, and to defend the North Sea and the Atlantic sea lanes. It was these considerations which ensured that the British were no less concerned to appease the Italians as the Germans in the late 1930s, in a vain attempt to detach Mussolini from Hitler; an objective which formed an important part of the background to their policy during the Spanish Civil War (which is examined below in Chapter 6).

By 1932 the Committee of Imperial Defence was advocating rearmament in the light of the Japanese threat. Within two years there was growing concern about the risk of war closer to home. From 1934 a programme of air force rearmament was undertaken directed against Germany. Neville Chamberlain, though aware of the need for this was, as Chancellor of the Exchequer 1931–37, unenthusiastic about the costs. 'What a fearful bill do we owe to Master Hitler, damn him!,' he complained in March 1936.[10]

Whilst this rearmament programme indicated a renewed military, as well as diplomatic involvement in the preservation of the stability of Europe, there was still considerable reluctance to contemplate the commitment of British power to the defence of the post-war peace settlement. One factor was a fear that the only power likely to benefit was Communist Russia. This was not only an influence on British policy in Spain. It also ensured that the British had little interest in negotiating agreements with the Russians directed against Germany, as the French had sought to in 1934–5, a stance which was only changed, too late to have any effect, in 1939.

Meanwhile, there was also a lack of public support for any British military commitment to defence of the European status quo. Rearmament and the beginnings of civil defence preparations in 1935 were indeed criticised by some in the Labour Party as an attempt to instil a war mentality in a reluctant public. There was no more enthusiasm for the prospects of war amongst the Dominions. This remained the attitude of both the Dominions and the public at the time of the Munich Agreement in October 1938. Hitler, after all, in urging the incorporation of the Sudeten Germans into the Reich, seemed only to be asking that the principle of national self-determination of Versailles, denied to them at the time, be extended to Germany. It was only after the subjugation of the remaining areas of Czechoslovakia in March 1939 had demonstrated Hitler's total disregard both for the principles of Versailles and of Munich that attitudes changed.

It was at this point that the British began to give the military guarantees that the French had sought in vain in the 1920s. Military conscription, albeit in a strictly limited form, was introduced for the first time in peacetime. By the end of the year British soldiers, for the second time in a generation, were again deployed in a Continental war. 'I did so hope we were going to escape these tragedies,' Neville Chamberlain wrote to the Archbishop of Canterbury, 'But I sincerely believe that with that madman it was impossible. I pray that the struggle will be short, but it can't end so long as Hitler remains in power.'[11]

From the beginning of the century Britain had been required, for her own perceived security interests, to play a greater role than hitherto in the maintenance of the stability of Europe. This was a necessity successive British governments sought to avoid or minimise. In the crisis provoked by the Fall of France in June

1940 it was, nevertheless, to lead to the grand, and futile, gesture of proposing Anglo-French Union. Others, however, including ministers and senior civil servants not connected with the War Cabinet, felt that the moral of Britain's inter-war involvement with the problems of European security pointed in a different direction. Lord Hankey, who had served as Cabinet Secretary from 1916–38, wrote to Neville Chamberlain on the following day, 17 June 1940:

The more I reflect on the events of recent years the more clearly I realize that the French have been our evil genius from the Paris Peace Conference until today inclusive. Heaven forbid that we should tie ourselves up with them in an indissoluble union![12]

There was, nevertheless, considerable popular interest in such ideas of federation in the face of the crisis of the 1930s. These enthusiasts shared in the general loss of faith in the League of Nations, which was marked by the declining membership of the League of Nations Union during the decade, and by the growth of pacifist organisations. They, however, were not rejecting the notion of collective security for the renunciation of war. To them the League had failed because it was an organisation of sovereign nation-states, and because it had proved unable to reconcile their squabbles. They therefore sought a closer political union.[13] In the context of an impending struggle against totalitarian dictatorships, these schemes generally focused on a union based upon the democracies of the British Empire and America. This did not mean that they did not have a European dimension. George Catlin, in 1941, even argued that Britain could play the same role in a European union as the USA might in a pan-American union.[14] The young men of Federal Union, remembered below in Chapter 7, were nevertheless somewhat unusual in focusing specifically upon the idea of a European union.

The experience of the Second World War was to give greater urgency to the idea of a European union amongst statesmen in several European countries. It was blessed in 15 major speeches by Churchill during his years in opposition between 1945 and 1951. European union commended itself to post-war statesmen, as it had to Briand, as a way of resolving Franco-German antagonisms and achieving a more permanent peace in Europe. British involvement in this process, however, except by way of encouragement, was not envisaged at this stage. Britain had been drawn into greater involvement in European affairs in the first half of the twentieth century because of its perceived need to play a greater role than hitherto in securing European stability. Such security interests did not mean that a power which retained extensive global interests and commitments felt obliged to participate in the European process; indeed some of the economic aspects of the initial plans for a European Coal and Steel Community seemed positively unattractive. It was only when the balance of opinion began to conclude that it was in Britain's economic interest that in 1961 the first effort was made to board the European train.

Notes

1. See George Catlin, *One Anglo-American Nation: The Foundation of Anglo-Saxony as Basis of World Federation: A British Response to Streit*, London: Dakars, 1941, p. 37; Sinclair Kennedy, *The Pan-Angles*, London: Longmans Green, 1915.

2. Daniel Pisk, *War Machine*, London: Yale University Press, 1993, pp. 115–35.
3. See for instance, Modris Eksteins, *Rites of Spring: The Great War and the Birth of the Modern Age*, London: Bantam Press, 1989; Samuel Hynes, *A War Imagined: The First World War and English Culture*, London: The Bodley Head, 1990; Alan Wilkinson, *The Church of England and the First World War*, London: SPCK, 1978 and; *Dissent or Conform? War, Peace and the English Churches 1900–1945*, London: SCM Press, 1986.
4. Including a Fascist International in which British fascists participated in the 1930s.
5. Alan Sharp, *The Versailles Settlement: Peacemaking in Paris 1919*, Basingstoke: Macmillan, 1991, pp. 43–4; Lord Robert Cecil, *A Great Experiment: An Autobiography*, London: Jonathan Cape, 1941, pp. 46f.
6. See Lord Robert Cecil to Lloyd George, 27 May 1919, Lord Robert Cecil Papers, British Library Add Mss 51076, ff. 43–6.
7. Quoted in Sharp, p. 49.
8. Made in a speech 'On the University Ideal' as Principal of the Fifth Congress of Universities of the British Empire, Cambridge, 14 July 1936, printed in Stanley Baldwin, *Service of our Lives: Last Speeches as Prime Minister*, London: Hodder and Stoughton, 1937, p. 58.
9. Jon Tetsumo Sumida, *In Defence of Naval Supremacy: Technology and British Naval Policy 1889–1914*, London: Unwin Hyman, 1989.
10. Gustav Schmidt 'The Domestic Background to British Appeasement Policy' in W. J. Mommsen and Lothar Kettenacher (eds), *The Fascist Challenge and the Policy of Appeasement*, London: Allen and Unwin, 1983, p. 103.
11. Chamberlain to Lang, 5 Sept. 1939, Cosmo Gordon Lang Papers in Lambeth Palace Library, London, vol. 191, f. 277.
12. Quoted in 'The Anglo-French Union Project of June 1940', in Max Beloff, *The Intellectual in Politics and other essays*, London: Weidenfeld and Nicolson, 1970, p. 197.
13. Clarence Streit, *Union Now*, London: Jonathan Cape, 1939, p. 21.
14. Catlin. p. 19.

1

Britain and European reconstruction after the Great War

Anne Orde

After the First World War, which was unprecedented in intensity and longer than any European war since 1815, the problems of reconstruction were themselves unprecedented.[1] They did not, however, generate many new ideas. Prevailing expectations of a rapid return to normality meant that little thought was given to the task of reconstruction. In November 1918 few people in any country were addressing anything but the immediate future problems of demobilising the armies and war industries. Those medium-term problems that were identified were expected to be dealt with fairly quickly. Bonar Law, for example, as Chancellor of the Exchequer, indicated to the American Treasury authorities six weeks after the armistice that he expected Britain's export trade to be back to a 'normal state of affairs' about the end of 1919.[2] The problems were also expected to be dealt with by the familiar mechanisms of relatively free-market liberal capitalism. There was little sense that new methods were needed. Government activity in domestic economies, and in international financial and economic relations, had of course grown greatly during the war. Such activity continued afterwards at a higher level than before 1914, in some countries much higher, in others less; but in most the aim was to reduce it. Except in Russia, socialists did not get much opportunity to put their ideas into practice; and in any case they had no plans ready for socialisation or a mixed economy. Even in Germany the strongest, and intellectually best equipped, of all European socialist parties could achieve from its 18 months' share in government nothing more far-reaching than the Stinnes-Legien agreement for industry-trade union cooperation in demobilisation and dismantling the war economy, works councils and the eight-hour day. Some industrialists and non-socialist politicians, such as Walther Rathenau in Germany and Etienne Clémentel in France, envisaged continuing forms of partnership between government and business. Some politicians and civil servants in France and Britain, such as Clémentel and Arthur Salter, envisaged continuing for a few years, or transferring to the new League of Nations, Allied cooperation in sharing raw materials. But the trend was the other way; the belief that bankers and businessmen were better equipped than governments to manage economic affairs proved predominant.

Nowhere was this belief more strongly held than in the United States, where it combined with a determination neither to be embroiled in European politics, nor to compromise the country's freedom of decision, and with a commitment to an open world trading system with no preferences or privileges. American refusal defeated all the proposals made after the armistice and at the peace conference for pooling war costs or sharing control of resources, or for intergovernmental cooperation in financing reconstruction. Private cooperation was forecast, but it could not be commanded and conditions in Europe were not such as to encourage anything beyond charitable relief. This was indeed given generously, but since the United States was now the world's largest source of finance, the lack of American official commitment was serious.

Faith in private enterprise was strong in Britain too, but tempered by a greater internationalism in financial and commercial circles and a closer involvement in Europe. The recovery of Europe was obviously in Britain's interest; for peace, stability and trade. As far as British government policy was concerned, ministers in the post-war coalition government, and their advisers, soon became convinced that the problems of restoring Europe were too great for private enterprise alone. Intergovernmental cooperation was needed for reconstruction, especially to set the smaller and new states of east central Europe on their feet. They did their best to persuade their American counterparts to join them in the effort. Immediately after the armistice they proposed an all-round cancellation of Allied debts. At the peace conference they proposed a comprehensive Allied policy on stabilising currencies and supplying capital and raw materials. J.M. Keynes, at that time a Treasury official, produced a scheme for rehabilitating European credit and financing relief and reconstruction by means of bonds issued by Germany on account of reparations, and by the other enemy states and the new states. These would be guaranteed by the major Allies and would be used as collateral for loans and the payment of debts between the Allies.[3] Keynes's scheme was open to the objection that it did not address French and Belgian problems; but the ground of American rejection was that Congress would not guarantee European bonds or authorise any joint effort. British advisers were also partly responsible for a proposal for a joint fund to help currency stabilisation and the purchase of raw materials in the new states of east central Europe, a proposal that was never even discussed by the political leaders. Having failed in all these efforts, and being concerned about Britain's own balance of payments, they hesitated to act alone beyond setting up a limited system of guaranteeing credits given by British exporters to purchasers in some east European countries. Direct government lending ceased in 1919: the only subsequent case of a British government credit to a European government was an interim one to desperate Austria in 1921–22. The government sent representatives to the Brussels financial conference of 1920, which declared the necessity of sound public finances, ending inflation, and freeing trade – advice which the British largely followed but which European governments, whilst paying lip service, mostly ignored in practice, continuing instead to finance reconstruction and buy social peace by inflation until it got out of control in 1922. After long hesitation, British ministers and officials played a prominent part in launching the financial reconstruction of Austria through the League of Nations. Subsequent League stabilisation schemes and loans for Hungary, Greece and Bulgaria enjoyed Treasury good will.

But on the two major problems central to European recovery (the shortage of liquid capital and the need to service new debts to the Americans) and falling wholly within government responsibility, British policy was hesitant and often inconsistent. Britain's own position imposed constraints. She was physically little damaged but had suffered severe financial and commercial losses. Much of her investments in the United States had been sold and the proceeds spent on the war. In 1919 income from invisible earnings did not cover the traditional adverse balance of trade. For her own reconstruction Britain needed to revive her export trade rapidly, and sell goods to the United States and other overseas countries who could pay cash and to whom short-term debts were owed, rather than to European countries which, whatever their future potential as customers, now required credit. Britain was still, and expected to be, a world provider of capital; but the demand for capital now exceeded the supply. New York now rivalled London as a world centre of finance. At the end of the war the government accepted the advice of an expert committee that the country should return to the gold standard at the pre-war parity; and it adopted a monetary policy appropriate to that aim. In addition to commercial borrowing, the government owed the United States government a war debt of some £760 million while being owed twice as much by the Allies; and it had a claim to reparation from Germany, fixed at the Spa conference in 1920 at 22 per cent of whatever might be received. Britain was still a rich country, and was regarded by foreigners as a boundless source of credit; but although no one as yet doubted her ability to recover fully, ministers and their advisers were conscious of the limits on her resources and the rising demands for social expenditure from the new democratic electorate.

It was certainly not easy to devise satisfactory policies on debts and reparations, and failures of understanding were not confined to Westminster and Whitehall: private experts did not do much better. But ministers found it extremely difficult to make up their minds among partially incompatible objectives, and so did not try to put awkward choices before the public. They were perpetually looking over their shoulders at the United States, hoping for a change of policy on debts which never came and which there was little serious reason ever to expect. They wished to cooperate with the United States on equal terms as creditors and providers. They did not wish to align Britain with the European Allies in confronting their common creditor. They were prepared to cancel all the Allied debts but not unilaterally. They wished to see Germany recover and play a full part in the European economy, but were not prepared to have Britain pay a disproportionate share of the cost. For about three years they went round and round among the problems, without coming to conclusions.

On one occasion only, in the winter of 1921–22, did Lloyd George take an initiative, without the United States, to bring all the problems of reconstruction, reparations, the pacification of Eastern Europe, and the restoration of Russia to the international comity together in one great conference. The problems were indeed interconnected as were all of Europe's political and economic problems. In order to pay reparations Germany needed to earn foreign currency. Her traditional markets in Eastern Europe were, however, fragile, their recovery delayed not only by economic weakness but by political instability and fear. Restoration of relations with Soviet Russia would relieve fear and open up possibilities of trade for Germany and others; but intense political suspicion and claims for unpaid debts and expropriated property stood in the way. The project was vast; the attempt to tackle it all together, although imaginative, was over-ambitious, for Lloyd George was virtually alone. In the event the French government refused to discuss reparations in a non-Allied body and so Germany could not be dealt with. War debts could not be solved in the absence of the United States. The Russian aspect then took on central importance, greater than the economic prospects warranted. Russia wanted very large credits, far more than was available even if an agreement could have been reached on debts and property. Even as a pump-primer, the international consortium, proposed for organising reconstruction and investment in Eastern Europe and Russia, was not credible. The grand design crumbled, leaving as the only outcome of the Genoa conference a project for international central bank cooperation.

As regards the allied war debts, before 1923 the British Treasury consistently advised cancellation whatever the United States did. It argued that much of the money would never be paid anyway, and that cancellation would free the Allies' credit, improve the prospects for British exports, and have a good effect on political relations. But ministers were either unconvinced, or too conscious, of how unpopular paying the United States would be while getting nothing from the Allies. In August 1922, having accepted that for the sake of Britain's credit in the world the debt to the United States must be paid and negotiations begun soon, the government issued the Balfour Note,[4] professing its desire for all-round debt cancellation and its readiness to abandon Britain's reparation claim as part of a general settlement; but failing these, offering to collect, from Germany and the Allies together, only as much as was needed to pay the United States.

The offer looked reasonable, even generous, to ordinary British eyes. Not so to the French, who observed at once that if they followed British exhortations to leniency towards Germany they would have to pay more to Britain themselves. Informed British opinion also criticised the Note. What was its point? Ministers do not seem to have thought that it would bring about a change in American policy; and there is very little evidence that it was intended as a bargaining counter in a serious attempt to bring about a general settlement of debts and reparations. It looks as though Balfour was simply publicising, in elegant prose, the ordinary resentment of the man in the street at Britain's unenviable position as simul-taneously a good debtor and perforce a lenient creditor. The government then, in January 1923, concluded an agreement for paying its debt to the United States over a period of 62 years. The terms were harder than those the Americans subsequently granted to other Allied debtors. An agreement was thought to be essential, and the terms were not thought to be impossible; but the instalments were an extra burden on Britain's balance of payments. After 1923 the option of cancelling the Allies' debts was still available, but was politically even more difficult to choose. Instead, in the debt settlements concluded with the various Allies after 1925, the principle of the Balfour Note was maintained; and if the Dawes Plan and the debt settlements had run their full term to 1986 Britain would have received as much as she had to pay the United States. No one expected the Dawes Plan to last for 62 years: it was only intended to be provisional, and revision was already being canvassed in 1926. The hope was that eventually reparations and debts might be scaled down together. As they were not, and since Britain had been paying the United States for four years before anything was received from the

Allies or anything much from Germany, there was still a substantial deficit when all payments ceased in the early 1930s.

Policy on reparations was equally confused. Having been quite as responsible as the French for the categories of damage listed in the peace treaty as payable by Germany, the government and much of British opinion soon concluded, with the help of work such as Keynes's *Economic Consequences of the Peace*[5] that the demands could not be paid in full or soon. But they were not willing to sacrifice any of Britain's percentage or agree to a priority for the repair of France's devastated northern region. They maintained instead that Britain's losses, although different, were as great as France's. Before the German liability was fixed and a schedule of payments was imposed in May 1921, Lloyd George alternated between seeking a quick agreement with Germany on a fixed sum – a course that would have helped stability but disappointed inflated expectations – and leaving it to time to moderate hopes and show what could be collected. After 1921 progress depended on inducing French governments to give Germany more time to re-establish her credit; but just as the Americans at the peace conference had criticised Allied demands but refused any inducement to moderation, so liberal Britons denounced French harshness but would not sweeten the pill of what they regarded as economic reason. Only on two occasions (the Balfour Note and the Bonar Law plan of January 1923) was the government willing to make tangible sacrifices for the sake of a settlement. Both offers were hedged about with difficult conditions. The Balfour Note was virtually meaningless without a change in United States policy: the Bonar Law plan[6] offered unilateral debt cancellation but maintained the British percentage of a reduced German liability.

It is of course impossible to prove whether or not unilateral cancellation of Allied debts or sacrifice of some of Britain's reparation claim would have led to better results. On paper each would have been costly. In practice, since Britain ended with a deficit as it was, the benefits of a more rapid settlement might have outweighed the losses. But successive governments, supported by political opinion, did not believe that such sacrifices were possible or needed. France was regarded as no worse off than Britain, and as bound to benefit if Germany were allowed to recover; so unpopular inducements were not thought necessary. Only when American influence and American money were at last brought to bear in the Dawes Plan and the London agreements of 1924 was Britain able to share in producing a settlement which, although provisional, led in turn to debt settlements, a few years of greater stability, and the completion of a real though fragile reconstruction.

Government was responsible for the parameters of public policy. Non-governmental institutions and private capital provided most of the actual resources devoted to reconstruction. The Bank of England occupied a halfway position between the two. Montagu Norman, the bank's governor throughout the inter-war period, was fanatical about central bank independence of government, and seems really to have believed that bankers, unlike politicians, were actuated solely by reason. But he worked closely with the Treasury, and his idea of where the dividing line ran between finance and politics may sometimes seem strange. It is hard not to see a strong political content in some of his actions and ideas, as when he took up the cause of rescuing Austria in 1922, or caused a London bank to refuse the Czechoslovak government an instalment of a loan issue in 1923; when he urged the House of Morgan to put pressure on the French government at the London conference of 1924, or when he half encouraged German ideas of using financial power to secure revision of the Polish frontier in 1926. In some cases Norman went against or beyond what the government would have chosen, in other cases he acted in line with government policy. Norman's policy was devoted above all to general monetary stabilisation and the restoration of Britain's financial position in the world. Stabilisation, after the chaotic conditions of the first post-war years, was a desirable goal from all points of view. The gold exchange standard which Norman promoted would have benefited sterling because countries would have kept part of their reserves in London: but the opposition of the Federal Reserve Bank of New York was decisive. Once he became convinced, in 1922, of the necessity of taking a hand in the financial reconstruction of Austria, Norman worked through the League of Nations to such an extent that by 1927 he was credited with dominating the Financial Committee and using it to further British financial imperialism. The reality fell short of this. Norman's ideas about reorganising east central Europe took no account of the aims of the countries concerned; however his ideas about outside control of national government expenditure were resisted by those governments able to do so. By 1927 Norman was having to yield to a conscious American exercise of financial power. Britain derived prestige from the work of the Financial Committee, but never dominated east central Europe financially, economically, or politically.

The pattern of British trade with Europe was not markedly affected by reconstruction after 1920. Britain imported more, by value, from Europe in the 1920s than she had done before 1914; but these imports were a slightly smaller proportion of the total import bill at the end of the decade, and exports remained fairly constant.[7] The trend towards greater reliance on trade with the Empire, that is associated with the 1930s, began in the previous decade. British capital had never since the mid-nineteenth century gone as much to Europe as to the Empire and the Americas. Of Britain's long-term investments overseas the percentage that was in Europe was rather higher in 1930 than it had been in 1913; but that percentage was still only 7.9 per cent as against 58.7 per cent in the Empire and 20.8 per cent in South America.[8] The largest single source of loans, of all kinds, to Europe in the 1920s was the United States. As part of the preparations for a return to the gold standard, the Bank of England imposed for several years a not wholly effective embargo on short-term foreign lending by British banks. In the first four years after the war, of all the European bond issues made in London and New York, over 70 per cent went to the countries of western and northern Europe and under 30 per cent to those of central and eastern Europe including Germany. The United States provided nearly 68 per cent of the total, Britain just over 32 per cent. But of Britain's share 40 per cent went to eastern and central Europe as against 20 per cent of the New York share.[9] After 1924 many more bond issues in both London and New York were for central and eastern Europe, thanks largely to German borrowing after the Dawes loan. In one class of lending Britain surpassed the United States. Of the loans issued under the League of Nations' auspices for Austria, Hungary, Greece and Bulgaria, almost half the total amount was subscribed in London.[10] In the inter-war years the credit of central and eastern European governments and institutions was not as good as that of northern and western Europe, while their need of outside help in reconstruction was greater.

Governmental loans, had they been possible, might have taken these facts into account. Private bankers, chiefly concerned with a good safe return for their clients' money, hardly could. But these figures suggest that British banks were quicker to recognise the need than American ones, or perhaps simply more adventurous.

Estimates of total European foreign borrowing in the 1920s can only be very approximate. Total international indebtedness has been estimated at £9 billion in 1924 and £12 billion in 1932. An estimate of foreign capital employed in different countries in 1930 gives Europe a net figure of £1,921 million, with Germany accounting for nearly half.[11] Estimates of the effect of all the borrowing and lending are even more difficult to make. Opinions differed at the time as to how productive some of the borrowing was. The war debts, equivalent to 65 per cent of the value of world trade in 1913, were a burden on the system even when they were not being paid, and payments after 1925 had a distorting effect on international capital movements. Yet whilst there was no substitute for borrowing, much of the capital for reconstruction came from countries' own resources. France had one of the largest tasks, but also greater resources than many. The French people paid for reconstruction out of their own savings twice as much as they received from Germany in reparation.

One way or another Europe reconstructed itself, and by 1927 it had substantially recovered in terms of food, raw material, and industrial production; and had even, in some respects, recovered its position in the world economy.[12] But the recovery was not uniform. Eastern Europe took longer than the west. Britain's growth in the 1920s was less than that of some other advanced countries; her overseas trade never fully returned to the 1913 level and her financial strength was never wholly restored. Furthermore, events after 1929 suggested that some of the recovery was not soundly based and was overdependent on credit.

In view of the incomplete nature of reconstruction, it is tempting to think that things would have been better if Britain had done more. But it is not wholly clear either that she was capable of doing much more or that what could have been done would have been decisive. Britain's main contribution would have been financial; the only method thought of at the time was the provision of loans. It was already being suggested in 1927 that the burden on the east central European countries of servicing their existing loans was too heavy, so that they would have had problems with payments even without the collapse of agricultural prices in the late 1920s and the financial crisis of 1931. If this is so, it becomes hard to argue that more outside lending would have solved the problem. It does, however, seem that British governments would have been wise to cancel the Allied debts and might have been able, had they tried, to convince public opinion that it was in Britain's interest to do so. Greater clarity of thought and policy in the first post-war years would hardly have come amiss.

It is equally tempting, and more useful, to compare the experiences of reconstruction after the two world wars. It seems plain that the second effort was more successful than the first. Five years after the end of the Second World War western Europe was launched on one of the longest periods of sustained economic growth in modern history. Twelve years or so after the end of the First World War Europe and the world fell into one of the deepest and longest-lasting depressions in modern history. The explanations do not all hinge on reconstruction, but it is possible to identify some important differences in the policies that were followed.

In the first place, most of the relief supplied after the First World War was given on credit. These loans added to the burdens of the receiving countries, and those that were not repaid were an obstacle to later borrowing. After the Second World War the bulk of relief was given in the form of grants, both in direct relief such as food and medical supplies and in rehabilitation resources to restart agriculture and transport. Another very significant difference was the virtual absence, on the second occasion, of inter-Allied debts. Lend-Lease did not entirely abolish the obligation to pay for goods and services, but it was agreed that goods destroyed in fighting the war should not be counted. Thus in the final accounting between the United States and Britain, the chief beneficiary under Lend-Lease, some $26–27 billion worth of United States aid was written off, leaving a liability of only $650 million to be paid.[13] Loans and credits were given to a number of countries immediately after the war, but the burden of debt incurred in a common cause did not hang over the international payments system and cause political ill feeling a second time.

The Marshall Plan is often credited with bringing about western Europe's recovery after 1947. The programme was undoubtedly a very important contribution, but it did not transform the task, nor did it apply to Eastern Europe. A more substantial difference may well have been that relating to Germany. Allied policy here was not at first any clearer or more benevolent than after 1918, but for various reasons it proved possible to start encouraging west German recovery earlier. Anglo-American policy on reparations was inspired by a determination not to repeat mistakes made after 1919; and new lessons seem to have been learned more readily. Perhaps most important of all, there was a real change in outlook, in general willingness to act quickly and for governments to take the initiative. In 1919 the United States government felt unable to ask Congress for power to extend credits once peace had been signed. Between July 1945 and July 1947 the United States government disbursed in Europe in one way or another $12,158 million.[14] Most of this money flowed back across the Atlantic in payment for imports. What made the difference was that it was put in early, at a point when private capital would not have ventured. The problems of reconstructing Europe after the two world wars were not all the same: not the least of the differences was in the climate of expectations.

Notes

1. See Anne Orde, *British policy and European reconstruction after the first world war*, Cambridge: Cambridge University Press, 1990.
2. Public Record Office, London, Treasury files, T1/12256/49893/18.
3. J.M. Keynes, *Collected writings*, London: Royal Economic Society and Macmillan, 1971, Vol. 16, pp. 429–36.
4. Cmd 1737 of 1922.
5. J.M. Keynes, *The economic consequences of the peace*, London: Macmillan, 1919.
6. Cmd 1812 of 1923.
7. Figures in B.R. Mitchell, *British Historical Statistics*, Cambridge: Cambridge University Press, 1988.
8. *The problem of international investment*, London: Royal Institute of International Affairs, 1937, pp. 142–4.

9. *Europe's overseas needs 1919–20 and how they were met*, Geneva: League of Nations, 1943.
10. Royal Institute of International Affairs, 1937, p. 232.
11. Royal Institute of International Affairs, 1937, p. 223.
12. *Memorandum on production and trade 1913 and 1923–27*, Geneva: League of Nations, 1929; *Memorandum on production and trade 1925 to 1929–30*, Geneva: League of Nations, 1931; B.R. Mitchell, *European historical statistics 1750–1980*, London: Macmillan, 1975.
13. *Survey of International affairs 1939–1946, America, Britain and Russia 1941–1945*, Appendix II, Royal Institute of International Affairs, London, 1953.
14. Alan S. Milward, *The reconstruction of western Europe 1945–51*, London: Methuen, 1984, pp. 45–8.

2

Was there a 'British' alternative to the Briand Plan?

Robert Boyce

One of the more interesting features of recent European historiography has been the rediscovery of a 'European' movement in the inter-war years. A few memoirs and articles appeared in the 30 years after the defeat of Nazi Germany, yet the movement scarcely figured in any of the standard accounts of the inter-war period.[1] One reason for the omission doubtless derives from the fact that Hitler's seizure of power discredited the European movement, and well before the outbreak of the Second World War interest in it dwindled to almost nothing. Some of the most dedicated Europeans in the 1920s had unwisely continued to pursue their cause in the 1930s after Hitler came to power. Some tainted it with appeasement, a few with wartime collaboration – Georges Suarez, biographer of the leading inter-war European, Aristide Briand, for example, was one of the first to be formally convicted and shot for his wartime activities.[2] In consequence, those involved in reviving the European movement after 1945 preferred to avoid reference to their somewhat tainted inter-war antecedents.[3] A second, more substantial, reason for the omission was however the tendency of historians writing in the aftermath of the Second World War to focus upon the war's origins and, looking backwards from that event, to treat the whole of the inter-war period as little more than the breeding ground for conflict. From this perspective, of course, the 'European' movement was of little or no account: nothing more than a conclave of political idealists and innocents, who could safely be ignored.

The past 20 years have seen a major shift in the way historians treat the inter-war period. Instead of looking backwards from 1939, many historians now choose to look forward from 1918 or to examine the 1920s as a decade worthy of examination in its own right. One consequence has been a greater emphasis upon the *dis*continuities in the course of inter-war history. Another has been the implicit recognition of the central importance of economic issues in the shaping of international affairs. As is now clear, politicians of the day were not indifferent to threats of war and aggression; but for most of the time – as at virtually every other time in modern history – their attention was focused mainly on bread and butter issues.[4] By the same token, in so far as threats to international stability did occur, they often appeared to come not from military aggression but rather from such problems as exchange rate instability, aggressively expanding US-controlled multinational business, foreign protectionism or mismanaged fiscal policy elsewhere in the international economy. These changes in historical focus, along with contemporary interest in the origins of the European Community, have brought about a rediscovery of the inter-war 'European' movement, which to an important degree was bound up with efforts to safeguard European industry and markets.[5] It is thus wholly credible that Sir Alfred Mond, chairman of Imperial Chemical Industries, Britain's largest corporation, should have observed in May 1927, after meeting leading businessmen and politicians in a half-dozen continental capitals:

It was quite remarkable, and I should not have believed it if I had not come so closely into contact with it. The idea that you must form some economic union of European countries, some form of joint action in industry. . .in taxation, in tariffs, and even further steps than that, in order to enable Europe to go on existing against the Continent of North America, is becoming almost axiomatic, almost a passionate faith.[6]

A few months later a Foreign Office official corroborated Mond's claim. The movement was 'a coming force – if not the force – in Europe; and I think most people in this country would be astonished to learn with what frequency it crops up in European speech and writing.'[7] And following the announcement in July 1929 that the French Prime Minister, Aristide Briand, intended to propose a plan for European federation, Paul Claudel, the French ambassador in Washington, reported that, 'Whatever the outcome, one may say that no international question has attracted so much discussion by the US press in recent years than the question of the United States of Europe.'[8]

The Briand Plan deserves a prominent place in history as the first instance of a formal proposal for European union from a major European power and as the direct forerunner of the present European Community. After informally consulting other European leaders in 1929, Briand, then both Prime Minister and Foreign Minister of France, publicly affirmed his intention to take the lead in promoting European unity at the Tenth Assembly of the League of Nations when it convened in September.[9] In the meantime he was tied up at The Hague where negotiations took place through August on the Young Plan, an ostensibly permanent settlement of the German reparations problem. Briand took up the European federation question in his address to the League Assembly in Geneva on 5 September, and shortly afterwards at a lunch that he held at the Hôtel des Bergues in Geneva for all the European delegates to the League. At the suggestion of his guests, he agreed to circulate a memorandum setting out his proposal in more detail, and then, when he had received the responses of the other 26 states, to report on the prospects for action to the Eleventh League Assembly a year hence.[10]

Briand's motives for taking this initiative were never made altogether clear, but they are transparent enough. One was the desire to organise resistance to American economic domination of Europe. It is important to remember that the initiative came before, not after, the Wall Street crash, when American multinational industry was benefiting from the boom to buy up European firms, US manufactured exports were increasing at a disturbing rate, and only a few weeks earlier a bill had cleared the US Congress calling for a further massive increase in

America's already excessive tariff wall. Briand, no expert in economic affairs, relied on the advice of Louis Loucheur, the industrialist-turned-politician who, since the breakdown of inter-allied economic cooperation in 1919 had advocated forming a European economic bloc, to serve as a counterweight to the industrial and financial strength of the Anglo-Saxon powers. Briand shared this aim,[11] and by 1926 key ministers and their advisers in France had accepted that their long-run goal must be 'an economic league of the European nations, leading eventually to a United States of Europe.'[12] As the American challenge intensified in subsequent years, British conservatives gave increasing consideration to organising the Empire into an economic bloc. In France it prompted Briand to think harder about providing a similar lead for Europe.[13]

Briand's other main motive was to tie Germany into a peaceful European structure before the ever-present danger of nationalism again arose to rule it out and revive the Franco-German antagonism. Briand was about to represent France at the forthcoming Hague Conference where he intended *both* to accept Britain's call for the early withdrawal of all Allied troops from the Rhineland, *and* to approve the new reparations settlement, the Young plan, which had been negotiated in Paris in the spring. The French were attracted to the Young Plan by the promise of guaranteed reparation payments, which would underpin their domestic financial stability and remove the need for higher taxes. The element of guarantee would be provided by Germany's commitment to make payments unconditionally on a specified part of the reparations total. The French intended to issue bonds against this commitment on the international markets, thereby obtaining immediate payment of the claim while also tying Germany's credit-worthiness to its willingness to continue reparations payments. This removed a major reason for continuing to station troops on German soil. But, as the French were aware, even the best laid plans could go wrong, and they were nervous about agreeing to withdraw the last of their troops from the Rhineland five years before being required to do so by the Treaty of Versailles, since this meant the abandonment of an important means of containing Germany.

Briand therefore turned to European federation as a *new* means of containment. As sketched out in the Memorandum that he circulated to interested governments on 17 May 1930, Europe would create institutions modelled on the structure of the League of Nations, with a Secretariat, an Assembly and a Council. In the first instance the new organisation would devote its attention to the elimination of trade barriers, the ultimate goal being a European common market.[14] Briand's hope was that the other European countries, however divided they might be in other respects, were sufficiently disturbed by the threat of American capitalist domination to join France in the mutual defence of the European market. Hence his statement at Geneva in September 1929 that the organisation would be 'primarily economic'.

Whether Briand's Plan stood any chance of realisation even at the moment of conception may be doubted, given the enormous diversity of regimes in Europe at the time.[15] The prospects diminished in October 1929 when Gustav Stresemann, the German foreign minister and one of Europe's most able statesmen, died; and further declined when the German coalition government led by the Socialist Hermann Müller gave way in March 1930 to a minority government led by the narrowly nationalist Heinrich Brüning. Even then it is just possible that something might have come of Briand's initiative had it received Britain's support. At this time, Britain's potential influence over the course of European affairs can scarcely be exaggerated. It was still the world's largest trading nation, and with its huge excess of imports over exports it provided a market of enormous importance for many of the Continental countries. It was also the one power capable of ensuring that any European structure was dominated neither by France nor Germany.

Briand's initiative, however, coincided with the advent of the second Labour government, which proved to be thoroughly unsympathetic to a specifically European initiative. The Labour government was zealously committed to free trade and the League of Nations, keen to improve Anglo-American relations, and almost pathologically francophobe. It regarded France as the main obstruction to an equitable reparations settlement, disarmament and European stabilisation. Briand's initiative seemed of a piece with post-war French policy, that is, an attempt by France to dominate Europe through an elaborate federal scheme. It also seemed certain to result in confrontation with the United States, thus destroying Britain's patient efforts to promote multilateral trade and dividing the world into exclusive and antagonistic blocs. The first reaction of William Graham, Labour's President of the Board of Trade, was to denounce Briand's initiative:

Whilst the American tariff which is now under consideration will undoubtedly be more protective than ever [he advised his Cabinet colleagues], there can be no question that we ought to indicate with the utmost clearness that we can be no parties to a policy which seeks to discriminate between different foreign countries and more particularly that we should not in any case be prepared to adopt a policy of discrimination against the United States.[16]

Graham was restrained by the Foreign Office, but he and other British ministers attending the League Assembly in 1929 damned Briand's initiative with faint praise and subsequently warned Briand of their apprehensions.[17]

During the winter of 1929–30 most of the countries in northern and western Europe took their cue from Britain. Briand did what he could to allay fears of the impact of his Plan upon the authority of the League, European-American relations, and the national sovereignty of the countries directly concerned. But despite his efforts, most of the replies to his Memorandum in June 1930, while uniformly polite, left little room for doubt that the Plan was impracticable. Briand was so discouraged that initially he refused to report the results to the League Assembly in September 1930. Eventually he was persuaded to do so, and a Committee of Enquiry into European Union (CEUE) was set up under the auspices of the League. This, however, was merely a face-saving gesture on Briand's behalf. As everyone appreciated at the time, the Briand Plan itself was dead.[18]

On the face of it, the demise of the Briand Plan was a decisive set back for the cause of European cooperation. Not only was there no other initiative of comparable scope or ambition before the Second World War, but the series of crises that occurred from the spring of 1930 markedly worsened relations between France, Germany and Britain, and left Europe dangerously unstable. The first crisis occurred in Germany where the economic slump had made government by parliamentary consent virtually impossible. From March 1930 the Brüning government resorted to government by decree, but succeeded only in worsening the deflationary spiral already devastating the economy. The Reichstag election of September 1930 resulted in startling gains for the Communists and Nazis and a sharp decline in support for the democratic parties. In March 1931 came the revelation of plans for an Austro-German customs union against which France vigorously protested, seeing the scheme as a thinly disguised attempt at *Anschluss*, which was illegal under the terms of the Treaties of Versailles and Saint-Germain and the guarantees offered at the time of the international loan of 1921.

The ensuing crisis triggered a run on the Austrian schilling, and France, by now the only country in the world with sizeable liquid assets to lend, deliberately withheld financial assistance until Austria publicly renounced the customs union scheme. British observers were infuriated by what they regarded as French recklessness. They grew even angrier when the financial crisis spread to Germany, and France again threatened to bring down the roof on everyone by refusing to support the moratorium on inter-government debts proposed by President Hoover, until Germany offered additional assurances of continued reparation payments. No sooner was this dispute resolved than the crisis shifted to London, forcing British representatives to go cap in hand to New York and Paris to request financial assistance. French authorities were annoyed at the way the Anglo-Saxon powers had sought to stave off a collapse of their commercial lending to Germany and Central Europe by insisting upon a suspension of inter-governmental payments, which affected France more than them. They were nevertheless prepared to co-operate in shoring up the pound, but to no avail. Britain's abandonment of the gold standard on 21 September 1931 caused intense humiliation within British ruling circles and the expression of open antagonism towards France and the United States, who were held responsible for this result. In Paris comparable frustration was felt when Britain refused to compensate the Bank of France for the massive losses it incurred in voluntarily trying to shore up sterling the previous summer. Thus provoked, France introduced a surtax on imports from Britain and other countries with depreciated currencies, which in turn brought threats of retaliation from London. And in January 1932 Chancellor Brüning aroused French fury when he announced that Germany could not resume reparation payments.[19]

The rise of political extremism together with the worsening of relations among the leading powers after 1929 swiftly reduced the chances of European co-operation in any form; and it seems reasonable to surmise that all possibility of effective co-operation virtually ended when Hitler became German chancellor on 30 January 1933. The World Economic Conference in the summer of 1933 – usually regarded as the climax of efforts to arrange a multilateral solution to Europe's economic crisis – thus came too late to reverse the drift towards war. Even so, it seems fair to say that the appearance and demise of the Briand Plan in 1930 was only the beginning of the story.

The Briand Plan might be described as an early example of the federalist approach to European unity.[20] Its rejection was a setback for the European idea. Yet, even after its demise the opportunity still existed for a less ambitious, non-federalist, 'British' approach to European co-operation. In the event, several of Britain's more important trading partners proposed precisely such an approach and looked to Britain for a lead. Virtually nothing came of these projects; but unlike those other 'missed opportunities' which are evident only to historians long after the event, this was a case where many British authorities openly advocated British support for initiatives of this sort. By the spring of 1932 senior British ministers accepted in principle the need for a flexible approach to multilateral trade liberalisation in Europe and beyond, including the limited use of regional trade preferences, which, if actually encouraged, would have anticipated the post-war 'British' approach to European co-operation.

The potential importance of such action can hardly be exaggerated. Given the narrowness of Hitler's 'window of opportunity' – his support was already waning by the latter part of 1932, as the German economy began to recover – any display of constructive co-operation among the European Great Powers in the preceding months would have contributed to the restoration of confidence, hastened the recovery, and might have closed the window altogether. Unfortunately, shortly after acknowledging the necessity to promote multilateral trade, the government acted against its own better judgement and turned away from Europe not only by associating itself in exclusive agreements with the countries of the British Empire but also by resisting similar regional arrangements within Europe. As a result, instead of lending new hope to Europe, Britain contributed to a further worsening of conditions at the very moment when Hitler was making his final bid for power. It seems no exaggeration to say that the British government's choice may well have been a mistake of world-historical proportions: a mistake due to little more than political self-indulgence, but one that would take a Second World War to put right.

To understand the logic of the events, we must go back to the latter part of the 1920s. Since the immediate post-war period when Central Europe nearly succumbed to political and economic chaos, the continental states had made good progress, first in stabilising their currencies, then, with this objective largely attained, in reducing the additional trade barriers thrown up in the aftermath of the war. But they could not proceed far on the trade side so long as the United States refused to co-operate while at the same time continuing to increase its inroads in markets overseas. Working through the Economic Committee of the League of Nations, the European states therefore sought a solution by drafting a clause, to be inserted in all future trade treaties, providing an exception to the most-favoured-nation principle for multilateral agreements among countries who agreed to reduce mutual trade barriers, so long as the agreements were open to all countries to join on an equitable basis. The clause, in other words, would allow for regional trade agreements, if they contributed to trade expansion rather than merely trade diversion, and were of a non-exclusive kind.[21]

The merits of the clause were obvious, but so too was the objection to it, namely that in allowing departures from the most-favoured-nation principle, it threatened to break up the system of international trade into separate and potentially conflicting regional blocs. This was a matter of great importance to countries such as Britain which, under free trade, had almost nothing to bargain with and relied upon the most-favoured-nation clause to ensure equitable treatment in foreign markets. The most-favoured-nation clause was the first item in nearly all British commercial treaties, and the Board of Trade jealously defended the principle against all preferential agreements. The only exceptions the Board would tolerate were for complete customs unions, such as between Belgium and Luxembourg, or for preferences between countries with long historical associations, such as the

Baltic states, Spain and Portugal – or the members of the British Commonwealth.[22] Despite the growing interest in European regional trade arrangements, the Board absolutely refused to contemplate further exceptions. In 1925 and again 1928 the Board flatly opposed any derogation from the most-favoured-nation principle to assist the economic recovery of the succession states of the Danube region.[23] However, in a misleading lapse British officials raised no objection to the plurilateral clause when it was discussed and approved by the League Economic Committee in the spring of 1929,[24] which raised hopes on the Continent of a change in British policy.[25] Perhaps encouraged by this development, Briand presented his proposal for European unity shortly afterwards at the Tenth League Assembly in Geneva.

British ministers attending the Assembly called for what they described as more practical action in the form of a tariff truce, to provide a breathing-space for multilateral tariff negotiations to begin. Britain's initiative led to a League-sponsored 'Preliminary Conference on Concerted Economic Action' in February 1930, where the tariff truce proposal received the support of the liberal trading nations of northern Europe. But it soon became clear that this was no more practical than Briand's initiative. The British Dominions and other primary producing countries in the developing world, whose revenues had been in steep decline since 1928 because of falling commodity prices, had refused even to attend the so-called tariff truce conference. Nor was the United States represented, and moreover it was about to demonstrate its disdain for a truce by introducing the Smoot-Hawley Tariff, the most protective tariff in US history. A radically scaled-down truce was eventually agreed at the League conference. But by the summer of 1930, with the new American tariff in place and protectionism and unemployment rising everywhere, even the British Labour government hesitated to ratify the truce, and approval only came when Philip Snowden, the Chancellor of the Exchequer and fanatical supporter of free trade, threatened to make it a resigning issue.[26]

Fear of Britain abandoning free trade in favour of an exclusive Empire protectionist bloc was a major factor in the decision of the Norwegian government to promote a more limited tariff truce among Europe's liberal trading nations at this time. Preliminary conversations were held at a meeting of Danish, Swedish, Norwegian and Dutch delegates to the Eleventh League Assembly at Geneva in September 1930. A further meeting was held in October at The Hague and in December at Oslo where, on 22 December, a convention was signed by ministers from the three Scandinavian countries, the Netherlands and Belgium together with Luxemburg.[27]

The actual provisions of the Oslo convention, as it was known, were modest enough. Signatories merely agreed to give at least a fortnight's notice before raising import duties or introducing new ones, and to give consideration to any objections or proposed amendments from other signatories, who had the right to denounce the convention if no satisfaction was received. Support for the convention, it may be noted, did not involve abandonment of the principle of unconditional most-favoured-nation treatment. Nevertheless, the convention was not a trivial gesture. Together the signatories accounted for nearly 9 per cent of world trade, more than France and roughly as much as Germany. And if scarcely a decisive initiative, the aim was the laudable one of initiating common action among the countries determined to hold back the rising tide of protectionism. Britain had been kept informed of the project from the beginning, and in early May 1931 Fernand van Langenhove, secretary-general of the Belgian foreign ministry, visited London to seek British support for the convention.

Van Langenhove was swiftly disappointed. After the arrival of Lord Tyrrell as ambassador in Paris in 1929, Foreign Office officials had been advised that the European movement was being taken seriously in France. They treated the reports with scepticism.[28] Early in 1930 Tyrrell reported warnings he had received that French leaders were divided on the way to proceed, and might seek a 'little European' solution, including Germany but excluding Britain, if Britain refused to accept a collective solution to Europe's economic and political crisis.[29] The threat was real enough, but when London made no effort to cooperate, the scales in Paris were tipped not in favour of a German entente but rather towards narrower national protectionism.[30] Only later was the Foreign Office obliged to deal directly with European initiatives, briefly in the late spring of 1930 when the Briand Plan was circulated, and again in the spring of 1931 when France approached London in a desperate attempt to devise a broad European solution to the economic crisis rather than leave Germany alone in the field with its scheme for a bilateral customs union with Austria.[31] Unfortunately, Foreign Office officials remained slow to appreciate the significance of these economic initiatives, and suffered embarrass-ment when belatedly they came round to support the French initiative, only to be repudiated by the Prime Minister.[32]

Van Langenhove was simply directed to the Board of Trade. There, senior officials remained totally committed to free trade and the defence of the most-favoured-nation principle. By their lights the Oslo convention seemed suspiciously like the French inspired initiative for the Danube region: that is, a regional association which threatened to undermine the most-favoured-nation principle and trigger the break-up of the world economy into exclusive blocs. This, they were sure, would be disastrous for Britain, whose global commercial and financial interests depended upon the maintenance of a multilateral payments system. On traditional free trade grounds, therefore, they rejected van Langenhove's approach almost out of hand. There is no evidence that ministers were even made aware of his visit.[33]

In the fourth week of June 1931 Walter Layton, editor of *The Economist*, went to Geneva as Britain's representative on a special sub-committee of economic experts of the Committee of Enquiry into European Union (CEUE). By this time Layton, like most British observers, had come to regard Continental Europe as hopelessly wedded to protectionism, and he set off reluctantly, believing that the other delegates would be indifferent to calls for trade liberalisation. He was therefore startled to find that there was indeed great interest in keeping the channels of trade open through regional or bilateral customs unions. The other delegates took the view that universal approaches, as exemplified by the tariff truce proposal, were impracticable while the United States and other overseas countries refused to join with Europe in negotiating a halt to the rise of protectionism. Unless the European countries were simply to throw in the towel and retreat into protectionism on a narrow national basis, therefore, their only alternative was to take the route indicated by the League of Nations Economic Committee in 1929 when it attempted to secure an agreed derogation from the most-favoured-nation principle for open-ended trade associations among countries prepared to liberalise trade among themselves. 'The point which interested everybody,' Layton reported, 'was the relationship between any such project and Great Britain.'[34]

Austria, Germany and France as well as the Oslo group of countries all indicated their readiness to extend automatic most-favoured-nation rights to Britain if Britain merely acquiesced in their respective projects. Nine months after the abandonment of the Briand Plan, three months after the start of the Austro-German Customs Union crisis, three weeks after the run had begun on German banks, and a week after Hoover had announced his proposal for a one-year moratorium on all inter-governmental obligations, the leading European countries still displayed a willingness to work together on the commercial front, to halt the slide into economic disaster. Layton, however, was in no position to offer British cooperation. The economic experts' report advocating a European common market,[35] received the support in principle of most countries in Europe, including France, Belgium, the Netherlands, Austria, Germany, Hungary, Yugoslavia, Poland and Lithuania.[36] But the British Board of Trade continued to insist upon the strongest reservations.[37] Before action could be taken, the financial crisis had swept away the Labour government and driven Britain off the gold standard.

The situation confronting British statesmen when sterling's enforced flotation was announced on 21 September 1931 was more ominous than at any time since November 1918. Everywhere trade was plummeting, unemployment was soaring, protectionism was on the increase and currency relations were a shambles, with half the world still on the gold standard and the other half following sterling off it. In Germany the banks were shut and a moratorium was imposed on foreign payments. In the United States cracks were appearing in the banking system. In Manchuria, Japanese militarists chose this moment to begin carving out their own exclusive economic bloc. As the permanent head of the Foreign Office had recently warned the Cabinet, for the first time since 1918 there was widespread talk in Europe of another war.[38] Until now, Foreign Office officials had been content to leave commercial issues to the Board of Trade and financial and monetary issues to the Treasury or Bank of England. They now squared up to this unprecedented crisis and in November 1931 set out a broad strategy for dealing with it.[39] Their approach rested upon two assumptions: first, that all the problems causing international tension – reparations, disarmament, German demands for treaty revision, the monetary crisis and the economic chaos in Europe – were interrelated and could not be solved in isolation; and secondly, that Britain's global interests made it incumbent that Britain provide a lead in overcoming the crisis. This, the Foreign Office believed, was possible if Britain was prepared to use the three major bargaining counters it had to hand. One was willingness to revive the 1924 Protocol so as to reassure France of British assistance in the event of conflict in Europe. The second was provided by the recent abandonment of the gold standard. Such was the anxiety of the countries still on the gold standard to see sterling return, the Foreign Office believed, that Britain could set very stiff conditions upon its agreement. The third and, for the Foreign Office, most important asset was access to Britain's home market. Not only was Britain still the world's largest importer, but, the Foreign Office appreciated, Britain's yawning trade deficit meant that many other countries were acutely dependent upon access to the British market for their own balance of payments stability.

The Office therefore urged the government to take full account of the international consequences of its tariff policy. In the words of the Foreign Office paper, 'A high protective tariff, combined with Empire preference, implies a measure of dissociation from Europe, a corresponding diminution of our influence over European affairs, and possibly a growth of economic antagonism.' From the standpoint of foreign policy, the Office deplored the prospect of a high and discriminatory tariff, which would trample on long-established foreign interests and be sure to provoke political as well as economic retaliation. It believed that holding out the inducement of keeping open the British market would, on the other hand,

incline the recalcitrant nations of the continent, and even, perhaps, the United States of America, to listen to our views on world recovery. *To our foreign policy, therefore, this tariff question is all important.* We urge that it should not be decided purely on grounds of domestic or Empire convenience; but that, especially in view of the present crisis, its efficacy as an instrument of foreign policy should be given the fullest consideration.

The Foreign Office readily acknowledged that using any or all of the three instruments raised extremely sensitive political issues. But, it argued, the danger of not using them was almost certainly greater. Europe was teetering on the brink, and Germany, potentially the most dangerous country, was becoming desperate.

People in this country [the Foreign Office] wrote seem to be unaware of the extent to which the future of 'civilisation' depends on what happens in Germany in the course of the next six months and of the grave doubt as to whether the upshot will be peace or war, recovery or collapse.

The strategy proposed by the Foreign Office was eminently sensible, indeed quite possibly the only way for Britain to proceed if it were to resume its leadership of the capitalist world. But having suffered a prolonged and acute crisis in the recent attempt to maintain the gold standard, ministers as well as Treasury advisers were extremely reluctant to risk a repetition and they therefore refused to contemplate restoring sterling to a fixed exchange rate on any terms for the time being. By the same token, 12 years of high interest rates and an overvalued currency had placed tremendous strain upon Britain's industries and had eventually provoked a widespread reaction against free trade and demands for protection, which were now heard loudly from the Tory backbenches. The pressure for a radical break with free trade and the introduction of a policy combining protection and imperial preferences became all the greater after the general election of October 1931, which saw a vast number of Conservatives returned and the formation of a largely Conservative National government. Nearly all the Tory backbenchers were protectionists, and it was no doubt the danger of such a course of action that had prompted the Foreign Office to put forward its crisis strategy in November.

Nine months later Britain adopted a policy of imperial protectionism at the Ottawa conference. The decision was widely anticipated, for the British government had been importuned constantly by the Dominions since the 1930 imperial conference and its Conservative members had firmly signalled their intention to move in this direction. Yet it is important to stress that there was nothing inevitable about the outcome of the Ottawa conference. In the first place, the National government was a coalition, the legitimacy of which depended upon the continued involvement of Labour and Liberal members, most of whom were in principle opposed to protectionism and exclusive imperialist policies. Had the Labour and Liberal members stood firm against imperial protectionism, the Tory majority could only have proceeded by abandoning the pretence of non-party government and going to the country for a new mandate, something they were extremely reluctant to do while the economic crisis continued. Secondly, the argument for trade protection had largely been removed by the abandonment of the gold standard. Protection was one means of shoring up the exchange rate when it was fixed on the gold standard; but by leaving sterling to find its own level, Britain's international payments would remain in equilibrium without resort to protection. This point was made repeatedly by Sir Herbert Samuel, the Home Secretary and a Liberal free trader, who was able to quote authorities such as Layton, Sir Josiah Stamp and J.M. Keynes in his support. As he argued, the only real value of an emergency tariff after September 1931 was as a means of bargaining for tariff reductions in Europe and elsewhere. In so far as a general tariff and preferences to the Dominions were conceded, there would be fewer means of negotiating trade liberalisation with foreign countries. His own hope was that Britain would provide renewed leadership in Europe by encouraging the formation of what he called 'low tariff customs unions' among groups such as the Oslo countries and in the Danube region; and he called for the reconsideration of Britain's rigid defence of the unconditional most-favoured-nation principle.[40] Intellectually he won the argument hands down, which was perhaps why he was so strongly disliked by his more imperial-minded colleagues. Conservative ministers insisted upon the need for an emergency tariff and the desirability of further preferences to the Dominions. But in Cabinet they were obliged to accept that the principal objective of policy must be the expansion of Britain's total trade, and they therefore agreed that no new preferences should be offered before the Ottawa conference, and then only in return for concessions beneficial to British trade.

Opposition to a retreat into imperial protectionism came from other sources as well. The Foreign Office, as described, loudly warned that a policy of imperial protectionism would aggravate the world crisis and jeopardise Britain's capacity for international leadership. The Treasury and Bank of England were clearly sceptical about the adequacy of relying upon Empire markets, which had never provided an outlet for more than a third of Britain's exports. They showed their scepticism by discouraging any reference to monetary policy at Ottawa: so far as they were concerned, Britain was a world economic power or it was nothing, and to retreat into the Empire was to risk the loss of two-thirds of its trade and overseas investment opportunities. Monetary policy, for which they shared responsibility, would remain designed to serve a global purpose.[41] Even the panel of industrialists (comprised of leading merchants and bankers as well as industrialists), which had been created by the government to advise it during preparations for the Ottawa conference pronounced against an exclusive imperial trade policy. J.H. Thomas, the Secretary of State for the Dominions and a keen imperial protectionist, was obliged to report to the relevant Cabinet committee that the need for a broader framework was being 'constantly mentioned by the Industrial Advisers'. Walter

Runciman, the President of the Board of Trade, similarly 'warned the Committee that the Government's Advisers tended more and more to insist on the vital importance of maintaining our foreign trade'. The industrial advisers, he and Thomas wrote,

were quite clear that the problems with which we were faced at Ottawa cannot be solved on exclusively Imperial lines. [They] suggested that it might be necessary to adjust our objectives on broader lines than hitherto contemplated, and to attempt to draw up what were described as the rules and regulations of an association of countries which others might join.[42]

In the preparations for Ottawa during the spring, the Cabinet committee addressed a series of questions, including whether Britain's delegates, before giving undertakings to the Dominions, should 'have regard to the effects on our trade with foreign countries and future commercial negotiations with such countries; and should they tell the Dominions that they must bear in mind these considerations?' The committee – which, it should be noted, included Neville Chamberlain, the Chancellor of the Exchequer and chief protagonist of an Empire policy – reviewed the situation in light of the industrial advisers' advice. It agreed that the questions must be answered in the affirmative.[43] A committee of depart-mental advisers meanwhile considered the possibility of a legal challenge if Britain went ahead with preferential arrangements at Ottawa. The view prevailed that it probably did not matter one way or the other. If challenged in court, preferences would probably be found to be incompatible with Britain's most-favoured-nation commitments contained in treaties with foreign countries. But no foreign country enjoying substantial trade with Britain was likely to raise a legal challenge because even after Ottawa its trade would remain too valuable to jeopardise.[44] The assumption in both committees was thus that Britain, while seeking a mutual *reduction* in Empire trade barriers at Ottawa, could not be drawn into agreements that would stand in the way of a policy of active trade expansion elsewhere.

As if to demonstrate the practical potential of such a strategy, France took the lead in renewing the scheme for Danubian economic cooperation based largely on trade preferences. For a few months Sir Frederick Leith Ross, the government's Chief Economic Adviser, supported the Foreign Office's call for a positive policy. 'The existing position is clearly so bad that I feel we ought not to place obstacles in the way of what is regarded as a really important step towards improving the position in Central Europe'.[45] The Board of Trade yielded a little and agreed to tolerate a modest level of cereal export preferences. But by April 1932 Leith Ross had reversed his position out of concern for Dominions opinion.

Is it advisable for us just before Ottawa to take the lead in proposing an arrangement in Europe prejudicial to their interests?

The Danube scheme appears to have been pushed by certain members of the League Secretariat, largely in the hope that it would help to establish a breach in the most-favoured-nation principle which might then be capable of further expansion, and might eventually provide a basis for a preferential system between the 'United States of Europe'. But here again, is it in our interests to support such a scheme? Our double relationship to Europe on the one hand and to America and the Overseas Dominions on the other hand makes our position peculiarly delicate, and if ever such a European preferential system became a matter of practical politics, this country would certainly have to sustain the greatest strain.[46]

Britain therefore hung back, arms folded, as France promoted the scheme at the Four Power conference in April 1932, and allowed the Germans and Italians to use spoiling tactics to block progress.[47]

Meanwhile, the Netherlands, Belgium and Luxemburg simultaneously formulated a new convention which they put to the Oslo group of countries in June 1932.[48] The new convention called upon signatories to make an annual 10 per cent reduction in import duties until they were no more than 8 per cent on manufactured products, 4 per cent on semi-manufactures, and completely eliminated from raw materials; for the unification of customs nomenclature; for the signatories to exchange the duty reductions on an unconditional most-favoured-nation basis among themselves; for the convention to be open to all other countries to join on equal terms; and for the benefits to be extended unilaterally to countries that offered comparable market access. This last provision was clearly included with Britain in mind, and indeed the authors of the convention acknowledged that it could not succeed unless Britain agreed to support it or at least raise no objections to it. Even then the Scandinavian countries were not prepared to be associated with the convention, on account of its break with the unconditional most-favoured-nation principle, until they were sure that Britain would approve. The Benelux countries therefore proceeded without them, and Paul Hymans, the Belgian foreign minister, put in a plea for support when he attended the Lausanne conference on reparations in July.[49]

The 'International Convention for the Reduction of Trade Restrictions', generally known as the Ouchy Convention after the town just outside Lausanne where it was signed by representatives of the Benelux countries, received a warm reception in many quarters in Britain. Walter Layton wired his congratulations to Hymans, declaring the Convention to be 'the first step to a European customs union'.[50] *The Manchester Guardian*, the *Financial News*, the *Financial Times*, the *News Chronicle*, the *Spectator* and the *Daily Telegraph*, all supporters of a liberal trade policy, similarly welcomed it, and so too did *The Times*.[51] At Lausanne Hymans sought out Runciman and Jules Durand, the French minister of commerce. Both expressed sympathy with the initiative without however committing themselves. Meanwhile van Langenhove sounded out William Brown, Runciman's private secretary, who intimated that Runciman would not raise objection to the Convention on grounds of breaching the most-favoured-nation principle.[52]

As Scandinavian representatives gloomily predicted, however, Hymans and other Benelux leaders were too sanguine about Britain's reception of the scheme.[53] At the Ottawa conference the following month, the British delegation found to its dismay that the Dominions were prepared to make no agreements except in return for guaranteed portions of the British market, while at the same time the only favours they intended to grant British trade would be at the expense of foreign countries. This meant trade diversion rather than trade creation: precisely the outcome the panel of industrial advisers had warned against and the Cabinet had rejected. The British delegation agonised over their predicament and privately raged against the Dominions for confronting them with demands that they knew made no economic sense. However, rather than return empty-handed and implicitly admitting that Imperial economic unity was, as their critics had long claimed, no more than an idle dream, they acquiesced in agreements with each of the Dominions which provided preferences at the expense of foreign countries.[54] To add insult to injury, they also joined in a statement that condemned, except in the most limited cases, regional trade agreements among foreign countries, such as the Oslo convention, which involved preferential treatment among the signatory countries.[55] One may surmise that Foreign Office officials winced on learning of the latter declaration, for as they privately acknowledged, it was the rankest hypocrisy for Britain to condemn others for seeking to do what had just been agreed to at Ottawa. At any rate, British policy had the effect of undermining support for the Ouchy convention. After convening the foreign ministers of the signatory states at The Hague in an unsuccessful attempt to hold them on course, F.B. von Blokland, the Dutch minister, wrote,

the British problem had played a major role. . . . Britain forms a bloc with the Dominions and has adopted an almost defiant attitude towards the Continent. . . . Britain also played a role in the sense that fear of Britain exercised a powerful influence over the Scandinavian delegates and that the shadow of Britain was constantly present like an uninvited and, in the circumstances, definitely unwanted guest.[56]

Students of British political history will be familiar with the aftermath of the Ottawa conference. The agreements aroused angry objections from the Liberal and Labour free traders within the Cabinet, and a minor crisis occurred when three of them – Snowden, Samuel and Sir Archibald Sinclair – resigned. This, however, was small beer compared to the impact of the agreements elsewhere in Europe and further abroad. Instead of providing a lead, as the Foreign Office and the Cabinet's panel of industrial advisers recommended, Britain had actually turned its back on Europe and even obstructed the alleviation of Europe's plight. Hopes that the Ouchy Convention might become the nucleus of an expanding trade bloc were destroyed. Confirmation that Britain would not tolerate preferential arrangements except those from which it benefited within the British Empire, together with invitations to the Scandinavian countries to prepare for bilateral trade negotiations with Britain, ensured that countries seeking to maintain or revive multilateral trade would do nothing to offend London. The Netherlands and several of the other Oslo countries were, however, sufficiently pessimistic of the results to begin to contemplate closer relations with Germany. Meanwhile Germany itself, with unemployment at nearly 25 per cent, experienced the politically devastating crisis that the Foreign Office had predicted the previous year. In July 1932, at the very nadir of the slump, the Nazi party made further gains in the Reichstag election, then with the economic decline at an end lost 2 million votes and 34 Reichstag seats in the election of 6 November. In retrospect it is evident that the tide had turned: Nazi support was declining throughout the country and its coffers were empty. Had the slump been even somewhat less severe or the recovery started earlier, the outcome might well have been different. But the situation was still obscure, and the result was to tempt conservatives to renew their invitation to Hitler to join the Nationalist party in government, and prompt Hitler to agree.[57]

Five years later Britain began to turn away from the Ottawa agreements and face up to the necessity for a continental military commitment. These shifts in policy, however, came only months before the outbreak of the war, and it is tempting to speculate that an economic or military commitment to Europe made earlier might have forestalled the conflict. It must be said that a continental military commitment lay so far outside British tradition as to be implausible in conditions short of acute crisis. An economic commitment, at least of a modest sort, is however another matter. From the end of the First World War British officials had actively promoted multilateral trade liberalisation, and from 1929 had been acutely concerned to hold back the tide of protectionism, particularly in Europe. Britain, as the world's greatest trading nation with interests in every part of the globe, naturally sought general acceptance of the most-favoured-nation principle in its unconditional form. But once it became clear that few European countries would join even in a tariff truce while the United States and other extra-European countries refused to participate, only two alternatives were left.

One was to continue to insist upon most-favoured-nation rights and watch the European countries retreat into narrow national protectionism, with the destruction of trade leading to mass unemployment, political extremism and the potential for international conflict, as liberals since Cobden had predicted would follow. The other was to seek to sustain international trade by agreeing in appropriate circumstances to the application of the most-favoured-nation principle on a conditional rather than unconditional basis, that is, where participating countries agreed to mutual tariff and non-tariff reductions, while keeping their agreements open to all countries prepared to make equivalent concessions. Had this required Britain to choose Europe over the Empire, then of course it would not have been practical politics in the early 1930s, but it did not. The principle, properly applied, would have served Britain's interests equally well by being approved by both groups of states.

The evidence suggests that most countries of Europe were ready and willing to proceed on the latter course, as Layton found to his surprise in 1931. It was advocated by the British government's business advisers in the spring of 1932, and the Cabinet's Ottawa Conference committee endorsed it in a general way. The Ouchy Convention, promoted by the Benelux countries in July 1932, offered precisely the framework for Britain's purposes: an open-ended, non-federal, liberal approach to the re-establishment of a European-wide market. Tragically, British ministers, more interested in their reputations at home than the wider interests of the country, overlooked it while allowing themselves to be bounced into the implicitly anti-European Ottawa project. One might well ask whether better leadership would have resulted in different choices with consequences sufficient to forestall Europe's slide into autarky and aggression. Of course, we shall never know. We do know that it was only after another 12 years and a second world war that Britain gained another opportunity to join its neighbours in constructing a prosperous, liberal Europe. Sadly, by that time the lessons of the inter-war years had been thoroughly obscured.

Notes

1. For example, C.E. Black and E.C. Helmreich, *Twentieth Century Europe, a History*, 3rd edn., New York: Alfred A. Knopf, 1966, a standard American university text, makes no

mention of the movement. Nor does D. Thomson, *Europe since Napoleon*, 2nd edn., London: Longmans, 1963, or even J. Joll, *Europe since 1870*, London: Weidenfeld and Nicolson, 1973, except cursorily in the context of the post-1945 movement (p. 461).

2. F. Siebert, *Aristide Briand 1862–1932: Ein Staatsmann zwischen Frankreich und Europa*, Erlenbach-Zürich: Eugen Rentsch Verlag, 1973, p. 512.

3. Thus, in March 1952, when the European movement was again vigorous, the twentieth anniversary of Briand's death passed unnoticed in Europe. *Ibid.*, p. 10.

4. Similarly reparations, an issue hitherto treated as a key security matter, is now also shown to have acquired its importance chiefly because of its effects on tax levels. B. Kent, *The Spoils of War; The Politics, Economics, and Diplomacy of Reparations, 1918– 1932*, Oxford: Clarendon Press, 1989.

5. See the useful but far from comprehensive bibliography in C.H. Pegg, *Evolution of the European Idea, 1914–1932*, Chapel Hill NC: University of North Carolina Press, 1983.

6. Sir Alfred Mond, *Industry and Politics*, London: Macmillan, 1927, p. 276.

7. *Documents on British Foreign Policy*, series 1A, vol. IV, London: HMSO, 1971, memorandum by M.H. Huxley, 8 September 1927, p. 8.

8. France, Ministère des Affaires Étrangères (hereafter MAE), Série Y internationale 1918–1940, vol. 639, Claudel to Briand, 13 September 1929.

9. France, *Journal Officiel*, Chambre de Députés, Paris: Imprimerie Nationale, 1929, statement by Briand, 31 July 1929, p. 2875.

10. League of Nations, *Official Journal*, Records of the Tenth Assembly, Plenary meetings, p. 36; France, MAE, série Y, no. 639, Claudel to Briand, no. 424, 13 September 1929.

11. Briand and indeed the whole French government strongly supported the policy of regional trade agreements in Europe 'comme une arme eventuelle contre le protectionisme des États-Unis.' France, MAE, série Y internationale, vol. 1398, Foreign Ministry to Serruys, 5 April 1929.

12. E. Bussière, *La France, la Belgique et l'organisation économique de l'Europe 1918–1935*, Paris: Ministère de l'Économie, des Finances et du Budget, 1992, p. 259.

13. As early as 1921 Briand had stated, 'We are caught between two formidable powers, the United States and Russia. It is indispensable to construct the United States of Europe with Germany.' Jacques Chabannes, *Aristide Briand, le père de l'Europe*, Paris: Perrin, 1973, p. 226. See also Siebert, *Aristide Briand*, pp. 515–16. On the American challenge of the 1920s, see R.W.D. Boyce, *British Capitalism at the Crossroads, 1919– 1932: a Study in Politics, Economics and International Relations*, Cambridge: Cambridge University Press, 1987, pp. 108–10 and passim.

14. League of Nations, Documents Relating to the Organisation of a System of Federal Union. VII. Political, 1931.

15. The most hopeful treatment is by Richard Lamb, *The Drift to War, 1922–1939*, London: Bloomsbury, 1991, pp. 43–45. Lamb blames 'British intransigence' for the failure of the Plan, but makes Britain's opposition less decisive than it actually was by identifying William Graham, president of the Board of Trade, and Lord Cecil, minister of state for the League of Nations, as enthusiasts for the Plan. Neither was enthusiastic.

16. Public Record Office, London, hereafter PRO, Cabinet (CAB) 24/205, C.P.209(29), memorandum by Graham, 15 July 1929.

17. R. Boyce, 'Britain's first "No" to Europe: Britain and the Briand Plan, 1929–1930', *European Studies Review*, vol. 10, no. 1 (1980), pp. 23–24.

18. Boyce, *British Capitalism at the Crossroads*, pp. 268–72.

19. R.W.D. Boyce, 'World Depression, World War: Some Economic Origins of the Second World War', in R. Boyce and E.M. Robertson (eds), *Paths to War: New essays on the origins of the Second World War*, Basingstoke: Macmillan, 1989, pp. 69–77.

20. Since Briand was always vague about his project it is difficult to be sure, but it seems likely that his intention, in the first instance, was to create a confederation of states.

However, he did seek to go beyond the traditional form of cooperation by creating common political institutions so as to promote an informal sharing of sovereignty. Like Jean Monnet, he anticipated that the habit of cooperation on the economic front and gradual economic integration would create the demand for political integration.

21. League of Nations, E.391, Comité Économique. 'La clause de la nation la plus favorisée dans les relations entre les accords plurilatéraux et les conventions bilatérales'. Rapport de M. Stucki.
22. PRO, Board of Trade (BT), 11/234, C.R.T.7094 (30), memorandum 'Commercial Policy', 5 April 1930.
23. PRO, Foreign Office (FO) 371/13587, C1427/718/62, Sargent to Board of Trade, 28 February 1929; ibid., C952/718/62, Sir H. Fountain (Board of Trade) to Foreign Office, 20 March 1929.
24. League of Nations, E/28ème session/P.V.1(1), Comité économique, Procès verbal de la première séance tenue le lundi 8 avril 1929 à 15 heures 30.
25. France, MAE, Société des Nations sous-série Secrétariat général, vol. 1402, Massigli circular letter, 18 March 1929.
26. PRO, CAB 23/65, 50(30)2, minutes, 2 September 1930.
27. G. van Roon, Small States in Years of Depression: the Oslo Alliance 1930–1940, Assen/Maastricht: Van Gorcum, 1989, pp. 6–11, 73 f.1.
28. PRO, Treasury (T) 160/392, F11300/03/3, Tyrrell to Henderson, no. 1034, 18 July 1929; ibid., Tyrrell to Henderson, no. 1077, 26 July 1929.
29. Boyce, 'Britain's first "no" to Europe', pp. 27–29.
30. Bussière, La France, la Belgique et l'organisation économique de l'Europe, pp. 331–35.
31. France, Ministère des Finances, B32290, 'Plan constructif français', 16 May 1931.
32. R.W.D. Boyce, 'Economics and the Crisis of British Foreign Policy Management, 1914–1945', in D. Richardson and G. Stone (eds), Decisions and Diplomacy: Essays in Honour of G.A. Grün and E.M. Robertson, London: Routledge, forthcoming.
33. PRO, FO 371/15689, W5150/1/98, Board of Trade memorandum to Henderson, C.R.T.1554/31, 2 May 1931.
34. PRO, FO 371/15697, W9109/7/98, Layton to Noel Baker, 15 July 1931.
35. League of Nations, C.510.M.215. 1931. VII, C.E.U.E./50, Report of the Sub-Committee of Economic Experts to the Committee on European Economic Union, 29 August 1931.
36. See for instance, League of Nations, C.33.M.17. 1932. VII, C.E.U.E./61, Austrian reply, 4 January 1932; ibid., C.E.U.E./62, Belgian reply, 4 January 1932; ibid., C.E.U.E./65, Yugoslav reply, 8 January 1932; ibid., C.E.U.E./66, Dutch reply, 12 January 1932.
37. PRO FO371/15699, W14012/7/98, Fountain (Board of Trade) to Foreign Office, 8 December 1931.
38. PRO, CAB 24/221, C.P.125(31), 'An Aspect of International Relations', memorandum by Sir Robert Vansittart, 14 May 1931.
39. PRO, CAB 24/225, C.P.301(31), 'Changing Conditions in British Foreign Policy, with reference to the Disarmament Conference, a possible Reparations Conference and other contingent Problems', 26 November 1931.
40. PRO, CAB 27/467, C.P.32(32), memorandum by the Home Secretary, 19 January 1932. See also CAB 24/223, C.P.243(31), 'The Present Situation', memorandum by the Home Secretary, 24 September 1931: CAB 27/467, B.T.(31) 2nd mtg., minutes, Balance of Trade committee, 8 January 1932; CAB 23/70, 5(32), appendix, 'Summary of Discussions on the Balance of Trade at the Cabinet on Thursday January 21, 1932'.
41. R.S. Sayers, The Bank of England, 1891–1944, vol. ii, Cambridge: Cambridge University Press, 1976, pp. 448, 450.
42. PRO, CAB 27/474, O.C.(31)53, memorandum by Dominions Secretary and President

of the Board of Trade, 7 June 1932. Representatives of all the peak industrial and commercial organisations were united in warning against a drift into narrow Empire agreements at Ottawa; see CAB 27/473, O.C.(31), 10th conclusions, 13 June 1932.

43. PRO, CAB 27/473, O.C.(31) 9th conclusions, 9 June 1932.

44. PRO, FO 371/16406, W3498/1167/50, minutes of Inter-Departmental Committee on Inter-Imperial Relations, 17 March 1932.

45. PRO FO 371/15208, C9461/8992/62, Leith Ross to Sir H. Hamilton (Board of Trade), 15 December 1931.

46. PRO, BT 11/223, C.R.T.2317(32), Leith Ross memorandum to President of Board of Trade, 14 April 1932.

47. *Ibid.*, C.R.T.2897(32), Sir J. Simon to Tyrrell, 21 April 1932.

48. van Roon, *Small States in Years of Depression*, pp. 39–44.

49. PRO T 160/486, F13017/1, Sir C. Wingfield to Simon, 28 June 1932.

50. *Ibid.*, pp. 45, 50–51.

51. See for instance, 'Freer Trade', *Manchester Guardian*, 21 June 1932; 'The Best News Yet', *News Chronicle*, 21 June 1932.

52. *Ibid.*, p. 52.

53. PRO, CAB 27/475, O.C.31(83), 'The Most-Favoured-Nation Clause in Commercial Treaties', 2 July 1932.

54. I.M. Drummond, *Imperial Economic Policy, 1917–1939: Studies in Expansion and Protection*, London: Allen and Unwin, 1974, p. 280 and passim; T. Rooth, *British protectionism and the international economy; overseas commercial policy in the 1930s*, Cambridge: Cambridge University Press, 1993, p. 95 and passim.

55. van Roon, *Small States in Years of Depression*, p. 79.

56. *Ibid.*, p. 53.

57. J.C. Fest, *Hitler*, Harmondsworth, Middlesex: Penguin, 1982, p. 348.

3

Britain and the World Disarmament Conference

Dick Richardson and Carolyn Kitching

Arguably, the problem of international disarmament was the most complex, intractable and potentially dangerous of any of the problems left unresolved by the Treaty of Versailles in 1919. Governments, statespeople, non-governmental organisations and individuals endeavoured for some 15 years to find an acceptable formula for international agreement. The climax of their labours was the World Disarmament Conference, held at Geneva from 1932–34. At this conference, Britain, and the other powers represented, discussed the momentous question of the distribution of world power and a realignment of the *status quo* based on the peace treaties of 1919. The failure of the conference marked a turning point in international relations. The post war world became a pre-war world.

Despite its importance, the problem of general disarmament between the two world wars has failed to interest historians, at least in Britain. Whereas the problem of naval disarmament has been well documented, most recently by Christopher Hall, the problem of general disarmament can be considered the least researched question of importance in twentieth century international history. It is almost 60 years since the World Disarmament Conference was the subject of a full-length published study – John Wheeler-Bennett's *Pipe Dream of Peace*. An equal length of time has passed since Rolland Chaput published a study of *British* disarmament policy in the inter-war period. Even academic articles on the subject are few and far between. The one major modern work, taken from primary sources, is Dick Richardson's *The Evolution of British Disarmament Policy in the 1920s*. As yet, there has been no full-length published study, or even a major academic article, on British policy at the World Disarmament Conference itself. The present paper aims to fill this gap.[1]

The dearth of secondary material on the disarmament problem can be explained by two main reasons. First, the amount of *primary* material available on the subject is so massive that it is almost a lifetime's work to research it adequately.[2] Second, with the significant exception of Richardson's study, there is an historical ortho-doxy on the subject stretching back to Wheeler Bennett and Chaput, which historians, inasmuch as they have tackled the disarmament problem at all, have felt unable or unwilling to challenge. Traditionally, the World Disarmament Conference has been analysed from the standpoint of orthodox diplomatic history, more especially in terms of the accession of Hitler to the German Chancellorship. Whilst not disparaging this approach, a number of considerations should be borne in mind. First, the agenda for the Disarmament Conference was set long before the Nazis achieved power. Indeed, the conference was in session for a full year (all but three days) before Hitler became Chancellor. German policy towards disarmament was firmly established under the Weimar Republic. Hitler merely took it over and refined it according to the perceived requirements of the day. If anything, the latest research, mostly undertaken in Europe, indicates that Hitler followed a softer line at Geneva than was advocated by his conservative predecessors and rivals and even his military advisers.[3] The present paper does not seek to duplicate this work, but to complement it by an analysis of *British* disarmament policy.

British policy itself has traditionally been approached from the standpoint of the armaments question in internal policy rather than the multilateral disarmament problem in external policy.[4] For example, the possible role of public opinion in 'imposing' a policy of unilateral arms limitation on the National Government of 1931–35 has been endlessly (and not entirely fruitfully) explored. Again, whilst not disparaging this traditional approach, there is a clear need for an alternative and complementary approach relating British multilateral disarmament policy to the technical and political problems of disarmament that formed the international disarmament agenda from the later 1920s onwards.

In the present paper, therefore, the question of British policy at the World Disarmament Conference is examined at two levels: the international problem, and technical policy. The first concerns the overall political problem emanating from the Treaty of Versailles in 1919. The second concerns the relationship of British policy on technical disarmament questions to the overall political problem. Within this framework, using the latest archival evidence from British sources, it will be shown that the traditional interpretation of British policy at the Disarmament Conference needs to be drastically revised.

The international problem

The problem of international disarmament in the inter-war years devolved from the Treaty of Versailles. Under Part V of the treaty, Germany was disarmed to the lowest limit consistent with the maintenance of internal order and the control of her frontiers. She was allowed to retain an army of no more than 100,000 men and was prohibited from possessing 'aggressive' weapons such as tanks, heavy guns, battleships over 10,000 tons, military aircraft and submarines. The Allied and Associated powers wanted to make it impossible for the new Weimar Republic to resume the policy of aggression which its predecessor had followed in 1914. However, to make the relevant clauses more palatable to Germany, it was stated in the preamble to Part V of the treaty that the arms reductions required were also intended 'to render possible the initiation of a general limitation of armaments of all nations'.

It was primarily upon the preamble to Part V of the Versailles Treaty that Germany was to base her claim for equality of rights with the other powers in the disarmament negotiations of the 1920s and early 1930s. Her interpretation, which was difficult to deny, was that the other nations had a moral, indeed legal, obligation to disarm in response to her own enforced disarmament. This interpretation was reinforced by the so-called 'Clemenceau letter' of 16 June 1919 by which the Allies stated specifically that the reductions required of Germany were

the first steps towards that general reduction and limitation of armaments which they seek to bring about as one of the most fruitful preventives of war, and which it will be one of the first duties of the League of Nations to promote.[5]

The Allies, however, did not put the same interpretation on the preamble to Part V of the Treaty, nor on the Clemenceau letter. They perceived that their obligation to disarm in 1919 was contained only in Article 8 of the Covenant of the newly-formed League of Nations, which stated that the maintenance of peace required 'the reduction of national armaments to the lowest point consistent with national safety and the enforcement by common action of international obligations'.[6] It was to be the duty of the League Council to formulate plans for 'the consideration and action' of governments.

If, in terms of legal obligation, it was from Article 8 of the Covenant that the discussions for a general disarmament convention devolved, in practice the impulsion behind the negotiations was the potential threat of Germany to the security system established by the Treaty of Versailles. As the years progressed, and German power grew in relation to that of Britain and France, more particularly as the United States isolated itself politically from European affairs, it became increasingly clear that, if the powers failed to negotiate a general convention, Germany would rearm unilaterally. In this sense, the disarmament problem was the problem of European security, and the problem of European security was the problem of German power.

Certainly this is how European statespeople and advisers perceived matters during the 1920s and early 1930s. At the same time, the disarmament question in practice was very much wider. There were genuine technical problems involved. There were the questions of political will and political leadership; of belief in disarmament and of perceptions of opposing parties' interests.[7] Above all, there was the question of whether or not the World Disarmament Conference could ever have been successful within its own terms of reference. It is often difficult for a handful of nations to reach a modicum of agreement on a restricted number of issues. For example, the five great naval powers were able to resolve the question of capital ships amongst themselves at the Washington Naval Conference of 1921–22, but failed to resolve the cruiser question, except for the imposition of certain qualitative limitations. In comparison, over 50 nations were represented at the World Disarmament Conference at Geneva, and the agenda covered all branches of the armed services, not simply naval armaments. This fact in itself gives some indication of the difficulties involved at the practical level – always given that the will to succeed was present.

By the time the Disarmament Conference assembled on 2 February 1932, international relations were in a state of confusion. Partly, this was a knock-on effect from the collapse of the international economy after the Wall Street crash of October 1929. But the rise of militarism and nationalism could be seen worldwide. In Germany, for example, the National Socialists had made significant gains in the Reichstag elections of September 1930. Democratic government had broken down. The Chancellor, Heinrich Bruning, was ruling by decree under Article 48 of the Weimar constitution. In South America, Bolivia and Paraguay were embroiled in their dispute over the Chaco. Even more alarmingly, Japan had embarked on a policy of military aggression in Manchuria. Effectively, the Japanese army was running the government rather than the government the army. This made it highly unlikely that Japan would sign a disarmament convention at Geneva. Yet if Japan refused to sign a convention, it was doubtful whether the Soviet Union would sign. And if the Soviet Union refused to sign, it was unlikely that the states on her western border – or, most important of all, Germany – would sign.

Nevertheless, even if a more general convention was unattainable, two possibilities remained. First, there might be an international convention restricted to a limited area (or areas) of armaments, for example a chemical weapons convention which extended the Geneva Gas Protocol of 1925. Second, there might be a general armaments convention restricted to western and central Europe. In the latter case, the central problem would be to equate the French demand for security with the German demand for equality of rights. This, indeed, was to be the essential feature of the search for agreement at Geneva.

The Franco-German demands were not incompatible. In fact, during the Lausanne conference in June 1932, there were direct talks between Edouard Herriot and Franz von Papen, French Prime Minister and German Chancellor respectively, for a disarmament agreement as part of a wider settlement covering the abolition of reparations and a Franco-German customs union. One of the principal reasons for these negotiations breaking down was the opposition of Ramsay MacDonald, the British Prime Minister, who was haunted by the spectre of a Franco-German alliance which would 'upset the balance of European power'.[8] However, the Herriot-Papen talks did not represent the mainstream line of advance towards a disarmament convention either for France or for Germany. Indeed, there was much opposition to the talks amongst nationalist forces in Germany in particular. At the same time, they illustrate the fact that the two continental powers were not averse to a disarmament agreement, recognising that through such an agreement they could both secure their interests. Both powers were prepared for an agreement, but preferred it to come through outside mediation rather than bilateral negotiation. Germany, in effect, wanted some kind of international endorsement of her equality of rights. France was prepared to reduce her military superiority over Germany, but only if she was given adequate compensation in the form of security guarantees by friendly powers.[9]

There were a number of possibilities. France could seek new or additional security guarantees from the United States, the Soviet Union, Italy, or Great Britain. She could seek to strengthen the collective security provisions of the League of Nations. She could press for tight provisions for verification in the proposed disarmament convention, and for automatic sanctions in case of violations of the convention. In practice, at various times and through various methods, she sought them all. For example, during 1931 she made approaches to Italy and the Soviet Union. Whilst not immediately bearing fruit, they were eventually to lead to the Laval-Mussolini agreements and Franco-Soviet alliance of January and May 1935 respectively. Primarily, though, France sought additional security guarantees from Britain, either directly, through military commitment, or indirectly, through the League of Nations or the disarmament convention. It would be too simplistic to suggest that the success or failure of the Disarmament Conference depended solely on Britain. But in practice, the resolution of Franco-German differences depended largely on the attitude adopted by British ministers on the question of security compensation for France.

The underlying problem faced by the British Government at the Geneva Disarmament Conference therefore was threefold. What should be the British attitude towards the German claim to equality of rights? What should be the attitude towards the French claim to security? And what compensations, if any, could Britain offer to France in return for reducing her margin of security over Germany? The answers to these questions had to be fitted into an international convention, within the overall context of Britain's worldwide security position. In this respect, the Government adopted a Eurocentric attitude. Despite the mounting crisis in the Far East, Britain more-or-less ignored Japan as far as the Disarmament Conference was concerned, except when the British delegation needed support on technical questions.[10] Similarly, while the Government attempted to maintain close relations with the United States, its prime objective was to prevent the Americans from putting forward proposals which adversely affected the British national interest. The Americans were regarded as untrustworthy, having an excessive rhetorical zeal for disarmament (especially in 1932, a presidential election year) whilst being unwilling to commit themselves to the European security system.[11]

The European problems facing the British Government at the Disarmament Conference were hardly new. They were intimately connected with the failed discussions for a Treaty of Mutual Assistance in 1923 and Geneva Protocol for the Pacific Settlement of International Disputes in 1924. They were apparent to the discerning from the moment the European security structure was settled at the Locarno conference of 1925. They had underlain the discussions in the Preparatory Commission for the Disarmament Conference during its four and a half years of labours from May 1926 to December 1930. However much successive governments tried to ignore them, or prevaricate, they would not go away. Neither the French nor the Germans would allow that to happen.

In practice, therefore, the discussions within the National Government concerning the Disarmament Conference were little more than re-runs of similar discussions in previous governments. An exception here must be made of the security and disarmament policy of the minority Labour administration of 1929–31. The Foreign Secretary in the Labour Government, Arthur Henderson, was much more favourable towards the concept of collective security and the possibility of increasing the powers of the League than his Conservative predecessors. He had even expressed sympathy with the idea of security compensations for France in return for concessions to Germany on disarmament, and his ability to gain the confidence of international statespeople had been instrumental in his being made chairperson of the Disarmament Conference.

The fall of the Labour Government in August 1931 represented a severe setback for disarmament. The chairperson of the Disarmament Conference no longer had the power of the British Government behind him, rather he was a solitary individual who could cajole and encourage the powers represented at the conference but effectively had no power to influence decisions. Moreover, there was much bad feeling between the incoming National Government and Henderson. Prime Minister Ramsay MacDonald adopted a particularly cold attitude towards his former Foreign Secretary. Largely this was because of the circumstances surrounding the demise of the Labour administration and Ramsay MacDonald's so-called betrayal of his former Labour colleagues.

On the surface, the fact that MacDonald remained Prime Minister appeared to offer hope that disarmament would be taken seriously by the National administration. Certainly MacDonald professed a sincere belief in disarmament, and had successfully promoted the London Naval Treaty in his Labour days. In 1932, however, he was little more than the nominal figurehead of a basically Conservative, anti-disarmament coalition with a majority of 497 in the House of Commons. Moreover, his ideas regarding the key problems facing the Disarmament Conference offered little hope that these problems could be resolved. He was scarcely an impartial arbiter of Franco-German differences, for, although he recognised the problems of France's feelings of insecurity, he was less than sympathetic to their demands for additional guarantees. He recorded in his diary on 24 January 1932 that the French were 'tricky, selfish and unscrupulous; they were out to dominate Europe and keep Germany underfoot' and that 'The diplomacy of France is an ever-active influence for evil in Europe.'[12] Such was his objectivity at the outset of the conference, though as the conference progressed he slowly began to accept that success would be possible only if some concession was made to the French view. Similarly, while he was rather more sympathetic to the general principle of Germany securing equality of rights, he was reluctant to assert this publicly, partly for fear of annoying the French and partly in case it might give rise to demands for equality of armaments rather than equality of rights. Thus rather than advocate a policy of active British mediation in the Franco-German dispute, he stated in a letter to the Air Minister, the Marquess of Londonderry that 'We need at Geneva, a policy quietly pursued without turning off our way to right or left. . .'[13] As late as December 1932, after Germany had left the Disarmament Conference for the first time, the British Prime Minister was still pursuing the same line. He commented lamely to French and German ministers that he wanted them to 'put their demands in such a way that Britain could say that she supported both sides'.[14]

Stanley Baldwin, Lord President of the Council, leader of the Conservatives in the National administration and effective power behind the scenes, took little interest in foreign affairs or disarmament but shared MacDonald's views of the French. He is reputed to have said to a friend 'One of the things that comforted me when I gave up office was that I should not have to meet French statesmen any more.'[15] He was particularly averse to French demands for increasing security through the League of Nations, and regarded the Geneva Protocol, so beloved by the French, as a 'quagmire'.[16] Although, during the 1920s, he regularly visited Aix-les-Bains, only a few miles from Geneva, he deliberately shunned the League and its proceedings. He was also opposed to French demands for security beyond the Locarno guarantees. The guarantees had been negotiated during Baldwin's second premiership, but he accepted them not so much because they represented an answer to the European security problem, but because they preserved Cabinet unity.[17] He would not willingly reopen the security question in the changed circumstances of 1932, even to secure a resolution of the disarmament problem.

The Foreign Secretary was Sir John Simon, perhaps the foremost lawyer of his time but with little experience of foreign affairs or disarmament.[18] He recognised the Franco-German problem very clearly and believed that Germany had 'quite a strong moral case, even if her legal one is invalid', but at the same time regarded the French concern for security as perfectly natural.[19] The problem was that he was unwilling to accept the logical policy for resolving the problem – active mediation between the two continental powers. Instead, he adopted the same line as MacDonald and Baldwin, pontificating in favour of Franco-German reconciliation whilst effectively leaving the two powers to their own devices. He later gained the reputation of being the most disastrous Foreign Secretary in the twentieth century. As regards the disarmament problem, that reputation is not undeserved.

If the three leading members of the Cabinet were united in not facing up to the real issues of the Disarmament Conference, the same can be said of most of the other members of the policy-making elite. Of many examples, perhaps the most illustrative is that of J.H. Thomas, Secretary of State for the Dominions. Representing his country at the opening of the Disarmament Conference, he was faced by a demand for greater security by the French Prime Minister, Andre Tardieu. His only comment, on hearing the translation of Tardieu's remarks was 'Oh 'ell'. This was translated back to Tardieu as 'Mr Thomas had listened with great attention and interest and would report faithfully to his colleagues.'[20] The fact was that Thomas, like MacDonald, Baldwin and Simon, either could not see the intrinsic link between security and disarmament, or was unwilling to accept its consequences.

At the same time, the existence of the Franco-German problem did not go unrecognised. Both France and Germany constantly referred to it. So too did Alexander Cadogan, the chief Foreign Office adviser on the disarmament problem. The Cabinet discussed it as early as 15 December 1931, during the run-up to the Disarmament Conference. Crucially, it was decided that Britain could not accept commitments in addition to Locarno which might involve the country in European war. The decision effectively sounded the death knell of the conference even before it had started. As Sir Robert Vansittart, Permanent Under Secretary at the Foreign Office and no lover of disarmament, pointed out in a note for Simon on 23 December 1931:

If His Majesty's Government take the Disarmament Conference seriously, then they must take the question of the security guarantee seriously also. If we are not seriously considering the question of the security pact, then our attitude towards the Disarmament Conference is not wholly sincere. We are giving it lip service only – knowing in our hearts that it is bound to fail.[21]

The Cabinet further discussed the question of guarantees on 13 and 20 January 1932, prior to the drafting of instructions to the British delegates at the Geneva Conference. But it avoided the real question at issue – French security in relation to Germany – by bringing up the question of a 'Mediterranean Locarno': French security in relation to Italy! Ultimately, even this concept was rejected, and so Britain entered the Disarmament Conference with no effective policy on the most crucial question facing the conference.

The extent of France's security demands depended on three factors which individually and collectively changed during the Disarmament Conference: the political persuasion of the French government; the nature of the German government; and the extent to which individual disarmament proposals reduced French military superiority over Germany. From the French point of view, the most desirable outcome was a system of collective security under the general auspices of the League but with non-League powers associated. Paul-Boncour put forward such a plan on 14 November 1932. Failing this, the French would have eagerly accepted either an Anglo-French alliance or military back-up to Locarno. Nevertheless, throughout much of the conference, France was willing to accept rather less in the way of compensation than any of these possibilities, providing the provisions for verification in the disarmament convention were tight enough.[22]

The French, of course, were in the unenviable position where they could not be precise about their security demands until they knew the precise nature of Germany's claim for equality. The Germans, however, followed a policy of reacting to other powers' proposals rather than putting forward proposals themselves. Both diplomatically and militarily, it was more advantageous to them to say 'not enough' to the proposals of other powers than to formulate a defined position. They wanted always to ask for 'more'. Germany, in fact, attempted to use the Disarmament Conference as a cover for the pursuit of her rearmament.[23] At only one point during the conference did they put forward a specific proposal for an overall settlement. This was in April 1932, when the Chancellor, Heinrich Bruning, endeavoured to gain a disarmament settlement at Geneva to preserve his precarious position at home. The Nazis had just made considerable gains at provincial elections in Prussia, Bavaria, Wurttemburg, Anhalt and Hamburg, and he determined to outflank them by returning to Berlin with an agreement securing equality of rights.

On 26 April 1932, Bruning put forward his proposals in a conversation with MacDonald and the American Secretary of State, Henry L Stimson, preparatory to a further meeting on 29 April which would include the French Prime Minister, André Tardieu. In private, at Stimson's villa at Bessinges, he insisted that he would be satisfied with a reduction in the period of service of the Reichswehr from twelve years to six and a reduction in the armed forces of France – though not to the German level – through the abolition or restriction of 'particularly aggressive' weapons. Equality of rights would be secured through the transfer of Germany's disarmament obligations from Part V of the Treaty of Versailles to the proposed disarmament convention, which might last for ten years. In return, Bruning was willing to consider an agreement along the lines of the Tardieu Plan of 5 February 1932 for an international force, with the ultimate objective of abolishing the weapons under its control.[24]

In the circumstances of the time, the Bruning Plan appeared to be very moderate. It satisfied Germany's claim for equality – temporarily at least – whilst assuring France of military superiority in Europe for a period of ten years. MacDonald and Stimson, while not specifically accepting the plan, agreed that the discussions of 26 April had helped 'towards immediately clearing away some of the fundamental obstacles towards ultimate agreement'.[25] Success depended on the negotiations with France scheduled for 29 April. Tardieu, however, was unable to journey to Geneva because of an attack of laryngitis (real or diplomatic, depending on the source) and two days later his government was defeated in the first round of the French general election. Any chance of agreement simply melted away.[26] Within a month, Bruning had been replaced by the more militant nationalist administration of Franz von Papen.

Opinions vary as to the possibility of an agreement based on the Bruning Plan. Many who were close to the personnel involved, for example the political commentator John Wheeler-Bennett and the military adviser to the British delegation, A.C. Temperley, believe the Bessinges conversations were a lost opportunity. Both attack MacDonald and Stimson for their failure to press Tardieu into attending the 29 April meeting.[27] Tardieu's position is interesting. He was a hard-line conservative, and was worried that any appearance of concessions on the German claim to equality might cause his defeat in the French elections of 1 May. Certainly it would have been difficult for him to backtrack on his security plan of 5 February in the middle of an election campaign. But that does not mean he was unwilling to make concessions if he had won an electoral victory. He was aware that Bruening might be replaced by a more aggressive nationalist, and from conversations at Geneva in March and April, it does seem that he was willing to reduce his security demands on Britain and the United States well below those put forward on 5 February.[28] As far as Britain is concerned, the indications are that MacDonald was relieved that Tardieu did not appear at Geneva on 29 April. He did not relish the possibility of being faced with security demands which, although pitched at a lower level than a month previously, might still be higher than those which the Cabinet had only recently rejected. In this sense, the Prime Minister's failure to press Tardieu to return to Geneva becomes understandable. His desire to avoid new security commitments was greater than his desire to promote disarmament.

The 'April episode' is extremely informative. Whilst ostensibly acting as mediator between France and Germany, Britain deliberately shunned this role. The explanation is simple. Any realistic proposal would raise the question of taking on a security commitment to equate French security with German equality. It was for this reason that the Disarmament Conference became bogged down during the summer of 1932, leading the new German government under Papen to withdraw from the Conference on 23 July on the grounds that no effective progress had been made towards an agreement securing equality of rights. Even after formally accepting the demand for equality, in the Five-Power declaration of 11 December 1932, the Government waited another three months before producing a disarmament plan of its own. Or rather the Government's junior ministers produced a draft convention in which their seniors had singularly little faith: the inappropriately-named MacDonald Plan.

The draft convention was formulated by the British delegate to the Disarmament Conference, Anthony Eden, together with Alexander Cadogan and the government's service and legal advisers in Geneva. Presented to the conference personally by MacDonald on 16 March 1933, it went some way towards meeting the German claim for equality of rights. But it proposed little more for French security than a consultative pact in case of a breach or threatened breach of the Briand-Kellogg Pact of 1928. The Government was still not prepared to make a meaningful concession on security to bring about a disarmament agreement. This is hardly surprising. As far as government ministers – as distinct from their junior advisers in Geneva – were concerned, the real reason for presenting the MacDonald Plan was to avoid Britain being blamed for the failure of the conference. As MacDonald himself admitted in a letter to the King, three days before presenting the plan at Geneva:

The British plan was a stop-gap, designed not to achieve disarmament, but to prop up a conference which everyone knew to be disintegrating.[29]

The Government's lack of belief in disarmament in general, and the British draft convention in particular, was further underlined on the day following its presentation, 17 March. Instead of staying in Geneva to push forward the convention, MacDonald and Simon departed for Rome for talks with Mussolini about a Four-Power Pact. Publicly, the Government continued to support the Geneva conference; privately, the majority of ministers acted on the assumption that it was dead. But they were unwilling to take responsibility for officially killing it.

As the conference progressed, the question of security compensation for France was to reassert itself on a number of occasions. But on each occasion, Britain's elemental response was that she could undertake no further continental commitments. Even after the drastic deterioration of international relations during the late summer and autumn of 1933, the Government was reluctant to broach the question of security. The French, by this time, were wanting 'guarantees of execution' – the application of sanctions – in the event of a violation of the convention. But on 20 September 1933 the Cabinet decided that all that should happen in such a case would be that other parties to the convention would be discharged from their obligations. In other words, states would be called upon to resume the arms race.[30]

Technical policy

If the underlying premises on which the Government based its disarmament policy were incompatible with the success of the Geneva conference, so too was Britain's position on individual issues of arms limitation. At Geneva, the British delegation became isolated, following policies which had little, if any, chance of being accepted; policies which, arguably, were against the national interest and which ran counter to the Government's overall aim of avoiding blame for the failure of the conference. At the same time, this is not altogether surprising. Even before the Disarmament Conference opened, it was clear that the Government's policy was to rest, not on the production of a programme based on the international realities of the time, but on the myth of Britain's unilateral disarmament. The Air Minister, the Marquess of Londonderry, for example, liked to give the impression that Britain had carried out a programme of disarmament in the years following the Versailles Treaty and that all that was required was for other powers to follow the British lead.[31] Nothing could be further from the truth. British arms reductions during this period had nothing to do with a quest for multilateral disarmament. They were practical measures taken only after careful examination of existing political, economic and strategic circumstances.[32] In practice, the Government was sceptical of multilateral disarmament, but adopted an armaments policy based on the concept of minimum perceived requirements.

At a time when reductions in government expenditure were perceived to be a panacea for all economic ills, most governments throughout the world formulated their armaments policies on a similar basis to the British. It is sometimes argued that, in the 1920s, Britain carried her arms reductions to a far greater extent than any other power, except for the states which had arms limitations forced on them by the peace treaties of 1919. In a quantitative sense, there is a germ of truth in this suggestion; in relation to plausible security threats, the matter is, to say the least, debatable. The myth of unilateral British disarmament in the 1920s has been exploded.[33] Still, at the outset of the Disarmament Conference, the main concern of the Government was that the British public accepted the myth. As MacDonald stated at a Cabinet meeting on 14 January 1932:

[The British programme] might be lacking in positive new proposals, but the sentiment and the intentions behind it were excellent. The delegation ought to emphasise the fact that we had not waited for the Disarmament Conference before disarming, and to describe the situation which had been reached as the results of our efforts. In this respect we had a magnificent case. Whether other nations believed us or not was not very material, provided that the whole case were put and reached our own public.[34]

A generous interpretation of this statement would suggest that Mac Donald had merely confused the armaments question in British domestic policy with the problem of multilateral disarmament in external policy. A less generous interpretation would suggest that British policy at Geneva was a charade, a public relations exercise masking the fundamental reality that Britain intended to increase her armaments.

Certainly this was the position of the service ministers and their departments. Whilst claiming that existing armaments were adequate to undertake existing commitments in Europe, for the purpose of the Disarmament Conference they suggested that additional armaments were necessary to obtain a minimum of security. But then, it had been a longstanding policy of the service departments to use disarmament conferences to advocate *increases* in armaments. For example, at the time of the Geneva Naval Conference of 1927, the Admiralty had claimed that Britain needed a minimum of 70 cruisers to ensure British security on the high seas – as against the 48 cruisers in commission and the 60 maximum that would be achieved at the contemporary building rate.[35]

At the World Disarmament Conference in 1932, the Government followed a policy of advocating reductions in armaments by France and a near standstill by Germany, whilst keeping schemes for increasing British armaments secret. When formulating the British draft convention in February 1933, Eden and Cadogan wanted to be open about British rearmament. For example, they included figures in the convention for British armaments as well as those of the continental powers. However, they were overruled by their superiors. The Ministerial Committee on Disarmament decided to omit the figures for Britain, since the figures involved increases for Britain but reductions for most other powers, France in particular.[36]

Britain's plans for rearmament did not simply concern effectives, they concerned tanks and military aircraft. Such plans placed the Government in a quandary. After formally accepting the demand for equality of rights for Germany in the Five-Power declaration of 11 December 1932, the hope was that Germany would limit herself to equality in principle, qualitative equality (the theoretical right to possess the same armaments as other powers, as distinct from quantitative equality) and equality of armaments. The Government acknowledged that the Germans had already undertaken a modicum of rearmament in breach of the Treaty of Versailles, but saw no reason why these limited contraventions could not be incorporated within a disarmament treaty. But the more Britain increased her armaments, the less chance she would have of constraining Germany's quantitative demands.[37] And the more concessions Britain made to Germany on quantitative matters, the more the French would raise counter-demands on security which the Government was not prepared to meet. However, the problem of British armaments was not simply quantitative; it was political and technical. In this respect, the Government was faced with a series of issues at the Disarmament Conference which exposed the contradictions of the British position and led to the British delegation becoming isolated at Geneva. Limitations of space preclude an analysis of all such questions, but an evaluation of three key issues – tanks, air disarmament and verification – will illustrate the point.

Germany was prohibited from possessing tanks and military aircraft under the terms of the Versailles Treaty. Yet, if equality of rights were to be accorded to her, there was no reason in principle why she should not be allowed to possess them. In the absence of a general prohibition of these weapons, therefore, the question at issue was the extent to which the Germans would seek to translate principle into practice. In April 1932, Bruning said he would be content with 'samples' of any weapon not prohibited by international convention, without specifying the exact quantity involved.[38] This was to remain the nucleus of Germany's demands under both Papen and Hitler.

Many delegations at Geneva supported the complete abolition of tanks, not only as a means of securing equality for Germany but as a means of disarmament. The United States supported abolition in the Hoover Plan of 22 June 1932. So too did Italy, the Soviet Union and the great majority of the smaller powers. Certainly, as a means of disarmament, abolition could be supported on two major grounds. It secured the elimination of a whole class of weapons which were regarded as offensive rather than defensive; and it was easier to verify than a mere restriction of tanks to an agreed number. Two major powers were opposed to abolition – Japan and France. The Japanese opposed abolition directly, but the French, very astutely, advocated the abolition of tanks in 'national armies' whilst allowing 'specialised contingents' under League of Nations authority to be armed with them – along with other heavy weapons.

Although the French objective on the tank issue was to retain a considerable superiority in *matériel* over Germany, there was at least a logic in their concept of an international force being equipped with heavier weapons than were permitted to national armies. The British position defied any such logic. The service line, accepted by the Government, was that light and medium tanks of a maximum of 16–20 tons provided necessary compensation for the manpower constraints of a voluntarist army. Far from wishing to abolish tanks, the services wanted to increase their number from some 208 to 550.[39] But adhesion to this line made British policy at Geneva untenable. If Britain claimed an increase in tanks, under the principle of equality a given number could hardly be denied to Germany. This in itself went against British policy, which sought to restrain rather than increase German armaments; for if rearmament were conceded to Germany, the French would demand increased guarantees of security. In practice, the situation was compounded because the Government defended the decision to retain tanks on the grounds that 16–ton tanks were 'defensive' whilst heavier tanks were 'offensive'.

Yet if 16–tons tanks were classed as 'defensive', Germany could legitimately demand an unrestricted number!

The Government was not entirely unaware of the predicament in which it had placed itself. Certainly Simon was aware of it as early as 3 November 1932.[40] The situation became serious when the British draft convention was being formulated. Something had to give. Britain had three main options: give up the retention of tanks; refuse to implement equality for Germany in respect of tanks; or accept a degree of German rearmament. The first course of action was considered impossible because of British security needs. The consequences of the second course – a possible German withdrawal from the Disarmament Conference only three months after being enticed back with the formal concession of equality – could not be faced. The decision, therefore, was to accept a degree of German rearmament and face a possibility of further French demands for security compensation. Under the MacDonald Plan, tanks with an unladen weight of over 16 tons would be prohibited, and all prohibited *matériel* – tanks *over* 16 tons – would be destroyed within three years of the convention coming into force.

In the British draft convention, Germany was accorded full equality of rights in tanks under 16 tons, although the Government hoped she would restrict her demands numerically. But as actual and suspected Nazi violations of the Versailles Treaty increased in number during the spring of 1933, the Germans made it clear that their demands for 'samples' would be higher rather than lower. The British on the other hand felt less and less inclined to agree to 'samples' at all. The Cabinet endeavoured to find a way out of its straitjacket, but its lame solution was to leave discussion of the question, inasmuch as it was possible, to the German, French and American delegations![41] It was a policy of vacillation: hoping for the best whilst anticipating the worst.

Throughout the World Disarmament Conference, Britain was isolated in wanting to retain tanks of 16 tons. The limit of 16 (occasionally adjusted to 20) tons was a purely artificial figure calculated to allow Britain to retain the tanks she wanted whilst expecting other states to eliminate their heavier tanks. In other words, together with Britain's associated but undisclosed quantitative demands, it was a question of the Government attempting to use the Disarmament Conference to improve Britain's world-wide power position: arms increases for Britain, arms reductions for others. There was simply no way the other powers would allow this to happen.

The position was very similar regarding air disarmament. In effect, the Government's air proposals, like the tank proposals, were designed to improve the relative power position of Britain. Whereas, at the time, Britain was the fifth-ranked air power, the Air Ministry hoped to use the Disarmament Conference to make Britain the top power. The idea was to demand equality with other powers in Europe and then claim additional aircraft for use in the Empire.[42]

Politically, it was impossible to put forward such a programme at Geneva, as the Air Minister, the Marquess of Londonderry, realised. His ploy, therefore, in the Government's pre-conference discussions, was to accept the theoretical need for qualitative restrictions on aircraft, whilst opposing all measures which did not fit in with the underlying objectives of the ministry. In this, he was so successful that, effectively, the Government entered the Disarmament Conference with no policy on air disarmament at all. On a number of occasions, the British delegates had to refer back to London for instructions. The result was that the agenda for air disarmament at Geneva was set by other powers, notably the United States with the presentation of the Hoover Plan on 22 June 1932. In his plan, Hoover proposed the complete abolition of bombing aircraft and aerial bombardment, though reconnaissance planes would be allowed. This question was to remain the key question for air disarmament throughout the remainder of the conference.

At first sight, it seemed that such a proposal was clearly in Britain's interest. Since Britain ranked as the fifth power in terms of military aircraft, the equalisation of air forces at the level of zero would theoretically improve Britain's relative position among the great powers. Besides, at a Cabinet Meeting on 5 May 1932, Baldwin had himself put forward a proposal for the abolition of military and naval aviation coupled with a scheme for controlling civil aviation.[43] The Foreign Office, War Office and Admiralty also supported abolition, the latter two departments because of inter-service hostility and a wish to deflect disarmament proposals onto the junior service.[44] However, by the time the Hoover Plan emerged, the Air Ministry view had prevailed, Londonderry having convinced the Cabinet that the internationalisation of civil aviation was impossible and that without control of civil aviation the abolition of bombing would be impossible. The ministry also pointed to the fact that using the air force 'for police purposes' in areas such as Iraq and the North West Frontier was far cheaper and more effective than using ground forces. Thus, when the Government circulated its 'Statement of Views' on the Hoover Plan on 7 July, Britain effectively rejected the American President's air proposals. Instead of accepting the abolition of the bomber, the Foreign Secretary suggested merely a quantitative restriction of the numbers of military and naval aircraft, together with a qualitative restriction on their unladen weight. Instead of a prohibition of bombing, he suggested that limits be laid down as to where bombing could be permitted.[45]

Yet, if bombers were not to be abolished, under the principle of equality Germany would have to be accorded the same theoretical rights to military aircraft as the other powers. This, clearly the Government did not want, partly as a matter of principle, partly because of the reaction of the French and the likelihood of additional demands for security. As with tanks, there was a need to square the circle. Consequently, in a Cabinet memorandum of 28 October 1932, Simon outlined a plan whereby Germany would be allowed theoretical equality but denied any aircraft at all in practice, pending an enquiry into the abolition of military and naval aviation and the internationalisation of civil aviation.[46] The Cabinet's proposals were set out in detail in the British draft convention of 16 March 1933, the MacDonald Plan. Except for troop-carriers and flying boats, aeroplanes were to be limited to 3 tons in laden weight, and each of the great powers assigned 500, with another 25 per cent in immediate reserve. Pending the international enquiry, Germany would not be allowed to possess any.[47] Bombing was to be prohibited 'except for police purposes in certain outlying regions', a reservation insisted upon by the Air Ministry but which negated the very objective of the proposal.

The British air proposals were so obviously designed for Britain's advantage that the Government rapidly became isolated at Geneva. The quantitative proposals would have taken Britain from fifth to first place in the ranking of air power. At one point, Allen Leeper of the Foreign Office calculated that, in effect, Britain was asking France to reduce the number of her aircraft from 1,800 to 500, and the other great powers proportionately, while the British Commonwealth figure would be raised from 1,000 to something in the region of 1,250–1,400.[48] Similarly, the qualitative restrictions were designed so that Britain would have to scrap only a handful of existing aircraft whereas other powers would have had to scrap many. But above all, Britain's 'police bombing' reservation was so patently insincere that it defied the imagination. What territories in the British Empire would have the rather dubious honour of being an outlying region? Were such regions to be specified in the convention? Would other states be allowed 'outlying regions'? On this issue, the British became the laughing stock of Geneva. As Temperley observed:

We were actually attaching more importance to preserving the amenities of being bombed for a few Pathan and Iraqi villages and to keeping the control of civil aviation in our own hands than to joining the rest of the civilised world in a practical attempt to remove the menace of the bombing aeroplane.[49]

Besides, there was never any hope that the Germans, having been granted theoretical equality, would forgo their claim for 'samples'. The only question here was the number that would be claimed. By the middle of May 1933, the Germans were estimated to have some 125 fighting machines in existence or under construction.[50] This being the case, they were likely to demand a similar number of 'samples' in order to cover their covert rearmament. In the circumstances, the continuing advocacy of an international enquiry into the possibility of abolishing all military and civil aviation, during which period the Germans were to possess no military aircraft whatsoever, was a substitute for a policy rather than a policy itself. Vacillation once again: hoping for the best, expecting the worst.

From a political point of view, British policy on the tank and air questions can be considered to be against the national interest. By isolating Britain at Geneva, the Government put itself in the very position it wished to avoid: that of assuming maximum responsibility for the breakdown of negotiations. But, even on military grounds, the British position can be criticised. Temperley's comment has already been noted. Basil Liddell Hart's conclusion goes even further. Writing in 1961, he argued:

If tanks and bomber-aircraft had been universally abolished in 1932 as was then proposed – and nearly agreed – and a system of international inspection established as a check on their revival, there could have been no successful *Blitzkrieg* in 1939–40.[51]

British policy was no different regarding verification itself. This question acted as a touchstone for the seriousness with which delegations approached the disarmament problem. Without proper verification provisions, there was no way of ensuring that a convention was being adhered to; no way of exposing a party which infringed the convention; no way, if necessary, of applying sanctions against a recalcitrant party. The French, throughout the World Disarmament Conference, pressed for the tightest verification provisions as a means of ensuring their security against Germany. During the summer of 1933, there were indications from both Paris and Geneva that France would relax her demands for formal security guarantees if the verification procedures were adequate. Lord Tyrrell, ambassador at Paris, suggested in a despatch of 7 June 1933 that verification was perhaps the key to an agreement at Geneva, with the French reducing their demands on other points of contention if the question of supervision was resolved to their satisfaction.[52] Eden, in Geneva, reached a similar conclusion and proposed that Britain make concessions to the French point of view.[53]

What the French were demanding were provisions for regular, periodic and automatic on-the-spot investigations built into the convention. Unless they could be satisfied that Germany would fulfil her obligations under the convention, there was no way the French were going to reduce their military superiority over Germany by any significant amount. From a disarmament point of view, verification can be used as a substitute for trust, and can itself *produce* trust. But the British armed services did not see matters this way. They were opposed to on-the-spot investigation, regular or otherwise. The Admiralty took a particularly strident line declaring that 'If countries act in good faith, supervision is unnecessary – if not, it is useless.'[54]

The service objections to verification were many. Verification would reveal British secrets – though not, apparently, the secrets of other powers, as Britain would be honest while other powers would not![55] It would infringe national sovereignty, require investigations into private companies, reveal a lack of reserves and essential defence preparations, undermine the Official Secrets Act and even (according to Eyres-Monsell) be 'rather degrading'.[56] Certainly the lengths to which the services would go in their efforts to oppose verification were extraordinary. On one occasion, a certain Capt. Bent of the Admiralty asserted:

from the point of view of language, a member of this country serving on a commission in Japan would have far more difficulty in obtaining information than a Japanese serving on a commission in this country.[57]

The attitude of the service departments towards verification was intrinsically connected with their attitude towards disarmament *per se*. They were opposed to disarmament, and therefore to verification. But logically, as they admitted, the most intense form of verification was the most effective from a disarmament point of view. Thus, if any real disarmament measures were to emerge from Geneva, it was likely that the most intense form of verification needed to be applied. In the circumstances, there is little wonder that the British services opposed continuous and automatic verification procedures with such tenacity. Agreement on verification might bring about agreement on disarmament!

At the outset of the Disarmament Conference, the Cabinet fully supported the service line regarding on-the-spot verification, regular or otherwise. However, as the conference progressed, under pressure from Geneva, the Government was forced to modify its attitude. In November 1932, it accepted the *principle* of on-the-spot investigation, but continued to oppose it becoming continuous and automatic. At the time, the British position was generally supported by the

American, Italian and German delegations, and there appeared to be no question of British isolation at Geneva. However, events in Germany during the summer of 1933 convinced both the Italians and Americans that continuous and automatic verification was essential if a disarmament agreement was to be obtained. The Americans accepted the principle in May, the Italians in September. The Germans, meanwhile, had accepted it in July 1933, and even the Japanese maintained a studious neutrality on the question. Britain was, quite literally, out on a limb at Geneva.

In September 1933, therefore, to outside observers and, more significantly, to the British delegation at Geneva, the British Government appeared to be the major obstacle to an international disarmament convention. The Government had boxed itself into a corner on the questions of tanks, air disarmament and verification. The Cabinet, even more unsure than ever as to how to handle the situation, sought a means of escape. It was offered by the French. The French, fully aware that the MacDonald Plan gave them no real security compensations in return for a diminution of their power in relation to Germany, produced their own disarmament plan, disguised as amendments to the MacDonald Plan. In effect, the five-year convention envisaged in the MacDonald Plan was converted into an eight-year convention divided into two equal parts. The first stage of the convention would constitute a four-year 'trial period' during which the verification procedures would be tested for effectiveness. It was only after these procedures had been declared acceptable that France would start reducing her armaments in order to facilitate equality of rights.[58]

During conversations in September 1933, the Americans and Italians accepted the French amendments. The idea was to present a united front to Germany: either accept the agreed plan or assume responsibility for breaking up the Disarmament Conference. For the British Government the French scheme was a godsend. The Cabinet was freed from its dilemma of being isolated at Geneva on the most important questions of disarmament. Britain could go along with France, Italy and the United States in a united front on the principle of the four-year 'trial period' whilst still maintaining reservations on the exact nature of the verification procedure and individual questions of armaments.

In one sense, ministers had a choice: continue with the MacDonald Plan for 'equality of rights' in five years, and face the concomitant demand for security from the French, or accept the French amendments as the basis of the convention. They chose the latter. But the demand for a 'trial period' of four years would effectively have put the Germans on probation, with no control over whether or not they had fulfilled their requirements at the end of four years. Equality of rights had moved further from their grasp – and they voiced their disapproval by walking out of the Disarmament Conference, and the League on 14 October. They had good reason to do so. In July 1932, Hitler's conservative predecessors had withdrawn from the conference because little or no progress had been made in some five months of discussion. In October 1933, Hitler could justifiably complain that the western powers, Britain in particular, had gone back on their word regarding equality of rights. If, as it seems, the British Government accepted the French amendments merely to escape their own dilemma and to place the onus of responsibility for the breakdown of negotiations on Germany, they were following a naive and dangerous course of action.[59] The predictable result was that not only did the conference fail but that Britain was seen to bear a great deal of responsibility for that failure.

Conclusion

In effect, Britain had no disarmament policy at the World Disarmament Conference. It had an armaments policy based on the myth of British unilateral disarmament and the desire to rearm. There was a distinction between rhetoric and reality. The Government paid lip-service to international disarmament for internal political reasons whilst following policies designed to improve Britain's position relative to the other major powers. It wanted to use the conference to legitimise British rearmament, in the same way that the German Government wanted to use the conference to legitimise German rearmament. British ministers wished to avoid being blamed for the failure of the conference. On no occasion did the Government evaluate, from the point of view of high political strategy, what gains, if any, Britain might make under a disarmament convention; or what losses, if any, it might suffer. The Cabinet did not even address the fundamental question of whether an international disarmament agreement, with adequate provisions for verification, might serve British interests better than the anarchy of the arms race (which was the realistic alternative.)

From the outset of the Disarmament Conference, the Government based its policy towards the international problem on the premise of no security guarantees in Europe additional to those given at Locarno. But this premise, firmly embedded in the Cabinet decision of 15 December 1931, effectively killed the conference before it had started. The chief problem facing the conference was the Franco-German problem; the problem of equating German equality with French security. The only realistic way in which this could be resolved was through Britain giving additional guarantees to France in compensation for a reduction in French superiority over Germany. Yet it was this concession which Britain continually refused. The most that Britain was prepared to offer was the consultative pact envisaged by the MacDonald Plan; but this was lip-service to the concept of security in the same way that Britain's disarmament proposals were lip-service to the concept of disarmament. There was little, if any, value in the consultative pact as far as the French were concerned. By refusing to take the problem of security seriously, in fact by trying to ignore it altogether throughout most of the conference, Britain ensured that the conference would not be successful.

Paradoxically, the nearer the Disarmament Conference came to success on individual technical points, for example on tanks and the abolition of military aviation, the greater became the gap between the necessities of an international convention and the political and military assumptions of the Government. The greater, too, the steps required by the Government to bridge that gap. The Government had no intention of bridging it. Instead, it followed a policy of vacillation, of avoiding decisions. Decisions required commitment, and any move towards German equality would require an equivalent commitment to French security. Conversely, a move towards French security would require an equivalent commitment to German equality. The Government was both unwilling and unable to square the circle.

If the Government had one overriding aim, it was to avoid responsibility for the anticipated failure at Geneva. The minutes of the Cabinet and Ministerial Disarmament Committee are littered with references to this aspiration. From the standpoint of the Cabinet – as distinct from Eden, Cadogan and Temperley in Geneva – the MacDonald Plan, Britain's one major contribution to the Disarmament Conference's proceedings, was primarily a face-saving device to avoid responsibility for failure. The Government's acceptance of the French amendments to the MacDonald Plan had a similar aim. It was an attempt to force Germany into accepting a disarmament convention on worse terms than under the MacDonald Plan; or, if she refused, into assuming responsibility for the break-down of negotiations. The move backfired. Not only did Germany withdraw from the Disarmament Conference, she withdrew under conditions whereby Britain acquired a major responsibility.

The conventional view of British policy at the Disarmament Conference is that the Government actively pursued a disarmament agreement at Geneva, and adopted the role of mediator between France and Germany. This perception must now be revised. Ministers misconstrued the nature of the disarmament problem and adopted policies on individual questions which had little or no chance of acceptance. They deliberately shunned the role of mediator. It was over 13 months before Britain produced a draft disarmament plan, or rather the Government's junior advisers produced a plan in which their seniors had no faith at all: the MacDonald Plan. Throughout the conference, British policy was one of vacilla-tion: hoping for the best, anticipating the worst, avoiding blame. In the light of Britain's rearmament proposals, disguised as disarmament proposals, it was a policy which verged on duplicity. The reality is that Britain must bear a much larger responsibility for the failure of the Disarmament Conference than has hitherto been assumed.

Notes

1. See Christopher Hall, *Britain, America and Arms Control 1921–37* Basingstoke: Macmillan, 1987; J. Wheeler-Bennett, *The Pipe Dream of Peace*, New York: Fertig, 1971 (reprint); Rolland A. Chaput, *Disarmament in British Foreign Policy*, London: Allen & Unwin, 1935; Dick Richardson, *The Evolution of British Disarmament Policy in the 1920s* London: Pinter, 1989. The latter should be consulted for a full bibliography concern-ing British disarmament policy in the 1920s.

   In addition to the above works, the following academic articles should be noted: Dick Richardson, 'Process and Progress in Disarmament: some lessons of history' in V. Harle & P. Sivenon, *Europe in Transition*, London: Pinter, 1989 and 'The World Disarmament Conference 1932–34' in D. Richardson and G. Stone (eds), *Decisions and Diplomacy*, London: Routledge (forthcoming).

   Chapters 3 & 4 of David J. Whittaker's *Fighter for Peace: Philip Noel-Baker 1889–1982* (York: Sessions, 1989) are informative and useful, but Noel-Baker's semi-autobiographical *The First World Disarmament Conference 1932–33*, Oxford: Pergamon, 1979, leaves much to be desired. A more informative memoir is that of Salvador de Madariaga, head of the Disarmament Section of the League of Nations Secretariat, *Morning without Noon*, Aldershot: Saxon House, 1974. An older memoir, still extremely useful is A.C. Temperley, *The Whispering Gallery of Europe* London: Collins, 1938. See also J.J. Underwood, *The Roots and Reality of British Disarmament Policy 1932–34*, unpublished PhD thesis, University of Leeds, 1977.

2. Madariaga once calculated that a single sub-committee of Sub-Commission A of the Preparatory Commission for the Disarmament Conference used enough League of Nations paper during its deliberations – which lasted only three months – to allow the Polish delegation to make the return journey from Warsaw to Geneva treading on League paper all the way!

3. See, e.g., Maurice Vaisse, *Securite d'Abord* Paris: Pedone, 1981. On German disarmament policy, see, e.g., Michael Geyer, 'The Dynamics of Military Revisionism in the Interwar Years: Military Politics between Rearmament and Diplomacy' in Wilhelm Deist *The German Military in the Age of Total War*, Oxford: Berg, 1985, also the first two chapters of Deist's *The Wehrmacht and German Rearmament*, Basingstoke: Macmillan, 1981. Further papers of note by Deist are 'Internationale und nationale Aspekte der Abrustungsfrage 1924–1932' in H. Roessler (ed.) *Locarno und die Weltpolitik 1924–1932* Gottingen: Musterschmidt-Verlag 1969; 'Bruening, Herriot und die Abrustungsgesprache von Bessinge 1932' in *Vierteljahrshefte fur Zeitgesichte*, vol. 5, 1957, pp. 265–72 and 'Schleicher und die deutsche Abrustungspolitik im Juni/July 1932' in ibid, vol. 7, 1959, pp. 163–76. See also E.W. Bennett, *German Rearmament and the West 1932–1933*, Guildford: Princeton University Press, 1979.

4. It is especially important to emphasise the distinction between the armaments question in internal policy and the disarmament question in external policy because ministers often confused them by their indiscriminate use of the term 'disarmament' to cover both aspects of policy.

5. Reply of the Allied and Associated Powers to the observations of the German delegation on the conditions of peace, *Papers relating to the Foreign Relations of the United States, Diplomatic Papers*, (hereafter cited as FRUS) Paris Peace Conference, 1919, vol. 6, pp. 954–6.

6. The Treaty of Peace, 28 June 1919, *Parliamentary Papers*, Cmd. 153 of 1919.

7. For a brief analysis of the importance of these five factors in international disarmament negotiations, see Richardson, 'Process and Progress in Disarmament: Some Lessons of History', in Harle and Sivenon, op. cit.

8. See Notes of an Anglo–French–German conversation, 27 June 1932, *Documents on British Foreign Policy 1919–1939* (hereafter cited as DBFP), series 2, vol. 3, no. 150. Also Edouard Herriot, *Jadis*, Paris: Flammarion, 1952 p. 345; Franz von Papen, *Memoirs*, London: Andre Deutsch, 1952, pp. 181–2.

9. For a fuller analysis of French and German policy at the Disarmament Conference, see Richardson 'The World Disarmament Conference 1932–34' in Richardson and Stone, op. cit. Also Vaisse, op. cit.

10. There is only one reference to the Far East and Japan in the Cabinet Minutes. The final conclusion was that the situation 'required further exploration' (document in the Public Record Office, London, hereafter PRO, CAB23/70, 19(32)2, 23.5.32).

11. On this point, with particular reference to the Hoover Plan of 22 June 1932, see, e.g., Noel-Baker, op. cit., ch. 10; Hall, op. cit., pp. 125–8; Underwood, op. cit., pp. 107–10.

12. Quoted in David Marquand, *Ramsay MacDonald*, London: Cape, 1977, p. 717.

13. Marquess of Londonderry, *Wings of Destiny* London: Macmillan, 1943, p. 56.

14. Record of a Five-Power Meeting, 6 December 1932, DBFP. series 2, vol. 4., no. 211.

15. Quoted in N. Rostow, *Anglo-French Relations 1934–35*, Basingstoke: Macmillan, 1984, p. 247.

16. Baldwin to Austen Chamberlain, 6 September 1927, *Austen Chamberlain Papers*, PRO FO 800/261.

17. See Richardson, *The Evolution of British Disarmament Policy in the 1920s*, ch. 4.

18. In his recently published biography of Simon, David Dutton notes Simon's desire for disarmament, on the grounds of reduction of expenditure, as early as 1922. David Dutton *Simon: A Political Biography of Sir John Simon* London: Aurum Press, 1992, pp.

57–8. This desire, however, is quite distinct from experience in actually achieving any such reduction.
19. Summary of Discussion on Disarmament Policy, Meeting 8 December 1931, *Simon Papers* PRO FO 800/285; Sir John Simon, *Retrospect*, London: Hutchinson, 1952 p. 186.
20. David Dilks (ed.), *The Diaries of Sir Alexander Cadogan 1938–45*, London: Cassell, 1971 p. 7.
21. Notes by Vansittart, 23 December 1931, *Simon Papers*, PRO FO 800/285.
22. For a full analysis, see Vaisse, op. cit.
23. On this point see Richardson *The Geneva Disarmament Conference 1932–34* in D. Richardson and G. Stone, op. cit.
24. Conversation among members of the American, British and German delegations, 26 April 1932, FRUS, 1932, vol. 1, pp. 108–12. Temperley, op. cit. p. 203.
25. Gibson to Acting Secretary of State, 29 April 1932, FRUS, 1932 vol. 1, pp. 112–14. Hugh Gibson was the principal American delegate to the Disarmament Conference.
26. On this point, see Deist, 'Bruening, Herriot und die Abrustungsgesprache von Bessinge 1932' in *Vierteljahrshefte fur Zeitgeschichte*, vol. 5, 1957, pp. 265–72.
27. Temperley, op. cit., p. 204; Wheeler-Bennett, op. cit., p. 34.
28. Gibson to Stimson, 17 March 1932, FRUS, 1932 vol. 1, pp. 54–59; Gibson to Acting Secretary of State, 21 April 1932, ibid., pp. 104–6; Basil Liddell Hart, *Memoirs*, vol. 1, London: Cassell, 1965, pp. 194–5.
29. Quoted in Marquand, op. cit., p. 754.
30. PRO CAB23/77, 51(33)2, 20 September 1933.
31. See Londonderry, op. cit., chs. 3–5.
32. See Richardson 'Process and Progress in Disarmament: Some Lessons of History', in Harle and Sivonen, op. cit. p. 38.
33. See Richardson, *The Evolution of British Disarmament Policy in the 1920s*.
34. Ibid., PRO CAB23/70, 3(32)3, 14 January 1932.
35. For an analysis of British policy at the Geneva Naval Conference, see Richardson, *The Evolution of British Disarmament Policy in the 1920s*, ch. 9.
36. See, especially, meetings 14 and 15 of the Ministerial Disarmament Committee, PRO CAB 27/505. It should be noted that the draft convention allowed a moderate increase for Germany (200,000 men against the 100,000 allowed under the Peace Treaty) but this quantitative improvement in the German position was offset by the qualitative deterioration imposed by the introduction of short-term service.
37. See, for example, PRO CAB 23/76, 38(33)3, 31 May 1933; PRO CAB 27/505, DC(M)32, 15th Meeting, 7 March 1933; PRO FO 371/17381, W2879/117/98, 2 March 1933.
38. Temperley, op. cit., p. 203.
39. PRO FO 371/17360, W6215/40/98, 30 May 1933.
40. PRO CAB 21/354.
41. PRO CAB23/76, 38(33)3, 31 May 1933.
42. PRO DC(P)36, CAB 16/102.
43. PRO CAB23/71, 26(32)2, 4 May 1932.
44. PRO CAB24/229, CP 164(32), CP 176(32) and CP 182(32), respectively.
45. League of Nations, *Records of the Conference for the Reduction and Limitation of Armaments: Conference Documents*, vol. 1, pp. 265–8.
46. PRO 24/234, CP 360(32).
47. The text of the British draft convention can be found in T.N. Dupuy and G.M. Hammerman, *A Documentary History of Disarmament and Arms Control*, New York and London: Bowker, 1973, pp. 221–38.
48. PRO FO371/17359, W5754/40/98, 6 May 1933.
49. Temperley, op. cit., p. 274.

50. PRO CAB24/239, CP 129(33), enclosure.
51. Basil Liddell Hart, *Deterrent or Defence*, London: Stevens, 1960 p. 250.
52. PRO CAB27/509, DC(M) (32)50.
53. PRO CAB24/242, CP 159(33).
54. PRO CAB27/509, DC(M) (32)15.
55. See ibid.
56. See, e.g. ibid; also PRO FO 371/17372, W13235/40/98, 19 November 1933. Eyres-Monsell's remark was made at the 17th meeting of the Ministerial Disarmament Committee, PRO CAB 27/505.
57. The remark was made at the first meeting of the Ministerial Disarmament Committee's sub-committee on supervision, PRO CAB 27/515.
58. *Documents Diplomatiques Francais 1932–1938*, Series 1, vol. 3, document no. 229.
59. PRO CAB 23/77, 51(33)2, 20 September 1933.

4

British reactions to the Jewish flight from Europe[1]

Louise London

Introduction

The exodus of Jewish refugees from Nazi Europe which took place in the years 1933 to 1939 was not a unified movement, but a series of flights and attempts at flight. Successive outbursts of anti-Jewish persecution in Germany and extensions of Nazi rule to new territories impelled more and more Jews, in different parts of Europe, to seek refuge abroad. In Britain, reactions to these developments followed a cycle of crisis and adjustment. Each new step in Nazi persecution of Jews caused a sharp increase in the pressure for admission of refugees, which was in turn met by a response at the level of policy. Home Office ministers and officials, pre-occupied above all with achieving firm immigration control, took the lead in formulating the government's response. They reviewed immigration procedures in the light of the new pressures and adjusted them if this was thought necessary. The adequacy of the system might then not be further examined until a subsequent crisis raised the question again.

This paper is concerned with objectives of British government policy on Jewish refugee admissions to the United Kingdom and with the extent to which those objectives were realised. It argues that the British response may be broadly characterised as one of containment: to confine the refugee problem to Europe, while letting some refugees come to Britain. The broad objectives of the government remained the same during the period, but its methods of containment changed. These changes are analysed in the paper, which divides the British response to the refugee movements of the pre-war period into two phases. The distinguishing factor between the two phases is that in the first phase the majority of would-be refugees were not required to obtain visas, while in the second phase a visa requirement was imposed. The earlier phase commenced in the spring of 1933, as refugees began to flee persecution in Germany. In this phase, which lasted just under five years, control was exercised without requiring holders of German passports to obtain visas. In each of the five years from 1933 to 1937 between one and three thousand refugees from Germany arrived at the ports without visas. Most sought entry as visitors and nearly all were admitted.

Developments which occurred in March–May 1938 marked the end of the first phase and the start of the second. In response to a new Jewish exodus after the Austrian *Anschluss* of March 1938, the British government introduced a crucial modification in immigration control procedures, designed to stem the flow of refugees into Britain. A system of mandatory pre-selection of refugees abroad was imposed. From May 1938, holders of German and Austrian passports were required to obtain British visas prior to setting out. In the months that followed, the onward march of Nazism on the Continent produced an expansion and intensification of the refugee crisis. A new refugee emergency in Czechoslovakia in September–October 1938, followed by the *Kristallnacht* pogrom in Germany in November and its aftermath of persecution, created further demand for refugee admissions to Britain. Many more Jews were now desperate to escape from areas under Nazi control. At this juncture, pressure on the British government to adopt a more generous policy reached an unprecedented level and, following Cabinet discussions, a number of changes were made in British admissions policy and procedures, in order to facilitate an increase in the rate of entry. The vast majority of the refugees who succeeded in obtaining a haven in the United Kingdom entered during the ensuing nine months. The Home Office later estimated that when war broke out in September 1939 some 78,000 refugees had been present in Britain, of whom perhaps 70,000 were Jews. The 78,000 refugees comprised 55,000 adult Germans and Austrians, 10,000 Czechs and 13,000 unaccompanied children, plus unspecified numbers of children who had come with their parents.[2] These figures represented a compromise between the government's response to the pressure for admissions and its aim of trying to maintain firm control over numbers. The numbers were far higher than had been intended. During the war, Home Office ministers and officials, anxious to reduce the number of refugees in the country, devoted much ingenuity to facilitating refugee emigration from Britain: by the war's end they had succeeded in bringing the numbers down by at least 13,000.[3]

The developments outlined above occurred within the framework of existing British immigration law and refugee policy. The next few pages of this chapter will attempt to place the response to the Jewish influx in context, by providing a short outline of British immigration law and the position of asylum seekers, followed by brief observations on the nature of British policy on refugees. The remainder of the chapter is devoted to the history of the controls on the refugees from Nazism.

Immigration Law and the position of asylum seekers

The Home Office had no departmental responsibility for the plight of Jews in Europe. It aimed to maintain firm control on refugee admissions to the UK, in accordance with its duty to enforce immigration control over aliens generally. Modern immigration controls in Britain commenced with the Aliens Act, 1905, the result of anti-alien agitation, much of which reflected hostility to recent Jewish immigrants.[4] The 1905 Act introduced selective port controls aimed at excluding destitute and diseased aliens. Included in the new law was a concession which permitted the entry of refugees who failed the standard poverty test.[5] During the First World War normal immigration was suspended; soon afterwards, under the

Aliens Restriction (Amendment) Act 1919, all legal protection for refugees was abolished, together with all rights of appeal.

The state nonetheless still possessed the right to grant asylum if it saw fit. Home Office spokesmen claimed that they exercised this discretion sympathetically, thereby ensuring that the pre-1905 tradition of granting political asylum was being maintained in practice.[6] This British tradition was repeatedly invoked on occasions when the country's response to refugees from Nazism was debated in Parliament and elsewhere. Pro-refugee groups argued that British policy should conform more closely to the tradition by being more generous. Home Secretaries of the inter-war period asserted that their policies respected the tradition of asylum, but the substance of what they said rarely amounted to more than saying that the government was treating refugees no worse than other aliens. Such claims by Home Secretaries that their policy continued the tradition as far as possible continue to the present day.[7]

The era of mass immigration for settlement had ended with the First World War. After 1919 a system of tight controls on all passengers formed an effective barrier against unwanted alien immigrants. The detailed requirements for admission were contained in the Aliens Order, 1920, under which most aliens needed to prove that they could support themselves, or that they had a permit from the Ministry of Labour if coming to work. Certain refugees were eligible under these requirements, but many more could not fit into the limited categories of entry in the immigration rules.

British policy on refugees

The British government did not have a refugee policy, nor a policy of asylum, but a policy of containment. The problem of Jewish refugees had been caused by Germany and it was felt that the German government had the prime responsibility for solving it. The British government had no strong domestic imperatives for finding a solution. Britain had near-impregnable sea defences against the entry of unwanted immigrants. Unlike countries of refuge on the European mainland, she was spared the difficult task of policing land borders. France, for example, found that problems of unwanted refugees overlapped with a pre-existing problem of illegal immigration. British policy-makers, cautious about undertaking new obligations in Europe, argued that none of the objectives of British foreign policy required the United Kingdom to solve refugee problems on the Continent. The Jewish refugee problem was not a British problem; the overriding aim was to avoid its becoming so.

To have a refugee policy at all was seen as giving hostages to fortune. The best way to preserve both sovereignty in the international sphere and freedom in domestic policy, so far as the refugee issue was concerned, was to keep policy on refugees to a minimum. To do otherwise, so British policy-makers argued, would only perpetuate the problem.[8] In the mid–1930s emigration arrangements funded by private individuals and charitable bodies were expected to succeed in disposing of, or 'liquidating' – to use a term favoured by certain experts – the refugee problem.

British policy aimed at discouraging the further growth of refugee problems in Europe. To this end, strenuous efforts were made to show that Britain would not be blackmailed into accepting the burden of unwanted Jewish populations, whether from Nazi Germany, Poland or Rumania, especially if Jews were forcibly expelled in a state of destitution. The Foreign Office therefore opposed British involvement in financing Jewish refugee emigration from German territory; it also opposed the large-scale expansion of opportunities for the permanent emigration of destitute refugees. Financial support for refugees would, it was feared, tempt the Poles and other governments to step up persecution of Jews, in the hope of making them leave. These principles provided the underlying logic for the Foreign Office's apparently ambivalent and contradictory approach to the work of the Intergovernmental Committee (IGC).[9] The IGC had been set up in mid–1938 by the Evian Conference on refugees. Its brief was to foster orderly migration, through persuading the German government to allow Jews to emigrate with enough capital to shield them from destitution. The IGC, however, failed to achieve tangible improvements in emigration opportunities: success in this field remained the preserve of non-governmental organisations.

Within the British government, aid to refugees was given low priority. Policy initiatives as well as administration were left to officials and to the voluntary organisations – Jewish, Christian and non-sectarian. Mere humanitarian consider-ations were not seen as a proper basis for policy but were subordinated to immigration policy.[10] The government utilised the existing restrictive immigration laws and rules to deal with the Jewish influx. In cases where the government was prepared to try to mitigate a particular aspect of the problem, or take a generous view of a particular case, it acted by means of discretionary exceptions. Concessions such as this did not set precedents and could be withdrawn or modified at will, thus avoiding the imposition of fetters on the government's sovereignty or freedom of manoeuvre. If British interests appeared to require moves to restrict refugee admissions, the necessary steps were taken. Britain, as government spokesmen constantly reiterated, was not a country of immigration for settlement.[11] Accordingly, for those Jewish refugees who entered the country, the role of the United Kingdom was generally perceived as being limited to that of a country of transit or first refuge.

The first phase: control without visas, 1933–1937

The Jewish exodus of 1933 presented the government with three options concern-ing British immigration procedures. One option was to modify the system to exclude refugees. A second was to facilitate their entry. The government chose a third alternative, which was to leave the system formally unchanged. The selection of the 'no change' option was consistent with the Home Office view that adequate powers were available to deal with the influx and that the additional restriction of re-introducing obligatory visas for all holders of German passports was therefore not necessary at this juncture.[12] Consequently, refugees holding German pass-ports could still present themselves for admission at British ports, without having first been obliged to obtain a visa at a British post abroad. The government's 'no change' policy was an interim decision, subject to review; in the event, it was left unaltered for nearly five years.

Yet, an initiative by leaders of Britain's Jewish community had led to an informal change of great significance. Jewish leaders were far from wishing to relive the experience of the years before 1905, when unrestricted mass Jewish immigration from Eastern Europe had been an embarrassment and a burden to members of the older-established Jewish community. On the contrary, the leaders of Anglo-Jewry were anxious to control and limit Jewish immigration, which they feared might provoke manifestations of anti-Jewish feeling.

Close cooperation over aliens matters between the Home Office and Jewish organisations was well established by this date.[13] A notable example of this co-operation was the Jews' Temporary Shelter (JTS) in London's east end, which handled the community's policy towards poor Jewish transmigrants. Officials of the JTS met transmigrants at the ports and interceded with the immigration authorities on their behalf.[14] Once admitted, many poor transmigrants were accommodated and fed by the JTS, whose concern extended to making sure that their guests left on the due date to continue their journey overseas.[15]

At the forefront of such Jewish charitable work for aliens was Otto Schiff, a Frankfurt-born city stockbroker, whose links with the Home Office were especially close. Schiff was President of the JTS at the time when German Jews first arrived in Britain fleeing persecution in early 1933 and he lost little time in founding the Jewish Refugees Committee. Shortly afterwards, Schiff joined three leading figures from the Jewish Board of Deputies in making an approach to the Home Office with proposals to contain the influx. The Jewish leaders asked the government to grant entry and extensions of stay to German Jewish refugees; in return, they offered on behalf of the Jewish community a guarantee to bear 'all expense, whether temporary or permanent accommodation or maintenance, . . . without ultimate charge to the state'; they also promised to look after refugees while they were in the country, and to arrange for their re-emigration.[16] Schiff had predicted that a maximum number of about 4,000 would come to Britain. However, the government, concerned about the unknown dimensions of the continuing exodus from Germany, decided against a relaxation of existing immigration controls. Jewish leaders were nevertheless told that their guarantee might be used in considering individual cases.[17]

The authorities had so far refused admission in only a handful of refugee cases. Nearly all suspected Jewish refugees were admitted; however, under a recent change in practice, they were being treated as problematic visitors. In the early 1930s the vast majority of aliens were still admitted to Britain subject to no immigration conditions of any kind. The imposition of 'precautionary landing conditions' – time limits permitting only a short stay and restrictions on taking employment – was generally reserved for the small minority of alien entrants whose cases appeared to present potential problems of control. The immigration authorities had, however, recently started to subject all German Jews to strict landing conditions of this type; and ministers decided that this practice should continue. A further precaution agreed at this stage was a requirement that new arrivals register with the police immediately, rather than after the usual three months.[18] Thus, although the existing system was still formally unchanged, it was being more strictly applied in the cases of suspected refugees.

However, in cases covered by the Jewish guarantee, permission could be granted more freely. Over the next five years the guarantee underpinned the admission of numerous refugees. For the Home Office, the great attraction of the guarantee was the offer of finance, which gave the government solid insurance against the risk of admitting refugees who might become destitute. It would even cover persons already admitted. Furthermore, the Home Office's undertaking to take the existence of the guarantee into account when considering individual cases did not bind it to admit anyone. Thus, it had incurred no specific obligations in connection with the guarantee, but had obtained instant benefits. The solution of the immediate problems of control and the limited influx which followed were regarded as satisfactory by the authorities. Yet the question of what would be done with refugees in the long run remained unresolved.

Cabinet ministers were aware that benefits might be obtained for Britain by offering a haven to distinguished Jews from Germany, where they faced persecution and the termination of their careers under the anti-Jewish laws of the Nazi regime.[19] However, the British government took no formal initiatives in this area itself. A new voluntary body, the Academic Assistance Council (AAC), later the Society for the Preservation of Science and Learning (SPSL), was founded by William Beveridge, then director of the London School of Economics, to help displaced scholars and scientists to come to Britain.[20] Only a minority of the academic refugees were allowed to take permanent jobs and settle. The majority could take only temporary jobs; they were increasingly advised to re-emigrate and many did so, for the most part going on to the USA.[21]

Despite high unemployment in Britain, Home Office and Ministry of Labour officials exercised discretion to let certain refugees enter employment, even if they could not comply with the regulations designed to protect the home labour force.[22] The authorities also agreed to a Jewish Refugees Committee training scheme designed to help young people already in Britain to acquire new skills which might increase their chances of emigration.[23] Publicly, the government maintained a cautious and conservative stance, reluctant to admit how many refugees were coming in, or how many were Jews. The Home Office did not wish to draw attention to *Jewish* refugees as a distinctive problem and refused to keep statistics on Jewish immigration, but obtained figures for its own purposes from the refugee committees.

The voluntary organisations co-operated closely with the Home Office. Officials developed friendly and informal links with a select group drawn from the refugee organisations and relied on them increasingly, both to manage refugee casework and to provide control. The authorities expressed confidence that, with the help of the voluntary organisations, they could cope with the refugees, who were largely of the professional classes, and many of whom could be absorbed.[24] As one Home Office official put it later, the refugees who came during the first five years had not occasioned 'any real anxiety either as regards number or quality'.[25] But British representatives vigilantly opposed any changes to international conventions on refugees which would oblige the United Kingdom to admit further refugees or to grant permanent settlement to refugees present in the country on a temporary basis.[26]

During the early years of the Hitler regime the belief that German anti-Jewish persecution might abate was widely held. The intermittent character of Nazi persecution, in which outbursts of violence alternated with legal discrimination, fed hopes of stabilisation, if not improvement.[27] In 1934, for example, such hopes led many Jewish refugees to return to Germany from abroad during a lull in extreme persecution; they included several hundred from Britain.[28] Records from the Jewish Refugees Committee (JRC) show that from 1933 to the end of the year 1938, out of 5,566 German refugees who re-emigrated from Britain, 2,304 persons – some 40 per cent of the total – returned to Germany.[29]

Widespread revulsion was felt in Britain at Nazi outrages against Jews.[30] Certain British observers nevertheless described Jewish unpopularity in Germany in terms which came close to accepting that anti-Jewish prejudice was natural.[31] After the *Kristallnacht* pogroms in 1938, for example, the Prime Minister, Neville Chamberlain, privately expressed himself unable to understand these acts of barbarity, which he condemned; he accepted, however, that prejudice against Jews was understandable and acknowledged that he himself felt it.[32] He appeared to accept Nazi anti-semitism as a fact of life and saw no need for it to lead to such an outrage as a pogrom. Nazi outrages stood in the way of Chamberlain's objective of establishing better relations with Germany. British foreign policy makers of the 1930s believed such relations were possible, if the extremes of persecution could only be contained. One of their main concerns was to contain the diplomatic repercussions of the refugee issue in order to minimise damage to Anglo-German relations.[33]

Anglo-Jewish leaders also hoped that Nazi persecution would abate. Such hopes faded, however, particularly after the Nuremberg laws of September 1935, which excluded Jews from German citizenship and social life. Jewish leaders decided to foster mass emigration of German Jews, launching the Council for German Jewry (CGJ) in early 1936, to help 100,000 younger German Jews emigrate overseas. But where to? Asylum in countries of first refuge such as the United Kingdom, which strictly limited new alien immigration, was seen mainly as a transitional stage for Jews from Germany. Jewish leaders and the British government gave high priority to keeping down numbers of refugees in the United Kingdom, which was intended to play only a peripheral role as a refugee haven. The consensus within the Anglo-Jewish leadership that the prime refuge should be Palestine enabled Zionists and non-Zionists, despite their differences, to co-operate in organising the settlement of German Jews in Palestine. In the early years the British government facilitated this process. Perhaps 40,000 Jews from Germany settled in Palestine prior to the end of 1937, compared with an estimated 10,000 then present in the United Kingdom. After this, however, the British government subjected immigration to Palestine to increasing restriction.[34] The Empire contained little else in the way of refuge. Jewish plans for organised schemes of refugee emigration from Britain and the Continent to the British dominions and colonial empire foundered on the objections of the governments concerned, although several thousand individual German Jews succeeded in entering South Africa and Australia.[35]

The second phase: from the Anschluss to the war

The imposition of visas

The start of the second phase, in which British controls were tightened through the introduction of mandatory pre-selection, came in March–May 1938, after the German annexation of Austria. The Home Office swiftly pushed through the reintroduction of obligatory visas for holders of German and Austrian passports.

The aim of this change was to control the pressure for entry as increasing numbers of Jews tried to escape from Nazi Europe. More and more refugee Jews were being made stateless, in law or in fact. This made them very hard to get rid of, once admitted to a country of refuge.[36] Furthermore, the Jewish refugee organisation had swiftly withdrawn its all-important guarantee from future arrivals, unless cleared with them first. This meant that future admissions of non-guaranteed refugees risked becoming a charge on the public purse, a development the Home Office was determined to avoid.[37] In early April, the Home Secretary, Sir Samuel Hoare, explained the new procedures, which had not yet been made public, to a deputation of Anglo-Jewish leaders. He warned that:

It would be necessary for the Home Office to discriminate very carefully as to the type of refugee who could be admitted to this country. If a flood of the wrong type of immigrants were allowed in there might be serious danger of anti-semitic feeling being aroused in this country. The last thing which we wanted here was the creation of a Jewish problem. The Deputation said they entirely agreed with this point of view.[38]

Otto Schiff, who was present, endorsed the reintroduction of visas, saying how difficult it was to get rid of refugees once they had come to Britain. He claimed that Austrians, especially, were largely shop-keepers and traders, with poorer re-emigration prospects than Germans.[39]

New instructions were issued to Passport Control officials in Germany and Austria. The new rules stated that applicants for visitors' visas who were Jewish, or who had 'non-Aryan affiliations', should be questioned closely about their intentions, since they were likely to be refugees. Once it had been established that a person was a suspected or self-confessed refugee, the case was categorised according to a two-tier system which had one rule for the unwanted masses and another for the privileged few. The rank and file of applicants whose occupations were in small-time commerce or the professions were normally to be excluded. However, visas might be given to an elite consisting of prominent individuals in the worlds of science, medicine, the arts, or the academic world, and to refugee industrialists who might invest in Britain.[40] The instructions thus reflected the continuing readiness on the part of the British government to permit and even encourage the entry of selected 'desirable' individuals from among the refugee masses. The Home Office also experimented, not very successfully, with methods of detecting refugees who posed as visitors.[41]

Long queues of desperate would-be refugees became a familiar sight outside British consular offices in the Third Reich. Applicants waiting long hours in the street provided obvious targets for harassment by local Nazis. Inside the consular buildings, insufficient staff struggled with unprecedented numbers of new visa applications.[42] Serious bottle-necks developed, in Vienna in particular. Complaints flooded in to the Foreign Office alleging mistreatment of applicants by officials.[43] The Home Office in London enlisted help from the voluntary organisations in handling casework and correspondence, but soon both the public and the private sectors were near to administrative collapse.[44]

At the Evian international conference on the refugee problem in July 1938 the British government claimed that humanitarian considerations had led it to adopt an 'even more liberal policy', yet no additions to the existing categories for admission were offered, despite hints of greater flexibility and generosity.[45] Nevertheless, during this period the Home Office, responding to the seemingly limitless demand in Britain for resident domestic servants, facilitated a greatly expanded immigration of Jewish refugee women to do such work, thereby combining humanitarian motives with self-interest, as Tony Kushner has pointed out.[46] Entry conditions for domestics were simplified, largely in order to economise on official manpower.[47] However, pre-selection remained the *sine qua non* for the Home Office. Refugees, even potential investors such as industrialists, were not to be let in even for short exploratory visits without previous investigation of their cases abroad. Discussing industrialists' cases, a Home Office official who was responsible for many aspects of refugee policy warned:

These unfortunate German Jews get up to all sorts of dodges in order to gain a footing in this country. . .once they are here they become refugees who cannot be got rid of.[48]

From Kristallnacht to the outbreak of war

Important developments in policy and procedure took place in the aftermath of the *Kristallnacht* pogrom of November 1938. The long-awaited overhaul of British admissions began. The Cabinet decided to speed up and simplify immigration procedures for refugees and to expand Britain's role as a temporary refuge. The huge backlog of refugee casework was also tackled. Chamberlain has not hitherto received sufficient credit for the shift to a markedly more generous policy of temporary refuge, which he told his Cabinet colleagues he regarded as necessary; despite objections from the Home Secretary, Sir Samuel Hoare, Chamberlain's view prevailed.[49] After this, admissions expanded dramatically.

New developments included the use of block visas, transports of unaccompanied children and the admission of large numbers of male refugees as transmigrants. British visas helped many Jewish men to obtain their release from German concentration camps, or to avoid detention altogether. In 1939 the Council for German Jewry set up a transit camp, on the site of a disused army camp in Kent. It was known as Richborough camp and eventually accommodated some 3,500 Jewish men who had been permitted to enter the country as transmigrants.[50] The Jewish organisation's figures, taken over a three-week period commencing in late December 1938, demonstrate the variable character of the immigration according to nationality, sex and category of admission. In this period, just over 1,000 new arrivals were registered by the German Jewish Aid Committee (as the JRC was re-named); of these, nearly two-thirds were Austrians. Forty per cent of the Austrians came for domestic service, which seems to explain why 66 per cent of the Austrians were female. Only 11 per cent of the Austrians were transmigrants. The figures for Germans, on the other hand, showed that 37 per cent were transmigrants, and that males predominated, making up 58 per cent of the total. Only 8 per cent of the Germans were domestics. The proportion of females among Austrians and Germans combined was 54 per cent – about the same as the proportion in the immigration as a whole.[51]

In November 1938 only 11,000 to 13,000 refugees were present in Britain, while well over 40,000 entered in the last nine months before the war. Yet throughout the period of expanded entry the principle of restriction through pre-selection remained intact.[52] Refugee organisations now had wide authority to select people for entry, but few refugees, whether children or adults, could come without guaranteed finance or sponsors; many had no access to either.[53]

The post-*Kristallnacht* policy of controlled expansion was successful in dramatically increasing the scale of admissions. However, the simultaneous reduction in refugee numbers through re-emigration which had also been part of the government's plan failed to materialise. The American authorities refused to modify their procedures to accelerate the admission of refugees who had come to Britain for eventual settlement in the USA.[54] To the consternation of the Home Secretary, refugee transmigrants accumulated in Britain, not leaving because there was nowhere for them to go.[55] Under the terms of the government's controversial White Paper of May 1939 Palestine's role as a refuge was restricted.[56] Home Office attempts to shift refugees from Britain to Palestine failed, since the authorities had suspended legal Jewish immigration in retribution for illegal emigration.[57] The search for other refugee havens abroad proved fruitless. New restrictions on entry reduced, but hardly stemmed, the flow of arrivals.[58] A last-minute decision to spend public funds on developing settlement opportunities abroad – in order to reduce refugee numbers in Britain – lapsed following the outbreak of war.[59] When war broke out the Home Office considered it had a refugee problem on its hands. Some weeks earlier, the near-bankrupt refugee organisations had called for a halt to new admissions.[60] In August 1939 the insufficiency of emigration opportunities led Jewish representatives to resist pressure to co-operate with Adolf Eichmann's accelerated timetable for the emigration of the remaining Jewish population of Vienna.[61]

Refugees from Czechoslovakia

The British response to refugees from Czechoslovakia after the Munich crisis of September 1938 provides new instances of the highly selective nature of British aid to refugees.[62] Guilt over British involvement in the enforced surrender of Czech territory to Germany led to the formation in October 1938 of a non-sectarian British refugee organisation, the British Committee for Refugees from Czechoslovakia (BCRC).[63] The BCRC was set up to aid refugees who fled from the surrendered territories and to help them find refuge abroad, in what was regarded as an act of atonement for British appeasement policy. The BCRC, in which Labour Party and TUC representatives played an active part, largely directed its sponsorship of refugees for British visas towards a limited number of persons it categorised as political refugees. These were mainly non-Jewish Sudeten German Social Democrats, plus persons from Germany and Austria who had previously sought refuge in Czechoslovakia. Individual Jews were included among political refugees, but Jews in Czechoslovakia, if persecuted merely because they were Jews, were treated as a low priority.

The British government reluctantly allocated a limited number of visas to BCRC cases, but intended that the bulk of the Czech refugee problem should be contained within what remained of Czechoslovakia, or dealt with by direct re-emigration overseas. Seeking to help the shaky Czech government, Britain advanced a huge sum of 4 million pounds to the Czechs for the resettlement of specified groups of refugees from the ceded areas. A secret provision in the agreement, finally concluded with the Czechs in early 1939, also covered assistance to Jews fleeing persecution in the Slovak areas. Later, when the Germans took control of the remainder of Czechoslovakia in March 1939, the British government froze the unspent balance of the fund and appropriated it to the task of carrying out the obligation to help refugees for which the fund had been established. In July 1939 the Czech Refugee Trust Fund was set up under Home Office auspices to administer the fund and take over the work of the BCRC, which had been allowed to continue its work until this point.[64]

Almost immediately after the 15 March takeover, the Home Office had become involved in directing the policy on how the funds were to be spent on refugee emigration to Britain. The Germans were pressuring Czech Jews to depart, but obstructing the departure of political opponents. The response of both the Home Office and the BCRC was to give priority to persons thought to be in danger from the German government. Home Office Permanent Under Secretary Alexander Maxwell proposed special arrangements to fund the continued illegal emigration of political refugees from Czechoslovakia.[65] In the selection of Jews, it was agreed to give preference only to those:

who might be considered suitable for emigration or for whose maintenance in Great Britain satisfactory guarantees were forthcoming.[66]

The opportunities for Jews from Czechoslovakia to come to Britain were therefore limited, especially since Anglo-Jewish bodies were reluctant to take responsibility for helping Czech Jews emigrate.[67] Maxwell told a Treasury official in May 1939 that Jewish organisations agreed:

that it would be a bad policy to encourage a general Jewish emigration from Czechoslovakia, and, while we cannot entirely exclude Jews, we ought, I think, to say that those who have left Czechoslovakia merely for economic reasons should not be selected for assistance.[68]

Jews were categorised as economic refugees, or racial refugees.[69] This meant that they were not allocated special visas and could only gain admission to Britain if they could qualify for the entry categories open to Jews from Germany and Austria. In late July, when Jewish emigration from Czechoslovakia was being placed under the direction of Adolf Eichmann, who was expected to use the same brutal methods he had employed in Austria, both Home Office and BCRC representatives opposed making British funds available for the involuntary mass emigration of 'non-political Jews'. They argued that to assist such emigration would play 'straight into the hands of the Gestapo and would be far more likely to encourage persecution and terror than to avoid it'.[70] The adoption of such a negative stance at a time when Jewish emigration was being strenuously promoted by the Nazis underlines the importance which British officials and refugee representatives attached to resisting pressure for forced expulsion of Jews from Europe.

Conclusion

Perhaps one in ten Jews who investigated escape to Britain succeeded in gaining refuge there before the war. This estimate is based on the number of enquiries about emigration in the files of the Central British Fund, which number over 500,000.[71] British admissions were highly selective. Jews seeking refuge found that persecution did not constitute a passport to admission. Yet some who did not strictly qualify under the immigration rules were still admitted through the exercise of authorities' discretion in their favour, if they were seen as desirable immigrants. What qualified people for entry was not the persecution they were trying to leave behind, but what they could bring with them. For some, capital assets were the key to admission; for others it was their youth. Jewish women who were prepared to turn their hands to domestic service could also enter. But persons over 45 were regarded as unsuitable for schemes of organised emigration and those who remained in Germany at the outbreak of war were mainly the elderly.[72]

In Britain the prevailing consensus was that, in defining the limits of refugee admissions, it was essential to maximise the benefits to the nation. Humanitarian considerations alone were seen as insufficiently compelling. Policies on refugees were evolved, but the Home Office pursued its narrow task of immigration control without a policy on the refugee problem as a whole. No department or body in British government was responsible for ensuring that consideration was given to helping refugees escape from Europe. The Home Office and refugee organisa- tions worked to limit commitments to refugees and refused to co-operate with Nazi pressure for forced emigration of Jews. The government's main aim was thus containment: of the size of the refugee problem; of the demand for emigration prospects; and above all, of their impact on Britain.

Large-scale Jewish refugee admissions stopped abruptly when the war started. The government now ruled out further alien refugee immigration to Britain, other than for purposes connected with the war. No help would be given to potential refugees to leave enemy controlled territory. There was a general ban on humani- tarian admissions: Britain's contribution to the refugee problem, it was said, was now to eradicate the Nazi regime which was its root cause.[73]

In 1940, as western Europe fell to the Germans and the possibility of invasion became real, panic about a possible fifth column led to mass internment of refugees, against Home Office wishes.[74] Deportation of internees in 1940 com- bined with re-emigration to the USA to reduce the numbers of Jewish refugees in Britain by perhaps one in five. At the war's end there remained of the pre-war arrivals perhaps 41,000 Germans and Austrians, including children (85–90 per cent Jewish) and 9,000 Czechs.[75] The Home Office pressed refugees to emigrate, and kept open its options on whether it would allow those remaining in Britain to stay on after the war.[76]

At the war's outset, ministers had explicitly renounced humanitarian consider- ations as a factor which should influence their response to refugees on the Continent. The country's war-time leaders did not subsequently allow such considerations to alter the course of British policy in a significantly more generous direction in response to the ample information available from mid-1942 about the Nazi programme of mass murder of Jews in Europe.[77] Assertions by Government spokesmen that Britain's national survival dictated relative inaction played an important part in deflecting a widespread campaign in support of saving Jewish people in Europe. The low priority the government gave to humanitarian aid is shown both by the degree of inaction and by the defence of this inaction by arguments which seemed not to acknowledge the decisive turn of the tide of war in the Allies' favour, treating even modest and apparently feasible proposals to save Jewish lives as a threat to the outcome of the war.[78] The number of Jews allowed into the United Kingdom during the war was negligible.[79] Before the war, as we have seen, Britain had offered a qualified welcome to over 70,000 Jews.

The themes raised in this paper have particular relevance for anyone concerned with how nations facing present day refugee crises weigh humanitarian considerations against presumed self-interest. Meanwhile, the historical debate continues about the record of 'bystander nations' on the plight of Jews in Europe.[80] Britain's record has always been controversial.[81] Nevertheless, the topic of the British response to the plight of Jews in Europe is notable – like the Holocaust itself – for its absence from the memoirs of all but a handful of prominent British politicians of the period.[82] However, in the last two decades it has started to receive the attention of historians, while the Holocaust is now established as a topic in the history national curriculum for schools. This chapter is intended to be a contribution to the understanding of the response to the Jewish refugee problem as a part of British history. It has tried to do this in such a way as to suggest that the British response to Jews in Europe raises not only issues of refugee policy and of Jewish identity and history, but also touches on questions at the heart of modern British identity, history and politics.

Notes

1. This article results from research financed by Queen Mary and Westfield College, London; The Central Research Fund of the University of London; the Memorial Foundation for Jewish Culture; the Economic and Social Research Council; the Harold Hyam Wingate Foundation; the Oxford Centre for Postgraduate Hebrew Studies and the British Academy. Crown Copyright material in the Public Record Office is reproduced by permission of Her Majesty's Stationery Office. The Neville Chamberlain papers are quoted by permission of Birmingham University Library.

2. Sir A. Maxwell (Permanent Under Secretary at the Home Office) to A.V. Hill, 16 April 1943, Public Record Office (hereafter PRO), Kew, London FO 371/36725, W11979/5711/48.

3. Carew Robinson, 'Alien Refugees', 30 March 1945, PRO HO 213/1009; Robinson, 'Alien Refugees', 10 May 1945, PRO HO 213/1008.

4. B. Gainer, *The alien invasion. The origins of the Aliens Act 1905*, London: Heinemann Educational, 1972; J. Garrard, *The English and immigration: a comparative study of the Jewish influx, 1880–1910*, Oxford: Oxford University Press, 1971.

5. Aliens Act, 1905, s.1(3).

6. Minutes by H. Scott, 19 November 1929, Sir J. Pedder, 14 December 1929, Sir J. Anderson, 2 January 1930, J. Clynes to Sir H. D'Avigdor Goldsmid, 5 February 1930, PRO HO 45/24765/423156/56; Clynes to J. Wedgwood MP, 22 July 1930, PRO HO 45/24765/423156/64.

7. See Sir John Gilmour, *Hansard*, 5th series, *Parliamentary Debates*, House of Commons, (hereafter *Hansard*), vol. 276, cols. 2557–2558, 12 April 1933; Sir Samuel Hoare, *Hansard*, vol. 333, cols. 2557–2558, 22 March 1938. In November 1991, for example, Kenneth Baker, then Home Secretary, speaking in support of proposed legislation which imposed new restrictions on asylum seekers, said that the government would 'continue to honour their commitment to people in that category' [i.e. to individuals persecuted on racial, religious or political grounds], and asserted that

'We have followed that noble tradition over centuries', *Hansard*, sixth series, vol. 198, col. 1087, 13 November 1991. Baker was speaking in a period when visa requirements and carriers' liability laws effectively prevented most refugees even from reaching Britain to apply for asylum.

8. P.M. Roberts, minute of departmental meeting, 5 December 1934, PRO FO 371/ 18462, R6930/5524/92, f.187; R.M. Makins, minute, 16 February 1935, PRO FO 371/19676, W1370/356/98, f.113; Makins, briefing for deputation, 'The League of Nations and refugees', 14 May 1935, PRO FO 371/19676, W4252/356/98.

9. For fuller discussion of these points, see L. London, 'British immigration control procedures and Jewish refugees, 1933–1942', London Ph.D 1992, pp. 160–92, 255– 62.

10. For statements by two Home Secretaries which emphasised the priority given to 'national' interests over humanitarian considerations, see references to statements by Sir John Gilmour, and Sir Samuel Hoare in n.7 above; see also Makins, minute, 16 February 1935, PRO FO 371/19676, W1370/356/98, f. 113.

11. See, for example, remark by Cooper in 'International Labour Committee, draft minutes of seventy-sixth meeting held at the Ministry of Labour on 17th May, 1938', PRO FO 371/22527, W7650/104/98, f. 85, p.1.

12. See remarks of Sir R. Scott (Home Office Permanent Under Secretary), AR(33) (Committee on Aliens Restrictions) Conclusions, 6 April 1933, PRO CAB 27/549.

13. Jewish representatives helped with repatriation of Belgian Jewish refugees after the First World War. The co-operation of Jewish organisations was facilitated by Jewish membership of Home Office committees concerned with aliens matters: see London, 1992, pp. 58–66.

14. Most came from Poland and Russia. However, for many years they did not require visas because they benefited from special exemptions for transit passengers from the usual visa requirements. See Aliens Act, 1905, s.8(1); Aliens Order 1920, Art. 4. Other Polish, Russian and Hungarian nationals required visas throughout the period covered in this paper.

15. L. London, 'Jewish refugees, Anglo-Jewry and British government policy, 1930–1940', in D. Cesarani, ed., *The making of modern Anglo-Jewry*, Oxford: Blackwell, 1990, pp. 163–90, esp. pp. 167–8.

16. 'Proposals of the Jewish Community as regards refugees from Germany', n.d., Appendix I to Sir John Gilmour, memorandum, 'The present position in regard to the admission of Jewish refugees from Germany to this country', 6 April 1933, PRO CAB 27/549.

17. Cabinet minutes (hereafter CAB) 23(33)5, 5 April 1933, PRO CAB 23/75; AR(33) (Committee on Aliens Restrictions) Conclusions, 6 April 1933; Report, 7 April 1933, PRO CAB 27/549; Cab. 27(33)8, 12 April 1933, PRO CAB 23/75.

18. Sir John Gilmour, memorandum, 'The Present Position in regard to the Admission of Jewish Refugees from Germany to this Country', 6 April 1933; AR(33) Conclusions, 6 April 1933; Report, 7 April 1933, PRO CAB 27/549; Cab. 27(33)8 12 April 1933, PRO CAB 23/75.

19. Cab. 27(33)8, 12 April 1933, PRO CAB 23/75; speeches by Sir John Simon, *Hansard*, vol. 276, col. 2810–2812, 13 April 1933 and Sir Herbert Samuel, ibid., col. 2807.

20. For the archives of the AAC and SPSL in the Bodleian Library, Oxford, see N. Baldwin, 'Catalogue of the archive of the Society for the Protection of Science and Learning', Oxford: Bodleian Library, 1988 (NR 31126); for analysis of these organisations' work see G. Hirschfeld, ' "A high tradition of eagerness. . .": British non-Jewish organisations in support of refugees', in W.E. Mosse, co-ordinating ed., *Second Chance. Two centuries of German-speaking Jews in the United Kingdom*, Tübingen, JCB Mohr (Paul Siebeck), 1991, pp. 599–610.

21. Ibid., p. 604; Esther Simpson (secretary of the AAC) Imperial War Museum, Department of Sound Records, *Britain and the Refugee crisis, 1933–47*, tape 4469; PK Hoch, 'Some contributions to physics by German Jewish emigrés in Britain and elsewhere', in Mosse, 1991, pp. 229–241.
22. Ministry of Labour, memorandum, 'Refugees from Germany irrespective of nationality', 3 Oct 1934, PRO LAB 8/78, discussed London, 1992, pp. 117–118.
23. Gomme, memorandum, 'Jewish refugees from Germany', 20 May 1933, PRO HO 45/21609/675231/1; memoranda and correspondence, 16–17 June 1933, PRO HO 45/21609/675231/2; Hoare to Schiff, 1 August 1933, PRO HO 45/21609/675231/3; correspondence between B. Davidson (JRC) and E.N. Cooper (Home office), 13–25 October 1933, PRO HO 45/21609/675231/4; the scheme is discussed in London, 1992, pp. 129–132.
24. See e.g. Holderness to Blight (LCC), 19 October 1933, PRO HO 45/15882/666764/46; S. Hoare(a Home Office official) to Makins, 15 May 1935, PRO FO 371/19676, W4255/356/98, f.18; A.J. Sherman, *Island refuge. Britain and the refugees from the Third Reich, 1933–1939*, London: Paul Elek, 1973, pp. 72–3.
25. Home Office memorandum (n.d.), sent by J.R.D. Pimlott to O.C. Harvey, 15 March 1938, PRO FO 372/3282, T3517/3272/378, f. 18.
26. S. Hoare to Makins, 15 May 1935, PRO FO 371/19676, W4255/356/98, f.18; Cooper, Home Office draft statement at opening of conference on German refugees, 21 Jan 1938, PRO FO 371/22525, W985/104/98. f.64; see generally London, 1992, pp. 142–6, 160–92.
27. H.A. Strauss, 'Jewish emigration from Germany. Nazi policies and Jewish responses (I)', *Year Book XXV of the Leo Baeck Institute*, London: Secker and Warburg, 1980, pp. 313–61.
28. See Jewish Refugees Committee statistics for May 1933–October 1934, SPSL, Box 116/2.
29. 'Report of activities of German Jewish Aid Committee (the new name adopted by the JRC in 1938) January 1st. 1938–February 1st. 1939', p. 6., Archives of the American Jewish Joint Distribution Committee (henceforth AJDC) for the period 1933–1944, New York, file 587.
30. The Foreign Office was sent details of a resolution passed by the Board of Studies in History of the University of London, recording 'shame and horror at the unexampled barbarity of the concerted attack on the Jews within the German Empire'. W.P. Morell to Secretary of State, 11 November 1938, PRO FO 371/21637, C13827/1667/62, f.21.
31. See, e.g. the views expressed in the despatches of the British Ambassador in Berlin Sir Horace Rumbold: Rumbold to Simon, 28 Mar 1933, PRO FO 371/16720, C3074/319/18, f.140; Rumbold to Simon, PRO FO 371/16722, C3594/319/18, f.1.
32. See Neville Chamberlain, letters to his sisters in Neville Chamberlain papers (hereafter NC), Birmingham University Library: NC to Ida, 10 November 1938, NC/18/1/1076; NC to Hilda, 30 Jul 1939, NC 18/1/1110.
33. Sherman, 1973, pp. 35–84.
34. London, 1990, pp. 167–8, 173, 174–9; London, 1992, pp. 96–103.
35. Ibid., pp. 103–113.
36. C.B. McAlpine, memorandum, 1 March 1938, PRO HO 213/94.
37. For the decision to make the policy change and the details of its implementation, see documents in PRO FO 372/3282 to PRO FO 372/3286, commencing Strang, memorandum of telephone conversation, 12 March 1938, PRO FO 372/3282. T3272/3272/378, f. 1, discussed in London, 1990, pp. 174–80; London, 1992, pp. 147–160, 193–230.
38. Home Office minutes of meeting with deputation, 1 April 1938, PRO HO 213/42.

The changes affected Austrian passport holders from 2 May and German passport holders from 21 May; one month's notice was deemed necessary in the latter case but none in the former, since the Austrian state was defunct.

39. Ibid.

40. Passport Control Department, circular, 'Visas for holders of German and Austrian passports entering the United Kingdom', 27 April 1938, PRO FO 372/3283, T6705/3272/378, f. 326.

41. L. London, 'British immigration control procedures and Jewish refugees, 1933–1939', in Mosse, 1991, 485–517, p. 504.

42. On 25 April 1938, 'Local Nazis forced Jews outside the Vienna Consulate to wash cars', *Jewish Chronicle*, 29 April 1938, p. 18; D. St Clair Gainer (Consul-General) to Under Secretary, 26 April 1938, PRO FO 371/21635, C3944/1667/62, f. 170.

43. Sherman, 1973, pp. 133–4.

44. Sherman, 1973, pp. 99–100, 124–5, 131–2, 155–8.

45. Lord Winterton, Speech, 6 July 1938, 'Intergovernmental Committee, Evian – July 1938, verbatim report of the first meeting, CI/E/CRI', PRO FO 919/8; see London, 1992, pp. 205–8.

46. T. Kushner, 'An alien occupation – Jewish refugees and domestic service in Britain, 1933–1948', in Mosse, 1991, pp. 553–577.

47. London, 1992, pp. 217–226.

48. Cooper to Roberts, 23 August 1938, PRO HO 213/270.

49. See Conclusions, Cabinet Committee on Foreign Policy, FP (36) 32nd meeting, 14 November 1938, PRO CAB 27/624; CAB 55(38)5, 16 November 1938, PRO CAB 23/96; on 15 November Chamberlain had seen a high-powered Jewish deputation, led by Viscount Samuel, a former Home Secretary, offering a new guarantee to underpin the admission of young people; for discussion see London, 1992, pp. 236–255.

50. See Central Council for Jewish Refugees, *Annual Report of the Council for 1939*, London, 1940, pp. 5–6.

51. GJAC report, cited n. 29 above.

52. Home Office minutes of meeting with deputation, 1 April 1938, PRO HO 213/42; Hoare, *Hansard*, vol. 342, col. 3082, 22 December 1938; Hoare, *Hansard*, vol. 345, cols. 2455–7, 3 April 1939.

53. See London, 1991, p. 510.

54. For details see PRO HO 213/115, PRO HO 213/116, PRO HO 213/117 and PRO HO 213/118.

55. See the minutes of Hoare's remarks at the January and March 1939 meetings of the Cabinet Committee on the Refugee Problem, PRO CAB 98/1.

56. *Palestine: A Statement of Policy*, Cmd 6019, London, 1939.

57. Sherman, 1973, pp. 242–243; B. Wasserstein, *Britain and the Jews of Europe, 1939–1945*, Oxford: Oxford University Press, 1979, pp. 1–39.

58. London, 1991, pp. 509–10.

59. Hoare, Interim report, Cabinet Committee on the Refugee Problem, CO 151(39), 7 July 1939, PRO CAB 98/1; Cab 37(39)11, 12 July 1939, PRO CAB 23/100; CRP (39) 6th mtg, 25 September 1939, PRO CAB 98/1; Sherman, 1973, pp. 242–250.

60. Cooper to Randall, 18 September 1939, PRO FO 371/24100, W13792/3231/48, f. 120; Sherman, 1973, p. 255; Wasserstein, 1979, pp. 81–2.

61. Bentwich, 'Report of visit to Vienna', 17 August 1939, Archives of the Central British Fund (hereafter CBF) for World Jewish Relief (microfilm), Wiener Library, reel 4, file 25.

62. See chapter, 'Refugees from Czechoslovakia after Munich', London, 1992, pp. 297–353; For the refugee crisis, see Sherman, 1973, 137–159.

63. For the origins of the BCRC see PRO HO 294/39.

64. For the history of the CRTF see PRO HO 294/5.
65. Minutes of meeting, 21 June 1939, PRO HO 294/50.
66. Lord Hailey to Maxwell, 14 April 1939, PRO HO 294/39.
67. H. Bunbury, 'The Problem of Jewish refugees from Czechoslovakia', 5 April 1939, PRO HO 294/39.
68. Maxwell to Waley, PRO T 160/1324/F13577/05/9.
69. See e.g. E Allen, 'Memorandum on emigration to the United Kingdom pending final settlement of persons coming from Czechoslovakia', 20 Aug 1939, PRO HO 294/52.
70. Memorandum of meeting on 29 July 1939, PRO HO 294/7.
71. This estimate was given by the CBF's Director in July 1990. Access to the CBF's case files is restricted.
72. Norman Bentwich, *Wanderer between two worlds*, London: Kegan Paul 1941, p. 29; Strauss, 1980, pp. 318–328.
73. Summary of Conclusions and Conclusions, CRP(39) 6th mtg, 25 September 1939, PRO CAB 98/1.
74. See F.H. Hinsley et al. *British Intelligence in the Second World War, Volume 4, Security and Counter-Intelligence*, London, HMSO, 1990, pp. 47–64.
75. See n. 3 above.
76. See records of inter-departmental and internal discussions, August 1944–October 1945 in PRO HO 213 1008 and 1009; Herbert Morrison, as Home Secretary, claimed repeatedly that if Jewish refugees were permitted to remain in Britain this would risk inflaming anti-semitism. See T. Kushner, *The persistence of prejudice. Anti-semitism in British society during the Second World War*, Manchester: Manchester University Press, 1989, pp. 152–162.
77. Wasserstein, 1979, pp. 183–221.
78. See e.g., arguments put forward by government spokesmen in parliamentary debates: Lord Cranborne, *Hansard*, Fifth series, *Parliamentary Debates*, House of Lords (hereafter *Hansard* (HL)), vol. 126, cols. 811–62, 23 March 1943; O. Peake and A. Eden, *Hansard*, vol. 389, cols. 1117–1204, 19 May 1943.
79. The proportion of Jews among refugees admitted in 1940–42 was 'quite small' according to Maxwell: Maxwell to Hill, 16 April 1943, PRO FO 371/36725, W11797/6711/48.
80. For a survey of the literature on this question see, M. Marrus, *The Holocaust in History*, New York: Meridian Books, 1987.
81. For a contemporary difference of opinion see the speeches of Viscounts Samuel and Cranborne, *Hansard* (HL), 10 December 1945. vol. 138, cols. 492–506, 524–533.
82. The refugee problem is mentioned by Samuel Hoare, *Nine Troubled Years*, London: Collins 1954; Herbert Samuel, *Memoirs*, London: Cresset Press 1945; Edward Winterton, *Orders of the Day*, London: Cassell, 1953. In *Herbert Morrison: an autobiography*, London: Odhams Press, 1960, the author justifies his record on internment.

5

Bishop Bell and Germany

Alan Wilkinson

English Christianity and Europe

'The history of the Church in other lands rings out for us a warning note. The sturdy common-sense of most English Churchmen will, I think, respond to that warning. . .Superstition does not fit in well with the national characteristics God has given us.'[1] So declared Randall Davidson, Bishop of Winchester, in 1899. Later when Davidson was Archbishop of Canterbury, George Bell became his chaplain. During the First World War (which coincided with Bell's period as chaplain), Davidson developed a more transnational understanding of the church. But here in 1899 he was still voicing his belief in an English version of Christianity which expressed and safeguarded the God-given English national character. In 1901 Mandell Creighton, the historian and Bishop of London, wrote in a similar vein:

The root idea of the National Church in England is simply this, that England can manage its own ecclesiastical affairs without interference from outside . . . I am not ashamed to own that I am an Englishman first and a Churchman afterwards.[2]

Such a confident belief in a self-sufficient church which would brook no 'interference from outside' made any transnational ecumenism impossible.

Centuries earlier the English Reformers, having learned much from Lutheranism and Calvinism, had then become preoccupied with the civil war and allowed the leadership of European Protestantism to pass to others. In any case, when after the Restoration, incumbents who would not accept either Prayer Book or Ordinal were ejected, it seemed to Protestants both in Europe and in Britain that the Church of England had made a decisive move in the Catholic direction. So by the eighteenth century, apart from occasional episodes such as Archbishop Wake's remarkable correspondence with the Gallican church, the Church of England was largely isolated from European Christianity: Protestant and Catholic.

The development of Anglo-Catholicism in the nineteenth century opened some doors and closed others. By reaching out to both Roman Catholicism and Eastern Orthodoxy, Anglo-Catholics began the long process of reducing the insularity of the Church of England and taking it stage by stage into Europe. The Lambeth Conference of Anglican bishops in 1888 paved the way for intercommunion with Old Catholics and Swedish Lutherans, both of which had retained apostolic succession. The lack of this and other Catholic features among German Lutherans and the Reformed made Anglican relationships with them much cooler and more problematical. In 1841 Frederick William IV of Prussia had attempted to introduce episcopacy into the Prussian church and unite it with the Church of England through the creation of a joint bishopric in Jerusalem. But the scheme was heartily disliked by both Anglo-Catholics and strict German Protestants. It foundered in 1881.

However it was through its biblical scholarship that Germany exercised its most potent influence upon the Church of England and the Free Churches before the First World War. Though some Evangelicals and Anglo-Catholics regarded German biblical criticism as destructive and godless, the influence of such scholars as Wellhausen, Schweitzer and Harnack was by no means confined to liberal churchmen. Nevertheless many shared the caution about German scholars expressed even by the liberal-minded Archbishop Frederick Temple: 'They did admirable service. . .but I was long ago convinced that the last word can never come from Germany'.[3]

When war came, many English publications depicted German Christianity as corrupted by paganism and liberalism. Anglo-Catholics and Nonconformists particularly disliked Lutheran erastianism. But before the war, most Anglicans and Nonconformists had felt a closer kinship with Germany, the home of Protestantism, than with France (identified with loose morals) or autocratic Russia. The creation of 63 Anglican chaplaincies in Germany by the end of the nineteenth century was a response to the growing popularity of Germany as a destination both for businessmen and tourists. No other foreign church had so many places of worship there. The German royal family, several of whose members were closely related to Queen Victoria, gave active support to these chaplaincies. So for 40 years the Empress Augusta regularly worshipped at the Baden-Baden chaplaincy. St George's Berlin remained open throughout the First World War because the Kaiser was its patron. Though the chaplaincies made Anglicanism better known in Germany, they were enclaves of Englishness rather than centres for ecumenical exploration.[4]

In 1907 the Kaiser paid a state visit to Britain. As a follow-up to this, a German delegation of about 130 Roman Catholic and Protestant churchmen visited Britain in 1908. In 1909 a similarly sized inter-denominational group from Britain visited Germany. Both visits were conducted in an atmosphere conducive more to euphoric speech-making than to confronting theological and political differences. Associated Councils of Churches were set up in Germany and Britain in 1910. At the annual meeting of the British branch in May 1914 Archbishop Davidson voiced his optimistic belief that the two Councils had practically achieved the mutual friendship which they had been created to promote.[5] On 17 July 1914, the Kaiser's Chief Court Chaplain wrote to Davidson to sound him out as to whether Anglicans would be likely to join in a celebration of the four hundredth anniversary of the Reformation. In his reply of 1 August the Archbishop revealed how far the Anglican pendulum had swung since the Reformation. The Church of England could not corporately identify itself with the celebrations (he wrote) because they might seem 'a declaration of a coherent and solidly united Protestantism against a coherent and solidly united Catholicism'.[6]

It was not until the 2 August 1914 Conference at Constance that anything ecumenical for the whole of Europe was attempted. Many delegates failed to arrive. Those who did so had to disperse the following day as frontiers closed. A German delegate said to an English Quaker as they parted on Cologne station: 'Whatever happens, nothing is changed between us.' However the organisation which emerged from this curtailed conference, significantly known as 'The World Alliance for Promoting International Friendship through the Churches', eventually did important work before flowing as a tributary into the World Council of Churches in 1948.

Thus for most of the period leading up to the First World War, the English churches were not orientated towards Europe. Anglicans and Nonconformists looked instead towards the Empire in which most of their work was concentrated. The Roman Catholic lines of communication ran to Rome rather than to Germany or France. It was only when thousands of British soldiers embarked for France in August 1914 that continental religion began to interact with that of the English, so that eventually (for example) the French wayside crucifixes they so admired were transmuted into quintessentially English war memorials for village churchyards.

The First World War

During the afternoon of 4 August 1914 whilst the Prime Minister was announcing in Parliament the British ultimatum to Germany; on the other side of the river George Bell was arriving at Lambeth Palace for three days of consultations about whether he should become a domestic chaplain to the Archbishop. His stay proved hectic because he was asked to assist in drawing up the official prayers and services for use in time of war. Some members of the public complained that they were not patriotic enough. But the Archbishop replied that he had received many requests that the prayers should not claim that God was on the British side. Thus in August 1914 Bell began a relationship with Germany which was to dominate the rest of his life.

Bell, born in 1883, the son of a parish priest, had been educated at Westminster school where he had special access to Parliament and the Abbey, the heart of the church-state nexus. After Oxford and Wells theological college he was ordained deacon in 1907, priest in 1908, and served as a curate at Leeds Parish Church, where he looked after a group of 200 artisans and tradesmen. The group's aim was not only devotional. In their meetings and his house visits they tackled leading social questions of the day. When he was young, he and his sister had usually been assigned the poorest parts of his father's parish to visit at Christmas.

Theologically Bell was nourished by Liberal Catholicism – a tradition which owed much to F.D. Maurice, theologian and Christian Socialist, and which had been definitively expressed in the symposium *Lux Mundi* (1889) edited by Charles Gore. In 1889, Henry Scott Holland, Gore's closest friend, founded the Christian Social Union (CSU) to promote social thought and action. In 1892 Gore founded the Community of the Resurrection (CR) which was identified with Liberal Catholicism, Christian Socialism, church reform and a reaching out to Catholicism, East and West.[7] At Leeds, Bell was surrounded by Gore's Liberal

Catholicism. His vicar's second cousin, a founder member of CR and CSU, lived at the Mother House of CR in Mirfield twelve miles away. Bell became a friend of Neville Figgis, a leading political thinker and prophet at Mirfield. Brought up as a Congregationalist, Figgis like Gore believed that the establishment smothered the prophetic vocation of the Church of England. At Mirfield also was Keble Talbot who in 1944 was to press for Bell's nomination to Canterbury and Bell knew his brother Neville who was a curate in Leeds when he was there. Their father was E.S. Talbot, a former vicar of Leeds, then Bishop of Southwark, one of Gore's closest friends, a confidant of the Archbishop's, a fervent supporter of CSU and a contributor to *Lux Mundi*. When Bell returned to Christ Church Oxford as a tutor in 1910, he and Scott Holland, now Professor of Divinity, collaborated on social issues. Having committed himself to a wide range of social concerns from settlement work to WEA lecturing, he worried that if he were to go to Lambeth he would be unable to continue this commitment. However the Bishop of Wakefield reassured him that he would have a great deal of scope for his 'social sympathies' and could be 'a link in some ways between the Archbishop and Labour'.[8] Bell also hesitated to go to Lambeth because, like Gore, he believed that the establishment must be modified. 'What I believe in is not the Church of England but the one holy catholic church,' wrote Gore.[9] Bell shared the Anglo-Catholics' conviction that the church was not, and must never be, the creature of the state. When he spent Christmas 1914 at Canterbury with the Archbishop, Davidson, he noted in his diary on 29 December that this was the day on which Becket was murdered and went to the Cathedral to visit the place of his martyrdom. Indeed Becket was to become increasingly influential in the twentieth century Church of England, reminding it that there are times when the church has to stand against the state.

From the very beginning the Archbishop placed great confidence in his new chaplain. Bell did not begin his duties until December, but in August Davidson welcomed his suggestion that he (Bell) should call together people from different churches and with differing views to meet at Lambeth in October. Bell himself believed that Britain had been morally bound to go to war. But *The War and the Kingdom of God* (1915), a remarkable Anglican symposium which he edited, struck a note quite different from the hyper-patriotism so common at the time. Bell wrote with deep feeling about the scandal of Christians fighting one another. He claimed

There is a greater cause than the cause of the patriot; a devotion higher than devotion to country or home . . . a Master more powerful and more sufficient than any earthly Lord . . .

The common loyalty of Christians to the Kingdom transcended nationality.[10]

The Archbishop was by temperament a conciliator. He believed that most problems could be solved with commonsense and give-and-take. Some politicians nicknamed him 'God's own Butler'. Yet when Dean of Windsor he had been strong enough to stand up to Queen Victoria, and as Archbishop of Canterbury had been denounced as an ally of revolutionary radicals when he voted with the Liberals to limit the powers of the Lords during the constitutional crisis of 1911.

During the First World War Davidson's moral stature and authority at home and abroad increased markedly as he strove to uphold and deepen a sense of the *Una Sancta* beyond national frontiers. By contrast jingoist clergy like Bishop Winnington Ingram of London preached a crude nationalist religion. The *Church*

Times deplored the fact that music by a German (Handel) was to be played at the requiem for Lord Kitchener and some congregations refused to sing German hymns or tunes. Davidson, despite his natural dislike for dissenters from the established order, nevertheless defended the rights of conscientious objectors. In face of fierce criticism he applied the Just War tradition to the conduct of the war, condemning reprisals, the bombing of civilians and the use of poison gas: 'we mean to come out with clean hands' he said. He asked in 1917: 'Do those who describe the terrible sight of little London children lying dead really want to see little German children lying slaughtered in like manner by us?' However, two facilities which were crucial to ecumenical communication in the Second World War were lacking: broadcasting and an official bureau for the churches in Geneva.

Instead, until the USA entered the war, American churchmen played a valuable role as couriers or postmen. One of them, Dr J.R. Mott, was asked by Davidson in October 1914 to pass to German churchmen in Berlin this message:

I, for my part, am resolved not to let these terrible international strifes impair a friendship and a community of thought and prayer which I have valued beyond words. That our German brothers and friends in the Faith of Our Lord Jesus Christ desire simply to be loyal to the cause of Our Master and of truth, I do not doubt for an hour.

From the German side in 1916, Dr Adolf Deissmann referred in one of his weekly letters to American Protestants to 'the noble Christian spirit of the Archbishop'.[11] Just before the Armistice in a sermon in the Abbey, Davidson spoke of how the Lord's Prayer crumbled barriers: ' "Our Father", "Pater Noster", "Notre Père" – yes, and "Unser Vater" '.[12] Bell later wrote with deep admiration of the Archbishop's war-time ministry:

His refusal to be carried away, whether in ultra-nationalism or ultra-pacificism (sic), begot a confidence in his judgement. There was something massive about him, massive and true. And throughout the four and a half years of the War . . . he spoke the brave, strong, and heartening words of a Christian bishop. He said nothing common, or mean – nothing vindictive.[13]

These comments indicate how much Bell admired the Archbishop's ministry during the First World War. Bell's own ministry during the second war showed how much he had absorbed Davidson's concept of the church as the conscience of the nation. He learned also from the Archbishop and from his time at the heart of the church-state nexus at Lambeth how to use the relationships with people of power which his position provided and how to use all the various means of influencing public opinion at his disposal – sermons, speeches in the Lords, letters to the press. People began to regard the Archbishop and Bell as a partnership and to realise how much influence Bell exercised. Davidson's new readiness to reach across national barriers was perhaps surprising in one who had hitherto been so committed to the concept of the National Church. It is impossible to say how much Bell influenced him in his war-time judgements (particularly as it was Bell who wrote Davidson's biography), though we do know that on occasion Bell supplied him with ideas and quotations. Davidson did, however, write all his own sermons. It is significant that though Davidson was really a Low Churchman his closest clerical advisers were all in the Catholic tradition – Archbishop Lang, Bishops Talbot and Gore, and Bell himself. All of them explicitly repudiated a nationalist Christianity.

Ecumenism between the wars

Though Bell had an ecumenical role behind the scenes at Lambeth, it was not until 1919 that he stepped onto the European ecumenical stage when he attended a conference arranged by the World Alliance near the Hague, as the Archbishop's observer. It was the first meeting since the war between German and Allied delegates. It was just after the Versailles Treaty had been signed. The atmosphere was tense. The Germans arrived and stood embarrassed until Bishop Talbot went to greet them, arms outstretched. German delegates eased the tension by declaring their condemnation of the invasion of Belgium. Some called it a 'spiritual peace conference'. Bell made a great impression on Archbishop Söderblom of Uppsala:

He hardly said anything except when he was asked. Then, after consideration he gave a thoughtful answer which always proved to be reliable. The face is dominated by two large, round eyes, which shine with the life and soul and indicate a rich inner life. In my opinion, no man means more for the ecumenical awakening than this silent Bell. This Bell never rings unnecessarily. But when it sounds, the tone is silvery clear. It is heard.[14]

In his turn Söderblom inspired Bell with a great vision of how ecumenism could be a gospel of hope to a divided and war-torn world.

It was often said during the war, outside as well as inside the churches, that if only the churches had been united across Europe, the war might never have broken out. In the post-war period the pursuit of the ecumenical vision evoked some of the same hope and idealism as the League of Nations, of which it was in many ways the ecclesiastical equivalent.[15] Ecumenism was practical penitence. So the Lambeth Conference of Anglican bishops, of which Bell was assistant secretary and to which he contributed behind the scenes, declared in 1920 that the war had brought home the weakness of the church: 'Men in all Communions began to think of the reunion of Christendom, not as a laudable ambition or a beautiful dream, but as an imperative necessity.'[16]

In 1922 the Archbishop, preaching the annual sermon before the opening of the League of Nations Assembly, described the horrors of war: 'And deliberately we say that, God helping us, there shall be no "next time".'[17] During the war both of Bell's two brothers and many of his former pupils and parishioners had been killed. He therefore shared the horror of another war and the determination to prevent it. Some reacted by becoming pacifists. Others, like Bell, were pacifiers, believing that there was a latent harmony between the nations which could be actualised by agreement.[18]

At the first ecumenical conference of Life and Work at Stockholm 1925, Bell helped to draft the message and publicly endorsed Söderblom's plan for a permanent ecumenical council. The message declared: 'We summon the churches to share with us our sense of the horror of war, and of its futility as a means of settling international disputes. . .'[19] At Stockholm there had been a good deal of tension between those, including Bell, who saw the Kingdom of God as at least partly realisable on earth, and those, especially the Germans, who took a more pessimistic view of society. Bell wrote: 'German theology tends to be the theology of vanquished men, and their conception of the Kingdom of God the conception of those who have despaired of this world.'[20] Stockholm had encouraged continuation of work and in 1927 Bell and Deissmann arranged an Anglo-German theological conference in Canterbury on the Kingdom of God. A second conference was held the following year in Germany. *Mysterium Christi*, the collection of papers given at both conferences, was published in 1930 and edited by Bell and Deissmann. Bell wrote in his contribution: 'Christian theologians are bound by the very principle of the Incarnation to make an effort to enter into the world's affairs.'

Six months after he became Bishop of Chichester Bell wrote in the Christmas 1929 edition of the *Listener*:

A wise old writer in the Apocrypha, describing the occupation of working men . . . ends up with these words: 'They will maintain the fabric of the world, and in the handiwork of their craft is their prayer.' . . . I whole-heartedly believe that the serious exercise of a man's art is itself an act of worship . . . I believe that the Church should always be ready to blow a trumpet for Education, for Health, for Science, for Art, and now for a National Theatre. She should also blow a trumpet for Peace and Justice, and . . . she should not be afraid, when need is, of denouncing authority in the wrong . . . 'I cannot praise', said John Milton, 'a fugitive and cloistered virtue . . .' Nor, least of all on Christmas Day, can I praise a fugitive and cloistered Church.

All Bell's main beliefs are here: the world created by God and hallowed by the incarnation is sustained by ordinary people through their work as prayer. Therefore the church must be concerned with every aspect of life. But its calling is not just to bless but also to challenge. In 1918 with R.H. Tawney and Bishop Talbot he had drafted perhaps the most radical report ever produced by the Church of England on industrial life. During the 1930s he initiated a programme of help from his diocese of Chichester to bring aid to the unemployed of Salford; joined a group to study the causes of and solutions to unemployment; took up the cause of Brighton council house tenants who were paying too much rent; and persuaded the County Council to grant their road workers trade union rights. It was characteristic therefore that the branch of the ecumenical movement, with which he was most involved between the wars, was called 'Life and Work,' which brought Christians together to tackle social problems

The boy who spent his pocket money on cheap editions of the poets was able as Dean of Canterbury to bring back religious drama into the Cathedral. Later he invited T.S. Eliot to write *The Rock* and *Murder in the Cathedral* which celebrated Becket's stand against the state. The innovative artistic work in Chichester Cathedral and other churches in the diocese was in part the result of having a bishop who was as ready to stand up for what he believed about religious art as he was in political, ecumenical and international affairs.

By the 1930s Bell was able to draw upon a wide range of personal and theological friendships from all over Europe. So after the rejection of the 1928 revision of the Prayer Book by the Commons he sought the views of a variety of German and Austrian Roman Catholics and Protestants about the consequent church-state crisis. He tried to keep up with the very different world of continental theology. His grasp of German was poor but he managed to get through a book by Congar, the Roman Catholic theologian, in the original French. His friend Fr Gabriel Hebert, the Kelham monk, fired him with enthusiasm for the movement for liturgical reform which was particularly strong among German Roman Catholics.

The German Church Struggle

Appropriately enough, Bell was in Berlin for a meeting at the end of January 1933 as Hitler came to power. The Nazi challenge to Christianity gave the ecumenical movement, and particularly Life and Work, a new impetus. Soon Bell was writing to German church leaders about Hitler's persecution of the Jews and attempts to suborn the church. Some of this correspondence he made public. Thus Bell emerged as the most important and best-informed Christian critic of the Nazis. The 'real *vox ecclesiae*' Brilioth, the future Swedish Archbishop, called him. Bell's right to interfere in the German church struggle derived from his chairmanship of the Council of Life and Work. But he ceased to be chairman in 1934. After that his ministry to Germany rested upon the weight of his personal moral authority. The German pastor in London, Dietrich Bonhoeffer, became his leading adviser on German affairs. However A.C. Headlam, Bishop of Gloucester and chairman of the Church of England Council on Foreign Relations, took a benign view of what was happening in Germany and clung on to his view despite all the contrary evidence. 'It is quite untrue to say that National-Socialism is incompatible with Christianity,' Headlam wrote in the church newspaper *The Guardian*, on 2 September 1938. Up to March 1939 when Hitler annexed the rump of Czechoslovakia, many English Christians and pacifiers wanted desperately to believe the best of Germany. They felt guilty for demonising Germans during the war and for the punitive aspects of the Versailles Treaty. They were terrified of making any kind of stand which might lead to another world war which they believed would cause even more suffering than the last. They were also very unwilling to believe any reports of atrocities in Nazi Germany – such stories did not fit in with their optimism about human nature. Moreover, had not many of the German atrocity stories during the war been shown up as Allied propaganda? Many felt that the Versailles Treaty had given the Prodigal Son of Europe good reason for running away from home. Now he had returned, what moral right had the rest of the family to ask him searching questions? In any case, was not Hitler a bulwark against the spread of godless communism?

Niemöller's arrest on 1 July 1937 dramatically focused the German church struggle for many British church people, though in fact he had supported the Nazis and at first welcomed Hitler. Bell wrote to the *Times* (3 July): 'What is his crime? The truth is that he is a preacher of the Gospel of God, and that he preaches that Gospel without flinching.' The absence of Niemöller and other German delegates from the second world conference of Life and Work at Oxford 1937, underlined its grave message sent to the German church, largely at Bell's instigation. In England there was a tradition among Anglicans and Free Church people that the Christian has a duty to protest against immoral action by the state, but in German Protestantism of the 1930s the number of conscientious objectors (for example) could have been counted on the fingers of one hand.

Bell's work for the German church was so multifarious that there is no room for a detailed account. For example in 1934 he started the year with a letter to the *Times* (7 January) protesting against the muzzling of German pastors by Bishop Müller and followed it with letters to Müller himself and the German ambassador. He met German church leaders in London who advised him to be silent. He issued an Ascension Day message to the German churches. He drew attention in the summer to the Barmen declaration which formed the basis of the Confessing Church. And in August he presided at the meeting of the Council of Life and Work in Denmark which under his guidance came out decisively in support of the Confessing Church, much to the fury of the official German church delegation. When the news leaked out, a Nazi courier flew in dramatically and tried to take over the delegation. Bell also persuaded the Council to co-opt Bonhoeffer. On his way home Bell called on leaders of the Confessing Church. In October having urged the leading members of Life and Work to issue solemn warnings to the German ambassadors in their respective countries against further repression, he himself went to make his own protest to the chargé d'affaires at the German Embassy in London. In November he met the German ambassador, Ribbentrop, and after a prompting from Bell the Archbishop of Canterbury also saw Ribbentrop twice at Lambeth. Not surprisingly, 'Chichester' became a dangerous word to use in Germany, and his friends there referred to him as 'Uncle George' instead.[21] All these efforts involved continuous correspondence. Yet he had a huge diocese to run and most evenings arrived home late from diocesan engagements. Though he rarely went to bed the same day that he got up, he always attended 8 am Mattins in his chapel.

There are some 320 volumes of the Bell papers at Lambeth; 52 are about international affairs ranging from bombing policy to Cyprus and from nuclear weapons to Turkey; 64 are concerned with the German church, including 10 volumes on refugees. This gives some idea of the strenuousness of Bell's commitment to the quest for social righteousness and to his ministry to the German people.

Refugees

As early as June 1933 the Archbishop of Canterbury (Lang) and other church leaders addressed a meeting of protest against the Nazi persecution of the Jews. In August, Bell received a heartfelt appeal for Christians with Jewish ancestry in Germany and information about their ill-treatment. Mrs Helen Bentwich, herself a Jew, secretary of the German Refugees Hospitality Committee, wrote to Bell in September:

Their position seems almost more tragic than anyone else's. The Jews belong to a community and are assured of the practical help and sympathy of Jews all over the world. . .But these non-Aryans are veritable pariahs and belong to no corporate body which unites them and have no political convictions in common to stimulate them.[22]

Bell now set to work to mobilise support. At Christmas the Archbishops of Canterbury, York and Wales, together with Free Church leaders, appealed for donations to help German refugees. But very little money was forthcoming. Bell refused to give up. In a broadcast in September 1936 he pointed out that the Jews had already raised £2m for their own people and were planning to raise £3m more. However the general British public remained uninterested.

Bell and like-minded bishops were not only concerned with Jewish Christians but also with Jews in general. Hensley Henson, Bishop of Durham, spoke out powerfully for the Jews in the Church Assembly in November 1935. At Bell's prompting he issued a public condemnation of any participation of British academics in celebrations at Heidelburg University in 1936, and in 1937 put such pressure on Durham University that it reversed its decision to send representatives to celebrations at Göttingen – both these German universities were violently anti-semitic.

Thus it was that Henson became a hero to British Jewry. However, Headlam when he condemned Nazi attacks on Jews in August 1933, added the anti-semitic imputation that many Jews were responsible for Communist and Socialist violence and were not 'a pleasant element in German, and in particular in Berlin life'.[23]

When the National Christian Appeal came to an end in the autumn of 1937, Bell tried another tack and formed a Church of England Committee for non-Aryan Christians in association with Save the Children and the Quakers. Among its achievements, to which the people of Bell's diocese contributed, was that 33 pastors with their families, some 90 people in all, were rescued and enabled to begin new lives in Britain; several of the pastors went on to exercise ministries within British churches. Bell continued to lament what he called in 1938 'the seeming apathy with which the fate of the Jews and the non-Aryan Christians is being regarded by people of the British Empire'.[24] But Bell was not only concerned to help Jewish Christians. He was the focus of concern and source of help for many other refugees. It was a time-taking and emotionally draining task. To resettle just one Rumanian woman, for example, took 127 letters.

Why were people so indifferent? Was it the result of lingering distrust of Germans mixed up with anti-semitism? Was it a consequence of the old adage that charity begins at home? 'Refugees Get Jobs – Britons Get Dole' was one newspaper headline. Would there have been a more generous response if the German churches had not been so silent about the treatment of the Jews? Or if the British government had not discouraged attention to the Jews' plight, fearing that a mass exodus would lead to the creation of a Jewish state in Palestine? Adrian Hastings contends that the concentration by Bell and others on the German church struggle (which was in any case much more ambiguous than realised at the time) narrowed their focus so that the far more terrible things going on in Germany got much less attention.[25] What Bell's ministry meant can be gauged by the story of a Jewish Christian, Werner Simonson, who because all his grandparents were Jewish, lost his post as a High Court Judge. He was unemployed and constantly harried. In March 1939 he set out for England with ten marks and two suitcases. Desperate for work he went to see Bell. 'His huge warm blue eyes reflected his love and inner peace and I felt a personal contact which made me lose all my fear and nervousness.' Eventually he was ordained in St Paul's Cathedral in 1942 at the height of the war. 'German Judge to be Curate in London' was one headline.[26]

When war broke out, Bell immediately sent a letter to all the refugees he had helped. He created the German Christian Fellowship to promote prayer between the Christians of the two countries with monthly services in both German and

English in London. When in 1940 almost all aliens were interned, Bell was furious that anti-Nazi refugees, many of them his friends, were included. He visited the camps in the Isle of Man and at Huyton. Later Franz Hildebrandt, the former assistant pastor at Niemöller's church wrote:

But who would have time for a few thousand refugees, when the fate of England and the West was in the balance? Who would speak and act for them, these virtually stateless people? Who else but the Bishop of Chichester?. . .He was almost speechless and could only stammer and stutter. . .The sight of the refugees in their new captivity was just too much for him.[27]

When he returned he raised their plight with great passion in the Lords. His efforts and those of others secured the release of a considerable number of refugees.

To Bell, the presence of German and Austrian refugees in Britain was not a burden but an enrichment of national life. He said in a broadcast on 18 May 1941 that the refugees could be used 'to encourage the opposition in Germany itself'. He electrified a group of German pastors by telling them that they would be given opportunities by the Church of England to preach about the witness of the Confessing Church. He made efforts to provide training for pastors and laymen so that they could return to church work in Germany after the war.

During the war Bell pressed those in authority to allow Jewish immigrants into Palestine. The Archbishop of Canterbury (Temple) stirred the Lords on 23 March 1943 when he initiated a debate calling on the government to take immediate measures to provide help to those in danger of being massacred:

The Jews are being slaughtered at the rate of tens of thousands a day. . .The priest and the Levite in the parable were not in the least responsible for the traveller's wounds as he lay there by the roadside, and no doubt they had many other pressing things to attend to, but they stand as the picture of those who are condemned for neglecting the opportunity of showing mercy. . .We stand at the bar of history, of humanity, and of God.[28]

In a later debate on refugees in the Lords on 28 July, Bell attacked the Bermuda conference on the subject for never mentioning the Jews in its communiqué. A recent government survey of the refugee problem throughout the world had given the impression that 'the systematic mass murder of Jews in Nazi-occupied Europe. . .was entirely forgotten'.[29]

The Second World War

Bell had a deeply compassionate heart. He had suffered grievously during the First World War. He desperately wanted the ecumenical movement to inspire the churches to rise above national interests. Like many of his fellow countrymen, Bell regarded the Versailles treaty as inequitable and believed that many of the German grievances against it were justified. It is not surprising therefore that though he knew more about the horrors of Nazism than any other British church leader, he supported appeasement. The word then had a noble and specifically Christian ring. It was as though the Elder Brother, once so convinced of his rectitude at

Versailles, was holding out a hand of penitence and friendship to the Prodigal Son. So on 27 September 1938, two days before Chamberlain flew to Munich, Bell wrote in the *Times*: 'Even a defeat in negotiation now, if we should be defeated, however humiliating, would be better than a war.'

In July 1939, knowing that war was imminent, Bonhoeffer with immense courage returned to Germany from America to pray and work for the defeat of his own country. Bell wrote at the beginning of September:

My dear Dietrich,
You know how deeply I feel for you and yours in this melancholy time. May God comfort and guide you. I think often of our talk in the summer. May He keep you. Let us pray together by reading the Beatitudes. *Pax Dei quae superat omnia nos custodiat.*
Yours affectionately,
George[30]

On Sunday morning 3 September 1939 in Chichester Cathedral the Dean with booming belligerency announced the outbreak of war. By contrast Bell walked quietly and alone from his stall, reminded the congregation to be Christians and to have compassion and forgiveness in their hearts throughout the war. In November he wrote at length about the function of the church in wartime. He evidently remembered how Gore in November 1914 had warned that it was easy to be swept along by the tide of patriotic fervour, but that when the war was over, everything would turn on whether 'there has been maintained and nourished amongst us the true counterpoise to war, the spirit of universal human brotherhood, the spirit which understands and seeks the Kingdom of God'.[31] So Bell began by recalling that though some had stood out against the nationalist fever during the first war, there was no 'counterbalancing force resolute enough to resist it'. The church in each nation became more nationalistic and 'failed to strike the universal note'. Bell went on to declare his conviction about the independent nature of the church's authority which owed much to the Anglo-Catholic tradition and echoed Newman's Tract 1 (1833):

So when all the resources of the State are concentrated, for example, on winning a war, the Church is not part of those resources . . . It possesses an authority independent of the State . . . It is not the State's spiritual auxiliary with exactly the same ends as the State.

He went on:

The Church then ought to declare, both in peace-time and war-time, that there are certain basic principles which can and should be the standards of both international and social order and conduct. . .The Church must be humble. It must acknowledge its own share in the guilt of the common injustice and lack of charity. Further, its witness must be disinterested and independent. . .It must not hesitate, if occasion arises, to condemn the infliction of reprisals, or the bombing of civilian populations, by the military forces of its own nation. It should set itself against the propaganda of lies and hatred. It should be ready to encourage a resumption of friendly relations with the enemy nation. . .The Church stands for the Cross, the gospel of redemption. It cannot, therefore, speak of any earthly war as a 'crusade'. . .The Church in any country fails to be the Church if it forgets that its members in one nation have a fellowship with its members in every nation.[32]

It was the charter of Bell's war-time ministry.

In the Lords in December 1939 Bell supported the offer by the King of the Belgians and the Queen of Holland to mediate. Bell's readiness to support a negotiated peace at this stage made some of his admirers in Britain and in Europe wonder whether he really understood Nazism after all.[33] Certainly refugee German pastors thought that English religion was too liberal-minded, too optimistic about unredeemed humanity and had no comprehension of the tragic and demonic elements in life.[34] Ulrich Simon, a Jewish refugee and then an Anglican priest, many of whose relations perished in concentration camps, as a great admirer of Bell commented that he 'had nothing of the charismatic leader. Never has there been a more normal human being. . .Bell's ordinariness and safe position in the established order enabled him to see the extraordinary and shoulder the unsafe, without at any time feeling the terror which falls on the unsheltered pioneers.'[35] However, Bell was not, and never had been, a pacifist. In a speech in the Lords about internment on 6 August 1940 he rounded on his critics:

I think I know the meaning of this war as well as most people. I have been an active and public opponent of Hitler in his attacks on the Churches and on the Jews since 1933. I desire the defeat of Hitlerism as strongly as anyone in this country.[36]

Germany and Nazism were not the same, he explained in *Christianity and World Order* (1940). This Penguin Special sold over 80,000 copies – a sign that it dealt with a theme of great contemporary interest and an indication of how well-known its author was. Bell contended that while the West could not make terms with Nazism, it could negotiate with Germany after a revolution. He commended the Pope's Five Peace Points of Christmas 1939 – a sign of his readiness to take advantage of the thaw in relations with Rome in the first part of the war. The distinction which he regularly drew between Nazis and Germans put him on a collision course with the followers of Vansittart in the government and press. It was this distinction which drew him into one of the most remarkable and controversial episodes of the war.

On 13 May 1942 Bell flew to Stockholm to visit the churches in Sweden. A fortnight later, to his amazement, Dr Hans Schönfeld, a German pastor and Director of an ecumenical agency in Geneva, turned up to see him. Bell had known him since 1929. Schönfeld told him of a growing and broadly based opposition movement to Hitler in Germany. He asked, if Hitler were overthrown and a government on a new basis established, whether the Allies would be willing to make terms. A few days later Bonhoeffer also arrived to see Bell. Bonhoeffer corroborated what Schönfeld had said and gave him the names of leaders of the opposition, including that of General Beck, for Bell to pass to the British government. Bonhoeffer believed that Germany deserved punishment and that a coup must be seen by the world as an act of penitence.[37]

When Bell returned in June he presented a memorandum about these events to the Foreign Secretary (Anthony Eden). He pointed out that the communication from the two pastors was a follow-up to that from von Trott and members of the Kreisau Circle which Visser 't Hooft, secretary of the embryonic World Council of Churches, had conveyed to the government in May. It had then replied that

Germany must be defeated first. Eden now responded to Bell with similar bleakness: 'I have no doubt that it would be contrary to the interest of our nation to provide them with any answer whatever.' Bell persisted but got nowhere. The Foreign Office was ready to go to great lengths to prevent people from knowing that opposition groups existed in Germany. So on 10 March 1943 Bell initiated a debate in the Lords in which he gave examples of opposition to Nazism in Germany without of course in any way referring to his recent contacts. In July 1944 the Bomb Plot against Hitler failed and many were arrested. Bell besought Eden in anguish on their behalf. Eden wrote on Bell's letter in red ink: 'I see no reason whatever to encourage this pestilent priest.'[38] There is a divine irony in the fact that when Eden wished to be contemptuous about Bell he reached for the phrase which according to tradition was used by Henry II about Becket, the martyr to whom Bell had expressed his devotion in those far-off days at Canterbury during Christmastide 1914.

To Bell and to his supporters, the presence of German and other refugees from Nazism in Britain and the existence of anti-Nazi groups in the occupied countries and even in Germany itself, made the war seem less like a war *against* Germany than a war *for* the true Germany. The ecumenical movement had created a much richer network of relationships than ever existed in the First World War and these could now be nourished through the embryonic World Council of Churches in Geneva, and through broadcasting. Weekly German services began to be broadcast by the BBC conducted mainly by refugee pastors. So Niemöller in Dachau heard from a fellow prisoner, an English officer who had a secret radio, about a broadcast service of intercession for him on his fiftieth birthday in January 1942. It had been conducted by the Archbishop of Canterbury and Bell had preached. Every Christmas of the war Bell broadcast a special message to Christians in Germany. In 1941 he said:

Do you remember that walk, Doctor, in a rather muddy field one spring afternoon with the Cathedral spire behind us, when we talked of the German Evangelical Church and its organisation? . . . I think of some of you in your homes in Marburg, Hanover and Berlin where you made me welcome . . . Martin Niemöller, my friend, I rejoice to hear your brave voice. I rejoice to hear your voice too, Bishop Wurm in Stuttgart, and yours, Bishop von Galen in Münster . . . Your fellow Christians everywhere are by your side.[39]

Bell, like his Archbishop in the First World War, tried to uphold the restraints of the Just War. When Hitler bombed Warsaw on 1 September 1939 the world was outraged. On 3 September a joint Anglo-French declaration instructed their forces to confine bombing to strictly military objectives. At Easter 1941 Bell called for renunciation of night bombing by all governments. He continued to press the government about food shortages in the occupied countries. In February 1942 Bomber Command adopted the policy of area bombing. Bell was isolated. Archbishop Temple, an old friend, could not support him in his protests, though Archbishop Lang and Headlam did. At prep school Bell's teachers had characterised him as faint-hearted, shy and inarticulate. Even at Lambeth the Archbishop felt he had to suggest the name of a possible bride because he thought Bell would be too diffident ever to propose. Yet his shyness, which continued, paradoxically enabled him to be more independent of the opinions of others. After some controversial speech he would ruefully point out to visitors to his study how huge was the pile of abusive letters, how small the number of appreciative ones. When he condemned the bombing of whole cities in his *Diocesan Gazette* in September 1943, the Dean withdrew the invitation to preach at the forthcoming Battle of Britain service in Chichester Cathedral. On 9 February 1944 Bell opened a major debate in the Lords on obliteration bombing. He insisted that a distinction between military and civilian targets was part of International Law:

Why is there this inability to reckon with the moral and spiritual facts? Why is there this forgetfulness of the ideals by which our cause is inspired? . . . The Allies stand for something greater than power. The chief name inscribed on our banner is 'Law' . . . It is because this bombing of enemy towns – this area bombing – raises this issue of power unlimited and exclusive that such importance is bound to attach to the policy and action of His Majesty's Government. I beg to move.[40]

Both Churchill and Bell had been horrified by the scale of the casualties during the First World War, but the same experience drove them in opposite directions during the Second World War. Churchill adopted obliteration bombing to avoid massive casualties among invading Allied servicemen. The result – the massive casualties among German civilians – outraged Bell. In addition Bell believed that the policies of obliteration bombing and unconditional surrender drove moderate Germans to support the Nazis. He felt deeply for aircrew, among whom were personal friends; he knew that some were sickened by their task.[41] But to other airmen he was an anathema. On one occasion, for example, he was due for a confirmation at a particular station. The chaplain requested transport. The adjutant responded 'Let the bugger bike'. Throughout the war Bell was immensely heartened by the constant support and advice he received from Captain Basil Liddell Hart, the military historian. In 1959 he wrote of Bell:

The wisdom and foresight of George Bell's speeches in the House of Lords. . .have now come to be widely recognised – and especially by military historians of the war. Hardly anyone would now question the truth of his repeated warnings about the folly of the Allies' unconditional surrender policy . . . George Bell, standing for the principles of his creed, came to achieve a far clearer grasp of grand strategy than did the statesmen.[42]

Having campaigned against the obliteration bombing of Germany throughout the war, Bell's condemnation of the dropping of atom bombs on Japan in 1945 had much more moral coherence and authority than condemnations from those who hitherto had been silent.

Just a month before the war ended, Bonhoeffer was executed. It was as though he had been the son Bell never had. Bonhoeffer's last message was not for his family or fiancée, but for Bell:

Tell him that for me this is the end but also the beginning. With him I believe in the principle of our Universal Christian brotherhood which rises above all national interests, and that our victory is certain – tell him too that I have never forgotten his words at our last meeting.

Bell preached at a broadcast memorial service in London on 27 July: 'His death is a death for Germany – indeed for Europe too. . .[43] Bonhoeffer's parents did not know of their son's death until they heard this broadcast.

Post-War Germany

During the war Bell was determined that the church should play a key role in the post-war reconstruction of Europe. Under his leadership the Church of England raised £250,000 for this purpose. Bell was delighted to help finance such projects as the rebuilding of the monastery at Monte Cassino and places for continental ordinands at English theological colleges. In May 1945, when war ended, Bell began exploring the resumption of contacts with the German Evangelical Church. In October, accompanied by Dr Gordon Rupp, the Methodist scholar, as interpreter, Bell set out from the Athenaeum in an army truck and flew to Stuttgart in a bucket-seated Dakota full of servicemen. On the way he composed, and Rupp translated, a challenging message for the German Protestant leaders. Though it began with warm ecumenical greetings, it went on to speak bluntly about the sufferings of the Jews and the deported peoples of Europe. In Stuttgart they joined a delegation from the World Council of Churches which had come to restore fellowship with the German church. In a charged atmosphere, Niemöller handed round what became known as the Stuttgart Declaration, signed by the 12 German Protestant church leaders. It included this passage:

With great pain do we say: through us has endless suffering been brought to many peoples and countries . . . we accuse ourselves for not being more courageous, for not praying more faithfully, for not believing more joyously and for not loving more ardently. Now a new beginning is to be made in our churches . . .

It was particularly difficult for Bishop Dibelius to agree to the crucial confession (quoted above) which had been added by Niemöller. Dibelius had experienced the terror of the Russian advance. He found it hard to have to point to the sins of Germany alone. He also anticipated that it would provoke a storm of criticism in Germany.[44] A few days later, 2,000 cold and gaunt people, many of them anxious and bitter, gathered in the blitzed Marienkirche in the Russian sector in Berlin. Four uniformed Christian representatives of the occupying powers stood beside the altar. Bell preached about the desperately sick man who needed the help of his four friends to bring him to the healing of Jesus. At Tübingen he heard a choir sing *The Messiah* – with the poignant words 'Comfort ye, Comfort ye, my people'. The bass soloist was a Roman Catholic priest lately released from concentration camp.

Such cathartic experiences helped the Evangelical Church to make a new beginning, to put aside revenge and hatred and to be received again into the ecumenical community. The German Roman Catholic Church, to its shame, never had the courage to make such a corporate declaration of guilt and penitence. It would have been very much more difficult to hand over such a statement if Bell had not been there to receive it, so universally loved and trusted was he by German churchmen. Later, an old German bishop, who was fatally compromised with the Nazis, refused to resign; no-one could persuade him to do so until Bell came out and talked with him on one of his many post-war visits. It is extraordinary that this reserved and very English bishop who could not speak German, and who came from the most wealthy and conservative diocese of the Church of England, should exercise a mediating role over matters great and small between Germany and the occupying powers, during the last chapter of a ministry to Germany which had begun in 1914.

Straight after the war ecumenical relationships with Roman Catholics were limited by the Vatican, but when Bell wrote *A Letter to my Friends in the Evangelical Church in Germany* in 1946, he included the German Roman Catholic Church equally with the Protestants as the source of a new birth for Germany.[45] In 1948 Bell explored ways of opening up dialogue between the ecumenical movement and Rome with a French Jesuit. In 1955 he called on Mgr Montini at the Vatican to discuss ecumenical collaboration and in 1956 encouraged a distinguished Anglican group to accept Montini's invitation to stay as his guests in Milan where he was now the Archbishop. A few months before he died in 1958 Bell called on the Pope. So in the post-war period Bell began the process of taking the Church of England into a new relationship with European Catholicism as well as with Protestantism. Yet he never lost his special relationship with Germany. In February 1946 he told the University of Basle which gave him an honorary degree: 'Germany is the very heart of Europe. Amputate Germany, and you will amputate Europe.' But he also added bluntly:

In Germany the Protestant and Catholic Churches both failed to give the nation that strong moral foundation which should have enabled them to make such a régime as the Hitler régime impossible. The Protestant Church in particular has been too detached from interest in social questions and too subservient to the state.

It was wholly characteristic that his last speech in the Lords in January 1958 was about Germany. In recognition of his remarkable ministry to Germany, the Federal Republic decided later that year to award him its highest honour. But the news arrived too late. He had died a few hours previously.[46]

The significance of Bishop Bell

This is not the place to discuss whether Bell ought to have become Archbishop of Canterbury. Both Archbishops wanted him as Bishop of London in 1945 and again in 1955, but first Churchill and then Eden refused for political reasons. Perhaps under the new system of appointments in which the church has a decisive say, he would have been given some such ecclesiastical recognition. Who can tell? Political friends tried to get him made a C.H. but their efforts were met with silence. His offence was that he had 'betrayed the "establishment" from within . . . and it was to the end unpardonable'.[47]

Bell is significant because of the sheer range and scale of his achievements. He was also (as I have argued elsewhere) a 'creative dissenter' who knew that he must be true to the subversive side of the biblical message, yet also knew that to be creative this meant knowing how to use the levers of power and being prepared to slog away at his homework – very different from the conformist who simply reflects the surrounding mood or the uncreative dissenter who mouths slogans, enjoys opposition and has no wish or capacity to exercise power.[48] In addition, Bell has become a symbol of how the church can be or might have been different. As such, Rolf Hochhuth used him in *Soldiers* (1961) to oppose Churchill – even though the personality of Bell in the play itself is a caricature. Ulrich Simon, the distinguished German Jewish Christian, wrote:

Bell re-enacted for the modern age what martyrdom had meant in the glorious past. He manifested that glory which the world crushes though it cannot live without it.[49]

Bonhoeffer is now commemorated in the Chapel of the Twentieth Century Martyrs in Canterbury Cathedral and in the Calendar of Portsmouth Cathedral. The Church of England added Thomas Becket to its Calendar for an annual commemoration in 1980. How long will it be before George Bell joins that list?

Bell's vision of a world, and particularly a Europe, united by a common allegiance to Christ and to a reunited church serving the wider concerns of his Kingdom, seems remote today when even many Christians accept that religious pluralism is enriching as well as theologically legitimate. But one must remember that Bell had much personal experience of how a common allegiance to Christ did in practice break down barriers of race, language and culture. He wrote in 1940:

I want to show that the Church is not one institution among many, but something given to man, owing its reality to God . . . I want to report how it has been developing as a world force . . . I want to show how it stands for something greater than the State or race or nation or class; and that it has a contribution to make different from the contribution of any other human organization.[50]

Though Bell was committed to the world church (hence, for example, his acute judgement in 1949 that Johannesburg was the second most important see in the Anglican Communion), his primary experience of the church was in Europe where the culture was still predominantly Christian. It was clear therefore if any religion were to provide a spiritual and moral framework for post-war Europe, that religion would be Christianity. Moreover, during and immediately after the war, European Christianity became very confident of its own centrality and effectiveness – hence the power of the Christian Democratic parties in Europe; thus in 1947 it seemed quite natural to everyone that Sir Stafford Cripps (who was close to Bell) as Minister of Economic Affairs could tell the Commons that Britain should 'refresh its heart and mind with a deep draught of that Christian faith which has . . . inspired the peoples of Europe'.[51]

Bell's work continues to bear fruit. The Conference of European Churches, established in 1959, now includes churches from Russia to Ireland. Without the financial help from the German Evangelical Church its work would have been impossible. A remarkable ministry of reconciliation, particularly towards Germany, has flowed from Coventry Cathedral ever since Christmas Day 1940, six weeks after the original Cathedral was destroyed by German bombs. The Roman Catholic Benedictine monks at Trier and the Anglican monks of the Community of the Resurrection at Mirfield entered into a covenanted relationship in 1983 after over 20 years of growing together. The Meissen Agreement (1988) between the German Evangelical Church and the Church of England brings them into a significantly close degree of communion. Since the 1960s, the movement for liturgical reform, which had excited Bell in the 1930s, has produced a remarkable convergence between Roman Catholic and Anglican worship, so removing the huge differences that used to be so marked when the English visited the continent.

Thus words which Bell quoted from his mentor F.D. Maurice were memorably fulfilled in his ministry and all that has flowed from it:

We shall tell them that their Fathers-in-God testify of a universal brotherhood, which has no limits of language or race, that they do not testify of the exclusion or the excision of any portion of the Church, but rather that all are one in Christ Jesus . . .[52]

Notes

1. G.K.A. Bell, *Randall Davidson*, London: Oxford University Press, Third Edition 1952, p. 262.
2. D. Nicholls, *Church and State in Britain since 1820*, London: Routledge and Kegan Paul, 1967, pp. 149, 152.
3. L.E. Elliott-Binns, *English Thought 1860–1900, the theological aspect*, London: Longman, Green and Co, 1956, p. 174.
4. P.W. Schniewind, *Anglicans in Germany, a history of Anglican chaplaincies in Germany until 1945*, Umkirch: Schniewind, 1988.
5. Alan Wilkinson, *The Church of England and the First World War*, London: SPCK, 1978, pp. 20–3.
6. Bell, *Davidson*, p. 732.
7. Alan Wilkinson, *The Community of the Resurrection, a centenary history*, London: SCM Press, 1992.
8. R.C.D. Jasper, *George Bell*, London: Oxford University Press, 1967, pp. 19–20.
9. Charles Gore, *The Religion of the Church*, London: Mowbray, 1917, p. 165.
10. G.K.A. Bell, *The War and the Kingdom of God*, London: Longman, Green and Co, 1915, pp. 5–6; Wilkinson 1978, pp. 256–9.
11. Bell, *Davidson*, pp. 832, 834, 918, 925.
12. R.T. Davidson, *The Testing of a Nation*, London: Macmillan, 1919, p. 157.
13. Bell, *Davidson*, p. 1152.
14. Jasper, p. 60.
15. Alan Wilkinson, *Dissent or Conform? war, peace and the English churches 1900–1945*, London: SCM Press, 1986, p. 67.
16. Lambeth Conference, *Report*, London: SCM Press, 1920, pp. 9–11.
17. Bell, *Davidson*, p. 1208.
18. Wilkinson, *Dissent*, pp. 85–136.
19. G.K.A Bell, *Documents on Christian unity (second series)*, London: Oxford University Press, 1930, p. 223.
20. Jasper, p. 68.
21. Ibid. Chaps 6, 11; Wilkinson, *Dissent*, pp. 99–100, 144–60.
22. Bell Papers, Lambeth Palace Library, London, vol. 27.
23. Wilkinson, *Dissent*, pp. 148, 160–5.
24. Jasper, p. 143.
25. Adrian Hastings, *A History of English Christianity 1920–1985*, London: Collins, 1986, pp. 344–5.
26. Wilkinson, *Dissent*, pp. 163–4.
27. Jasper, pp. 148–9.
28. F.A. Iremonger, *William Temple*, London: Oxford University Press, 1948, pp. 566–7.

29. G.K.A. Bell, *The Church and Humanity (1939–1946)*, London: Longman, Green and Co, 1946, pp. 124–5.
30. Jasper, p. 243.
31. Wilkinson, *Community of the Resurrection*, p. 142.
32. Bell, *Church and Humanity*, pp. 23–7.
33. Hastings, p. 343; Kenneth Slack, *George Bell*, London: SCM Press, 1971, p. 81.
34. Wilkinson, *Dissent*, pp. 223–7.
35. Ulrich Simon, *Sitting in judgement 1913–1963*, London: SPCK, 1978, p. 85.
36. Bell, *Church and Humanity*, p. 43.
37. E. Bethge, *Dietrich Bonhoeffer*, London: Collins, 1977, pp. 660–76; Jasper, pp. 266–75; W.D. Zimmermann and R.G. Smith (eds), *I knew Dietrich Bonhoeffer*, London: Collins, 1966, pp. 193–211.
38. P. Meehan, *The unnecessary war, Whitehall and the German resistance to Hitler*, London: Sinclair-Stevenson, 1992, pp. 304–39.
39. Bell, *Church and Humanity*, pp. 67, 69; Wilkinson, *Dissent*, pp. 252–3.
40. Bell, *Church and Humanity*, pp. 130, 140–1; Wilkinson, *Dissent*, pp. 265–72.
41. L. Mason, ' "Soldiers" and Bishop Bell', *Crucible*, March 1969, pp. 34–7.
42. Jasper, p. 284.
43. Bethge, pp. 830n, 833.
44. O. Dibelius *In the service of the Lord*, London: Faber, 1965, pp. 259–60.
45. Bell, *Church and Humanity*, p. 189.
46. Jasper, chap 15; E. Gordon Rupp, *I seek my brethren: Bishop George Bell and the German churches*, London: Epworth, 1975.
47. Edward Carpenter, *Archbishop Fisher*, Norwich: Canterbury, 1991, pp. 217–20, 225; Slack, p. 124.
48. Wilkinson, *Dissent*, pp. xiii–xv.
49. Simon, p. 86.
50. G.K.A. Bell, *Christianity and world order*, Harmondsworth: Penguin, 1940, pp. 12–13.
51. Wilkinson, *Dissent*, pp. 279–86, 306.
52. Quoted in Bell, *Christianity and world order*, p. 47.

6

Appeasement and Non-Intervention: British policy during the Spanish Civil War

Enrique Moradiellos

From the very beginning of the Spanish Civil War of 1936–1939, the policy followed by the Conservative-dominated British Government towards the conflict has and continues to be the subject of acute political and historiographical controversy. To a great extent, such controversy reflects in turn the enormous and divisive impact of the war upon British political life and public opinion; an impact which is only comparable in modern times to that of the French Revolution more than a century earlier.

No doubt, the main reason for the strange and passionate British interest in the civil war lies in the timing and duration of the Spanish tragedy: which paralleled the deepening crisis of the European situation and the descent of Britain towards the Second World War. In fact, to the contemporary British witness, the importance of the conflict derived from its symbolic and analogical nature: either because it was considered as a rehearsal for the impending war of Democracy against Fascism or as a premature phase of the ineluctable clash of the West with Communism. In both cases, there was a clear understanding of the intimate link between the Spanish struggle and the general European crisis of the late 1930s. An editorial in *The Times* accurately reflected this fact: '[Spain] may be regarded as a distorting mirror in which Europe can see an exaggerated reflection of her own divisions.'[1] Within the Foreign Office, Sir George Mounsey, Assistant Under Secretary in charge of the Department of Western Europe, when acknowledging in an internal memorandum the Spanish conflict and its international repercussions said: 'It is one of the gravest menaces, if not the gravest, which the world has had to face since the Great War.'[2]

This notwithstanding, historians of British foreign policy in the 1930s have tended to neglect or overlook, the essential connection between the Spanish war and the European crisis. They have also tended to view the British response to the conflict as a marginal and peripheral policy, clearly separated from the general continental policy of the British Cabinet. In other words: they have tended to dissociate the policy of Non-Intervention in Spain and the policy of Appeasement in Europe. However, as this chapter will attempt to show, the Spanish policy of the

British Government was an essential and constituent part of their general policy towards the European crisis of the late 1930s.

The starting point of any interpretation of British policy in the Spanish Civil War would have to be the clear fact, agreed by all historians, that British policy had a crucial influence on the course and final outcome of the Spanish war. In particular, it was very favourable to the Insurgent Army in practical terms and a serious obstacle to the war effort of the Republican Government. Such was, certainly, the effect of the policy of collective Non-Intervention promoted by the French and British Governments from August 1936, and officially adopted by all European Governments when they subscribed to the Non-Intervention Pact and participated in its London Committee of supervision.

The application of Non-Intervention worked against the Republic in two ways. In the first place, it meant the imposition of an embargo on arms and munitions to both sides without a parallel recognition of their belligerent rights, thus putting the legitimate Government and the rebels on the same footing in this key respect. Secondly, this embargo was applied basically against the Republic, because Germany and Italy continued their vital support to the rebels despite signing the Pact, while Britain nevertheless upheld the embargo and was followed under duress by France and other European Governments. So a system of aids and inhibitions was created which was fatal for the Republic in the long term and could never be counteracted by Soviet help.

Despite their public protestations of impartiality, British officials were very conscious of the prejudicial nature of unconditional support for the policy of Non-Intervention. In January 1939 Sir Robert Vansittart, Chief Diplomatic Adviser to the Foreign Office, admitted privately: 'the whole course of our policy of Non-intervention – which has effectively, as we all know, worked in an entirely one-sided manner – has been putting a premium on Franco's victory.'[3] On the insurgents' side, Pedro Sainz Rodríguez, a monarchist leader and first minister of Education of General Franco, also acknowledged this fact in his memoirs:

Many Spaniards, disorientated by the anti-English propaganda of the Franco regime, honestly believe that we gained our victory exclusively through Italian and German aid; I am convinced that, though this did contribute, the fundamental reason for our winning the war was the English diplomatic position opposing intervention in Spain.[4]

The importance of the United Kingdom's attitude to the Spanish conflict derived from its economic and strategic interests in Spain and from its position as a leading European and imperial power.

As regards British interests in Spain, three crucial points should be borne in mind: 1) that the naval base in Gibraltar was crucial to British control of the Mediterranean and communications with India – its security was essential for Imperial strategy and depended on Spanish goodwill; 2) Great Britain was Spain's most important trading partner, accounting for 25 per cent of Spanish exports and providing 10 per cent of its imports; 3) British capital accounted for 40 per cent of foreign investments in Spain, largely concentrated in the iron and pyrites mining industries.

Given the extent of those interests, the British Foreign Office followed with attention the critical situation in Spain since 1931, when the oligarchic monarchy was toppled by a democratic Republic bent on a programme of social reform. To summarize very briefly, the persistence of social and political upheavals, particularly after the electoral victory of the Popular Front in February 1936, convinced the British authorities that Spain had begun a process of revolutionary crisis, probably fostered by the Comintern, which the Republican Government was unable to resolve or contain. So, by June 1936, the Foreign Office had all but given up any hope of a constitutional solution in Spain, and expected either a military intervention to restore order and avoid anarchy or some sort of leftist social revolution.[5]

The crystallisation of this image of the Spanish crisis was parallel to the beginning of the British policy of rapprochement towards Fascist Italy, as part of the general policy of appeasement in Europe. The origin of such a policy lay in the difficult dilemma which the British authorities were then confronting in their strategic and diplomatic planning. Since the start of the economic depression, an overextended and enfeebled British Empire was threatened in three different and distant points by powers hostile to the *status quo*: Japan in the Far East; Nazi Germany in Central Europe; and Italy in the Mediterranean. Furthermore, Britain had neither the economic nor the military resources to confront alone the three potential dangers at the same time. Nor could she have relied upon the support of a debilitated France or an isolationist America. In such conditions, appeasement was a diplomatic strategy designed to avoid the hostile convergence of the three powers by reducing tensions with the nearest (Germany) and weakest (Italy).

Therefore, from June 1936, the main objective of British diplomacy was to restore harmonious relations with Italy in order to stabilize the Mediterranean situation and to avoid an Italian alignment with a potentially hostile Germany combined with Japan. Strategic considerations alone seemed to demand such a course, but there was also the strong desire to prevent an arms race whose financial demands would endanger the economic recovery and the social and political stability of Britain and its Empire. In addition to these two factors, there was also British suspicion of hidden Soviet intentions and the conviction that any war would provide ample opportunities for the expansion of communism. These were, in essence, the main pillars of the British policy of appeasement during the late 1930s.[6]

It is clear, then, that prior to the eruption of the Spanish Civil War, the anti-revolutionary preoccupation about Spain and the search for a Mediterranean entente with Italy were twin considerations at the Foreign Office. They were to establish the essential framework for the British reaction to the conflict, which began on the 17 July 1936 with a large military insurrection against the Republican Government.

The partial failure of the coup in many areas, including Madrid, transformed it into a bloody civil war. Since neither side had the means to wage a full-scale war, both were immediately obliged to look for foreign support. General Franco, soon to be head of the Insurgent Army, asked Mussolini and Hitler for help, which secretly arrived by late July. The Republican Government, hampered by total dislocation of the State apparatus, sought support from the new Popular Front Government in France. Both sides tried to gain the indirect help of the British Government. These facts forced the British Cabinet to respond urgently to the crisis, especially because the whole policy of appeasement would be endangered if the French ally were to help the Republic while Italy and Germany were support-ing Franco.

The British response to the crisis was to adopt a policy of tacit neutrality (that is, never formally proclaimed) which was, nevertheless, clearly benevolent towards the military insurgents. The essential aims of that policy were to avoid giving any direct or indirect help to a Government side whose legality was held to conceal a revolutionary purpose, and to avert any possibility of confrontation with rebel forces of counter-revolutionary persuasion. Not in vain, British diplomats in Spain had warned that 'no government existed today' and 'there were military forces in operation on the one hand, opposed by a virtual Soviet on the other'.[7] The extent of the anti-revolutionary feeling created by the Spanish crisis among the British authorities is clearly revealed by this statement by Sir Maurice Hankey, Cabinet Secretary:

In the present state of Europe, with France and Spain menaced by Bolshevism, it is not inconceivable that before long it might pay us to throw in our lot with Germany and Italy.[8]

The policy of tacit and benevolent neutrality was immediately implemented in four key respects: 1) by the refusing of facilities to the Republican fleet in Gibraltar, which was neutralized for the rest of the war; 2) by the imposition of a secret embargo on arms to the Republic; 3) by pressure on the French Government in order to prevent it giving any help to the Republic; and 4) by the avoidance of any confrontation with Germany and Italy due to their support to Franco. Awareness of the British position and consequent fears contributed significantly to the French reluctance to support the Republic and convinced Hitler and Mussolini that limited and covert aid to Franco would not provoke energetic opposition from Britain and might bring political and even strategic advantages.[9]

In this context, the Non-Intervention Pact signed in August 1936, with its corresponding embargo on arms and munitions, provided the necessary diplomatic cloak and shelter required by the British policy of tacit neutrality. Furthermore, by its mere existence and apparent efficacy, the Pact and its Committee of supervision became an essential means to safeguard the diplomatic aims established by the Foreign Office: to confine the war within Spain, and at the same time, restrain the intervention of the French ally, while avoiding any alignment with the USSR and any confrontation with Germany and Italy over their support to Franco. Stanley Baldwin, the Prime Minister, had given an early and clear-cut directive to Anthony Eden, the Foreign Secretary: 'On no account, French or other, must (you) bring us into the fight on the side of the Russians.'[10]

Thus, for the British authorities, from the beginning, the collective policy of Non-Intervention contained an element of fraudulence, in that its real aim was not the one declared – the prevention of foreign intervention – but rather the safeguarding of the political aims indicated above. As a Foreign Office memoran-dum acknowledged: 'we have considered the continued existence of the Agreement and of the supervising Committee as of more importance than the actual efficacy of the embargo itself'. Non-Intervention was thus perceived as the ideal means to carry out a policy clearly defined by Winston Churchill in a private letter to Eden:

It seems to me most important to make Blum [the French Premier] stay with us strictly neutral, even if Germany and Italy continue to back the rebels and Russia sends money to the Government.[11]

The political strategy formulated by the Foreign Office in late July and August 1936 was based on two conditioning factors mutually reinforcing one another:

The first factor was the preference for a victory of the military insurgents, who seemed to be less dangerous for British interests in Spain and Europe than the victory of a Government perceived as presiding over a process of bolshevisation. The following judgement by a Foreign Office analyst encapsulated the general impression within official circles:

. . .[reports from Spain] show quite clearly that the alternative to Franco is Communism tempered by anarchy; and I further believe that if this last régime is triumphant in Spain it will spread to other countries, and notably France.[12]

The second factor was the need to preserve a high degree of social and political consensus in Britain, where the trade union strength of Labour, along with growing popular and intellectual support for the Republic, precluded policies more favourable to the insurgents (such as official neutrality or direct assistance). This fact was discovered early by the Portuguese Government, when they asked confidentially of the Foreign Office what it would do to avoid 'the establishment of a communist regime in Spain' and received the following answer: 'England would not intervene militarily in Spain, whatever situation developed in that country. The British Government would not have the support of public opinion.'[13]

The equal importance of both conditioning factors was summed up in a private statement by David Margesson, Conservative Chief Whip, to the Italian representative in London:

Our interests, our desire is that the [military] revolution should triumph and Communism be crushed, but on the other hand, we do not wish to emerge from our neutrality. . .This is the only possible way of counteracting labour agitation.[14]

Parallel to those conditioning factors, the British political strategy was constructed on two implicit assumptions:

The first assumption was the expectation that the war would be short, given that the inexpert and badly supplied workers' militias fighting for the Republic would not be able to contain the advance of an experienced regular army supplied by two European military powers. Therefore, the conquest of Madrid was thought to be a matter of weeks and a suitable political occasion for the public declaration of neutrality. Not in vain, Military Intelligence had predicted by mid-August that 'prolonged resistance (in Madrid) is therefore unlikely', while the Foreign Office maintained 'the hope that the Civil War would be of short duration'.[15]

The second assumption was the conviction that the 'diplomacy of pound sterling' would be enough to recover the benevolence of a future military regime, because such a regime would have to seek help in the City of London in order to finance the post-war reconstruction of Spain. An early report by the Commercial Secretary at the Embassy confirmed this long-standing premise:

. . .When the war is over Spain will be in need of imports considerably above her normal requirements. . .,will be short of foreign exchange and there will be grave need for extensive foreign credits. . .In any case the obvious country in which to obtain such foreign credits will be Great Britain.[16]

Only within the framework of the political strategy indicated, can a crucial and often overlooked aspect of British policy towards the Spanish war be best appreciated: it represents a specific and regional version of the general policy of appeasement in Europe. The fact is that British non-intervention conformed systematically to the parameters established by that policy.

Until December 1936, there was total agreement in the Foreign Office and the Cabinet as regards the profile of British policy in Spain. Criticism of Non-Intervention was reduced to small sections of public opinion, the vacillating Labour Opposition and Left-wing parties. Towards the end of the year, however, the international and domestic situation began to change substantially.

In the first place, the republicans were able to hold on in Madrid, thanks mostly to Soviet military aid which began to arrive in October. Secondly, Hitler and Mussolini decided to intensify their material and diplomatic support for Franco. By the end of 1936, they had both concluded that Franco's victory could not be achieved merely by sending war *materiél* and a few technicians, but demanded a full-scale Army Corps. The result was the despatch of the 5,000 strong German Condor Legion, and the 40,000 men of the Italian *Corpo di Truppi Volontari*. Thirdly, the blatant intervention by the Axis powers strengthened public sympathy for the Republic and forced Labour demands for strong action and cessation of the arms embargo to the Spanish Government. These developments implied the partial breakdown of British political strategy, for they destroyed the assumption of a short war and ruined the confinement of the struggle which the Non-Intervention system had achieved.

The British Government was therefore obliged to readjust their Spanish policy to the new conditions of a long war and massive intervention by the Axis powers. It was in this process of analysis and reappraisal that the first splits appeared in the Cabinet and the Foreign Office over the required response to the changes, giving rise to two distinct phases of British policy between 1937 and the end of the war.

The first phase lasted from January 1937 to February 1938. In this period, the Spanish policy of the British Government reflected a precarious balance between the views of Anthony Eden, the Foreign Secretary, and the majority of the Cabinet, led by the new Prime Minister, Neville Chamberlain.

The Foreign Secretary was increasingly worried by the growing expansionism of the Axis Powers and their potential threat to British interests. He therefore favoured a firm policy of Non-Intervention in order to confine the Spanish war and foster an international mediation which would prevent the establishment of a regime in Spain closely connected to the Axis. Eden came to consider Spain as the touchstone of the policy of rapprochement to Italy. Consequently, he thought that any Anglo-Italian agreement would have to be conditional upon Italian proof of goodwill in Spain (by withdrawing Italian troops or supporting a mediation). In January 1937 Eden explained to the Cabinet the basis for his new policy of taking a strong line in Spain:

The Spanish civil war has ceased to be an internal Spanish issue and has become an international battle-ground. The character of the future Government of Spain has now become less important to the peace of Europe than that the dictators should not be victorious in that country. . .In this condition I consider it imperative that we should spare no effort to put a stop to intervention in Spain.[17]

Contrary to Eden, Chamberlain thought that there was a real possibility of splitting Italy from Germany (due to their latent antagonism in Austria and the Balkans) and that this strategic and diplomatic aim was sufficiently important to run some risks for the sake of it in Spain. In Chamberlain's view, Italian help to Franco could be tacitly condoned because there remained for Britain the lever of pound sterling diplomacy for the post-war reconstruction. In a Cabinet meeting of March 1937 he declared:

It had to be remembered that we were dealing not only with the Spanish insurgents, but, behind them, with the Germans and Italians. General Franco was not a free agent. No doubt he hoped to win, but hardly without assistance from the Germans and Italians. Consequently he was unlikely to agree to any undertaking which was unacceptable to the Germans and Italians unless we were able to do something disagreeable to him in return. The Germans and Italians would not allow him to do so. To insist up to the point proposed in the Secretary of State's Memorandum therefore, was not only useless but must lead to a very serious situation with Germany and Italy. If and when General Franco had won the Civil War, however, the situation would be very different, and no doubt he would be looking round for help from other countries besides Germany and Italy. That would be the moment at which to put strong pressure upon him,. . .that would be the time for action.[18]

Due to these underlying tendencies, the Spanish policy of the British Cabinet during 1937 showed ambiguous and contradictory features. On the one hand, there were initiatives clearly inspired by the policy of stiff measures advocated by Eden: the establishment of a land and naval control of Non-Intervention; the non-recognition of the Francoist blockade of Bilbao; and, foremost, the Nyon Conference which stopped the piratical attacks in the Mediterranean against the international merchant shipping (which was the work of Italian submarines trying to blockade the Republic by sea). On the other hand, following Chamberlain's view, there was a continuous tacit tolerance of Italo-German aid to Franco, a firm negative to any French help to the Republic and a persistent search for a way to ameliorate Anglo-Italian relations.

By February 1938, with the Nazi *Anschluss* of Austria on the horizon and Mussolini offering to begin the negotiations for an Anglo-Italian Agreement, the difference of opinion between Eden and Chamberlain reached a climax.

Eden suspected that Mussolini desired a diplomatic victory to counterbalance his abandonment of Austrian independence. He thought this abandonment re-vealed a secret deal by which Germany was to have a free hand in Central Europe in return for supporting Italian expansion in the Mediterranean. Therefore, it was more important than ever to make Spain the test-ground 'of Italian good faith and good will' as regards Britain. Meanwhile, he remained convinced of the need to condone some French aid to the Republic because Franco's victory 'would increase the likelihood of some early adventure elsewhere by the Dictator States' whereas 'prolongation of the war for another six months would increase the strain on Italy'. For his part, Chamberlain assumed that Mussolini was really anxious about the German arrival at the Italian northern frontier and was trying to restore his previous policy of 'equidistance' between Berlin and London. Consequently, he favoured the immediate opening of negotiations for an agreement without allowing the marginal Spanish problem to interfere in Anglo-Italian relations. During the ensuing debates, the rest of the Cabinet followed the Prime Minister's view and the result was Eden's resignation. He was replaced by Lord Halifax at the Foreign Office.[19]

The second phase in the Spanish policy of the British Cabinet lasted from February 1938 to April 1939.

After Eden's resignation, any practical idea of mediation or effective Non-Intervention in Spain was abandoned in favour of a quick reconciliation with Italy. Clear proof of this was given by the fact that there was only one meeting of the Non-Intervention Committee during the whole year. Furthermore, in order to facilitate the agreement with Italy, the British Cabinet actively promoted the end of the civil war by a victory for Franco, primarily by pressing the French Government to close their frontier to the transit of Soviet war *materiél* for the Republic. At the beginning of June 1938, the British Ambassador in Paris told Georges Bonnet, French Foreign Secretary, that his government were:

. . .unable to appreciate why the French Government are unable to carry out their undertakings under the Non-Intervention scheme and prevent the passage of munitions across the French frontier to Barcelona. It would be most unfortunate if sympathy with France in this country were on that account to decline. On the other hand it will be most regrettable if we cannot reap the fruits of our agreement with Italy, and this cannot take place until some settlement has been achieved in Spain.[20]

Mostly as a result of this pressure, by mid-June 1938 France closed its Spanish frontier and cut off the last and only channel of war supplies to the beleaguered Republic. British pressure continued unrelenting as is revealed by this private letter of the British Ambassador in Paris to Lord Halifax by the end of June:

I am going to see Daladier [the French premier] tomorrow morning and shall do this ('to impress upon him the absolutely vital importance that His Majesty's Government attached to the continued closure of the Pyrennese frontier'), for I feel it is very important to support Bonnet in every possible way in what I now believe to be his genuine fight to keep that infernal frontier closed. He tells me there are about eight Soviet ships in the offing, bursting with war *materiél*, which the Russians are terribly anxious to shoot into Spain. If they succeeded the war would go on for months more.[21]

The Anglo-French abandonment of the Spanish Republic was definitely sealed in September 1938, when the German-Czech crisis was resolved by the Pact of Munich and the consequent partition of Czechoslovakia. Lord Halifax implicitly recognized this fact in the House of Lords when he said in November:

It has never been true, and it is not true today, that the Anglo-Italian Agreement had the lever value that some think to make Italy desist from supporting General Franco and his fortunes. Signor Mussolini has always made it plain from the time of the first conversations between His Majesty's Government and the Italian Government that, for reasons known to us all – whether we approve of them or not – he was not prepared to see General Franco defeated.[22]

Against this background, the Cabinet approved the legal recognition of Franco's Government in February 1939, more than a month before the end of the war. Some analysts, like Sir Robert Vansittart, opposed such a move by voicing their concern at the prospect of a malevolent Francoist Spain: 'We should have a potentially hostile Power lying on some of our most vital communications.' But the prevailing view at the Foreign Office and the Cabinet still thought the alternative was even worse:

It would be a great mistake to suppose that moderation and discipline would characterize it [the Republic] once the immediate military necessity for moderation and discipline were removed. . . . The forces of indiscipline, anarchism, extremism and jacquerie in Spain are extensive, old and strong; and I think that they would render impossible the existence of the sort of administration Negrín [Republican Premier] purports to envisage as a consequence of defeat or disruption of the Whites. The main reason why the war goes on is the same as the reason why it started. It started because civil government under the Frente Popular broke down and let loose widespread jacquerie. Franco and his friends saw no way to stop this, indeed it was clear that there was no way to stop this short of an armed rising . . . Both sides are heroic and remorseless. Both have had their hecatombs. But the Reds started this competition in slaughter – and the Red atrocities were more atrocious than the White.[23]

In order to placate any public outcry over the fate of the Republic and Labour animosity against the official policy, Chamberlain advised his ministers to maintain the maximum political prudence towards what should appear a fait accompli:

. . .great care would have to be taken in dealing with the matter in public pronouncements in a cautious and guarded fashion. For example, we must avoid showing any satisfaction at the prospect of a Franco victory.[24]

In conclusion the evidence clearly suggests two main points about the British policy of Non-Intervention in the Spanish Civil War. First of all, that long before the *Anschluss* with Austria and the Munich Agreement, the Spanish conflict had served as the principal stage for the implementation of the British policy of appeasement in Europe. Secondly, by the same token, that Spain had developed into the main argument for the viability of appeasement within official circles and among public opinion.

The only essential difference with the *Anschluss* and Munich was that acute anti-revolutionary preoccupations remained part of the analysis and decision-making process of the British authorities until the Spanish problem disappeared. If due attention is not paid to this political-ideological element, one carefully concealed in official circles, it becomes impossible to understand the policy of inactivity in the face of the increasing strategic risks to the security of an area vital to the defence of the Empire; an area and country which was not and could not be a German or Italian sphere of influence (as Austria) nor was it 'a far away country of which we know nothing' (as Czechoslovakia). It seems clear that the sacrifice of a perceived Red Spain was deemed a reasonable price for Italian goodwill and the hope of preserving European peace, and as a result, the British Government washed its hands of the Spanish Civil War.

Notes

1. 'Europe and Spain', *The Times*, 8 September 1936.
2. Minute, 13 August 1936. Foreign Office Records, Public Record Office (hereafter PRO), Kew, London.
3. Memorandum by Vansittart, 16 January 1937. PRO FO 371/24115 W9673.
4. P. Sainz Rodriguez, *Testimonio y recuerdos* Barcelona: Editorial Planeta, 1978, pp. 234–5.
5. On Anglo-Spanish relations before and during the civil war, there are three basic studies: Jill Edwards, *The British Government and the Spanish Civil War*, London: Macmillan, 1979; Douglas Little, *Malevolent Neutrality: The United States, Great Britain and the Origins of the Spanish Civil War*, Ithaca, N.Y.: Cornell University Press, 1985; Enrique Moradiellos, *Neutralidad Benévola: el gobierno británico y la insurrección militar española de 1936*, Oviedo: Pentalfa Ediciones, 1990.
6. L.R. Pratt, *East of Malta, West of Suez. Britain's Mediterranean Crisis*, 1936–1939, Cambridge: Cambridge University Press, 1975; G. Schmidt, *The Policies and Economies of Appeasement. British Foreign Policy in the 1930s*, Leamington Spa: Berg, 1984; Paul Kennedy; *The Realities behind Diplomacy. Background Influences on British External Policy*, London: Fontana, 1981.
7. Telegram from the commercial secretary at the Madrid Embassy, 21 July 1936. PRO FO 371/20523 W6575. On the general course of the conflict, see: Hugh Thomas, *The Spanish Civil War*, London, Harmondsworth: Penguin Books, 1977; Paul Preston, *The Spanish Civil War*, London: Weidenfeld and Nicolson, 1986.
8. 'The future of the League of Nations, by Sir Maurice Hankey', 20 July 1936. PRO FO 371/20475 W11340.
9. Geoffrey Warner, 'France and Non-intervention in Spain', *International Affairs*, 38, 1962, pp. 203–30; Glynn Stone, 'Britain, Non-Intervention and the Spanish Civil War', *European Studies Review*, 10, 1979, pp. 129–49; Ismael Saz, *Mussolini contra la Segunda República*, Valencia: Edicions Alfons el Magnànim, 1986; John Coverdale, *Italian Intervention in the Spanish Civil War*, Princeton: Princeton University Press, 1975; Angel Viñas, *La Alemania nazi y el 18 de julio*, Madrid: Alianza Editorial, 1977; Robert Whealey, *Hitler and Spain. The Nazi Role in the Spanish Civil War*, Lexington: University Press of Kentucky, 1989.
10. Quoted in Thomas Jones, *A Diary with Letters, 1931–1950* Oxford: Oxford University Press, 1954, p. 231.
11. Quoted in Martin Gilbert, *Winston Churchill*, vol. 5 London: Heinemann, 1976, p. 782. The previous quotation is from a Foreign Office memorandum, 16 November 1936. PRO FO 371/20585 W15624.
12. Minute by Gladwyn Jebb (Western Department), 25 November 1936. PRO FO 371/20570 W15925.
13. Telegram from the Portuguese Chargé d'Affaires to Lisbon, 22 July 1936. *Dez Anos de Política Externa. 1936–1947*, vol. III, document no. 24, Lisbon: Impresa Nacional, 1964. On popular sympathies, see the result of the public opinion polls by Gallup: on average, 58 per cent of those questioned declared themselves in favour of the Republic; against 8 per cent in favour of Franco, and 34 per cent who didn't answer. *News Chronicle*, 28 October 1938.
14. Quoted in Ismael Saz, *Mussolini*, pp. 204–5.
15. Summary of Information, 14 August 1936. Records of the War Office, Directorate of

Military Operations and Intelligence, file 1576. PRO WO 106/1576. Memorandum, 16 December 1936. PRO FO 371/21383 W3018.
16. Report by Mr. Pack, 30 October 1936. PRO FO 371/20519 W1419.
17. Memorandum by Eden, 8 January 1937. Records of the Cabinet Office, Cabinet Committee on Foreign Policy, file 628. PRO CAB 27/628.
18. Cabinet Minutes, 3 March 1937. Records of the Cabinet Office, Cabinet Minutes and Conclusions, file 87. PRO CAB 23/87.
19. *Documents on British Foreign Policy*, 2nd Ser. vol. XIX, nos. 561, 568, 573, appendix I and II, London: H.M.S.O., 1982; A. Eden, *Facing the Dictators*, London: Cassell, 1962, pp. 579–91; John Harvey (ed.), *The Diplomatic Diaries of Oliver Harvey*, London: Collins, 1970, pp. 92–97. Eden's quotations are extracted from his remarks in the Cabinet meeting of 29 September 1937. PRO CAB 23/89.
20. Foreign Office telegram to Sir Eric Phipps and vice versa, 7 and 8 June 1938. PRO FO 371/22659 W7332, W7352.
21. Sir E. Phipps to Lord Halifax, 29 June 1938. Records of the Foreign Office, Private Collections, Halifax Papers, file 323. PRO FO 800/323. See also the Foreign Office internal note 'Account on what happened when the French frontier was closed in June last', 19 January 1939. PRO FO 371/24116 W1855.
22. *Parliamentary Debates. House of Lords*, 3 November 1938, col. 1624.
23. Memorandum by Mr. O'Malley (First Secretary at the Embassy in Spain), 7 January 1939. PRO FO 371/24147 W1415. Sir George Mounsey and Sir Orme Sargent (Assistant Under Secretary of State in charge of Central Europe) expressed their agreement with O'Malley's conclusions. Vansittart's views were stated at a Cabinet Committee on Foreign Policy, 23 January 1939. PRO CAB 27/624.
24. Minutes of the Cabinet Committee on Foreign Policy, 23 January 1939. PRO CAB 27/624.

7

Federal Union

Sir Charles Kimber

Peace in our time, he said, but his or mine
For I am 26 and he is 69

I believe these words to be much more than a savage commentary on a pathetic old man. To me, they go a long way towards illuminating the events of those fateful years between Versailles and Munich.

Although the Great War tore huge gaps in the generation containing those who were preparing themselves for government, those gaps were not enough to stop the survivors in Germany and Italy from throwing out the old men who had governed them before the war and taking over. In Britain and France on the other hand, the survivors saw victory as mission accomplished, duty done. They wanted only to return and cultivate their gardens. Politics could be left to those who understood it; they might be old and many of them hard-faced profiteers, but at least they had seen the country through.

In both Italy and Germany, nationhood had only recently taken the form of a unified nation-state. To the new men who took over, defeat was a national humiliation. To restore pride and respect for a new found national identity Fascists and Nazis saw only the need to dramatise and prove it in a display of national strength and disciplined conformity.

In both Britain and France on the other hand, nationhood needed no proving; both had been unified nation-states for too long, their nationhood forged in wars against each other. Loyalty to the state had been nationalised.

To all four nation-states the right to go to war to preserve or assert its identity and status was considered the final proof of its sovereignty. The feudal virtue of prowess in battle was proof of the virility of the nation's manhood; and territorial aggrandisement illustrated national superiority.

Here in Britain the generation which had been too young to fight saw things differently. We had taken to heart Nurse Cavell's last words, 'Patriotism is not enough, I must have no bitterness for anyone.' Like George Orwell we had come to recognise the difference between patriotism and nationalism. 'My country right or wrong' was not for us. War was no proof of manhood; empire no proof of national superiority.

Many of us joined the Peace Pledge Union launched by Canon Dick Sheppard in October 1934 and swore never to fight again. Others joined the Communist Party in the belief that in Communism there was the basis, not only of a fairer society, but also of a world in which national rivalry was no more. When the Spanish Civil War broke out many went to fight in the belief that the Republican cause transcended nationalism. We also put our faith in the League of Nations and joined the League of Nations Union. In the Covenant of the League we saw Europe's true memorial to those who had been killed. The Covenant of the League enshrined the idea of collective security. It was a revolutionary notion. Its signatories were to abandon the age-old practice of kings and emperors who had formed alliances in order to balance power between themselves. Instead governments were now committed to outlaw war itself by undertaking to band together against any nation which threatened to go to war. It took Italy's attack on Abyssinia to bring home to us how naive we had been to believe that the old men, brought up in the old ways, had ever had the smallest intention of changing their policies and honouring the Covenant.

When over 10 million of us voted in the 1935 'Peace Ballot' to impose sanctions, including 6 million who favoured military sanctions[1] – the truth of Rudyard Kipling's wartime verse from the trenches echoed down the years:

If any question why we died
Tell them because our fathers lied

It was, in my view, the last occasion on which Britain had the chance to lead in world affairs. The Hoare-Laval Pact and Baldwin's sealed lips concealing a lie felt to us as squalid and shameful as any episode in this country's history.

At the time, as a prelude to what I hoped would be a career in politics, I was working in the press and political relations office of an oil company. A school acquaintance, Derek Rawnsley, was similarly employed in another company and we used to meet frequently – often with others – for lunch. The talk, inevitably, almost always turned to the international scene – to what had gone wrong. Gradually we were forced to realise that although the Covenant of the League might have been regarded by us as a sacred vow – as it had by its sponsor, President Woodrow Wilson – the old men who were our governors had never taken it seriously. As men who exercised sovereign powers in the name of their entire nation, however small a proportion of its people their policies represented, they saw themselves as heirs to the absolute sovereigns who were their predecessors. Since sovereigns had always known what to do with treaties when they became inconvenient, there was no need for them to break precedent. In short, because the League had relied for its effectiveness on the promises of rulers of sovereign nation-states, it had been founded on sand. Without authority and powers of its own the League was fatally flawed.

Such were our perceptions at the time. Conversations of this kind were, of course, taking place all over the country in those years. There was an awfulness so far beyond credulity about the top Nazis which was paralysing. Faced by Neville Chamberlain's well-intentioned obstinacy great numbers of us were left suspended between disbelief and hope, helpless, as in a nightmare, to change what happened. I think it was Harold Nicolson who said of Chamberlain that 'he entered foreign affairs like a curate entering a pub for the first time'.

Munich, however, to coin a phrase, was one treaty too far. Rawnsley by now had left his oil company and was running two businesses of his own; one from an office in Bloomsbury's Gordon Square. Neither business had anything to do with politics, but when the Munich conference was announced he rang me and said, 'Look, we must do something. If you leave old Muddlitup (our name for my choleric employer) you can have a room here and we can get something started.' So, the following week I found myself in an elegant Georgian drawing room entirely bare except for some matting on the floor, a desk, a chair, a telephone and some blank paper.

I drafted a statement of our ideas after much discussion during which we were joined by a third partner, Patrick Ransome. He was a freelance journalist who had studied international law. We circulated the final version to friends, inviting them to a meeting in Gordon Square. We got a barrel of beer in and about 60 turned up. They were enthusiastic and very much approved the idea of launching an organisation. Better still, they contributed enough money to have a statement of aims printed and circulated. I picked out 400 names from *Who's Who* of men and women who were, or had been, active in international affairs and wrote by hand to each enclosing the statement under our adopted title, Federal Union.

The response was astonishing for its volume, variety and standing. Since Rawnsley was occupied with his businesses the job of interviewing those who responded, in order to discover what help they would give, fell to Ransome and myself. It was while we were interviewing Harold Butler of the International Labour Office that he told us about the forthcoming publication of Clarence Streit's *Union Now*. Streit was the Foreign Editor of the *New York Times*. In his book, after demolishing the case for international organisations based on national sovereignty, he went on to propose an immediate Federal Union of 15 democracies with which to confront the Axis bloc. His 15 democracies included not only the neutral European countries, but also the British dominions and the USA itself.

Whilst we recognised the power with which he argued the case against national sovereignty, the three of us who had launched Federal Union thought that Streit's proposal of an immediate union of such a kind was totally unrealistic. We also thought it undesirable. We were not anti-Yank, but Europe to us had a special identity, and it was as a European institution that we had criticised the League and were seeking to replace it. In our printed statement, however, we had not proposed any founder members by name; instead we had simply suggested that those prepared to join at once should do so as a nucleus which others could join later. Since everyone's attention was focused on Europe we simply assumed that, like us, everyone else would take it for granted that the Federal Union we were proposing would be European. It was to prove a serious mistake.

Among those who approached us – after first having sent a scout to vet us – was Lionel Curtis. He was a founder of Chatham House and had been one of Lord Milner's celebrated so-called kindergarten of bright young men during the Boer War. Messianic by nature – he was known as the Prophet – federalism to him was a sacred cause and his massive book on the subject was entitled *Civitas Dei*.[2] He brought with him Lord Lothian, who had been with Lloyd George at Versailles and was known as an appeaser, although this was an attitude he abandoned after Munich. He too had been one of Milner's kindergarten.

Ransome and I, by now, had seen a pretty wide variety of people and we decided to invite some to form a Panel of Advisers. Those who accepted were Wickham Steed, a former editor of *The Times*, Kingsley Martin, the then editor of the *New Statesman*, Barbara Wootton, the then head of Bedford College and later one of the first life peeresses, Curtis and Lothian. It was a mixed bag, but an influential one. At its first meeting it was agreed that I should draft a brief 'statement of beliefs', for which each member should canvas signatures from amongst the great and good of his or her acquaintances.

In the meantime I had been planting letters in the press giving Federal Union's name and address. As a result a rising tide of letters began to flood into Gordon Square. Their general themes were immensely encouraging. For example; 'You have put into words what I have been thinking for a long time. What can I do? I enclose a donation to help.' In reply we told them to do as we had done: call a meeting of friends, write to the press, form a branch and recruit members. We produced additional literature such as form letters, notes for speakers, answers to questions and we started *Federal Union News*.

Just as the panel of advisers was a mixed bag, so too were the signatories to the statement of beliefs which they obtained and also those who wrote in to join the organisation. The signatories included few active politicians. Ernest Bevin, the General Secretary of the Transport and General Workers' Union and Richard Law, Conservative MP and an Under Secretary for Foreign Affairs at the time, were important exceptions. There were men of science, such as Lancelot Hogben and Julian Huxley; men of religion including William Temple, the Archbishop of York, and the Moderator of the Free Church Federal Council; writers and journalists, including J.B. Priestley and Ritchie Calder; economists of various hues, of whom Lionel Robbins was perhaps the best known; militarists such as Liddell Hart and General Swinton and pacifists such as C.E.M. Joad[3] and Canon Charles Raven, Master of Corpus Christi, Cambridge.

The growing membership was also a mixed bunch. Some had been convinced by writers such as H.G. Wells, Bertrand Russell and Norman Angell that national sovereignty was the fundamental problem and cause of wars and therefore dreamt of a world federation. Others, once Streit's *Union Now* and W.B. Curry's later best-selling Penguin Special, *The Case for Federal Union*[4] had been published, saw Anglo-American Union as the objective. Those of us who had started the organisation soon found it difficult to keep the idea of a Union which was confined to Europe to the fore. This variety of proposed unions added a further difficulty; how to prevent the term 'federation' from degenerating into a 'cause' behind a catchword.

The task was made more problematic because both Curtis and Lothian, who were the most active of our advisers, were totally sold on Streit. Although, as secretary of Federal Union, I was acutely aware of the differences in the membership, I did not know the extent and single-mindedness of Curtis and Lothian's activities. I did not know, for instance, that Curtis had told Lothian that he proposed to use the three young men as Milner had used his kindergarten; neither did I know that Lothian was writing to everyone as though Federal Union had been started to promote Streit. I also had no idea that when Curtis later found that we were not to be used by anyone as Streit's British mouthpiece, he deliberately set out to have me replaced by his own nominee as secretary.

By the time that war broke out – a year after Munich – it was clearly time to disband the Panel of Advisers in favour of a properly constituted Council representing a membership committed to an explicit statement of objects. A conference of representatives from such branches as had then been formed approved a constitution and a statement of objectives which I had drafted and by which all members were to be bound. The statement did not contain the word 'federal'; instead it spoke of a Union of peoples, 'with a common government for common affairs and national self-government and national affairs'. Given the range of opinions within the membership it had proved impossible to suggest a set of founder members by name.

Throughout the winter and spring, during the phoney war, Federal Union grew rapidly and in spite of the blackout, public meetings throughout the country drew large audiences culminating in a Queen's Hall meeting as packed as ever it had been for the last night of the Proms. Within 18 months of the decision to launch an organisation Federal Union had over 200 branches and a membership count in the tens of thousands.

With the outbreak of war came a further important development; Sir William Beveridge fulfilled a promise he had made when we started. With Ransome acting as its secretary he organised a research institute made up of a series of discussion groups. Papers were submitted and discussed by leading specialists of the day. The economists included Lionel Robbins, James Meade, Lowell Dickinson, Evan Durbin, Harold Wilson[5] and Friedrich von Hayek. K.C. Wheare, Ivor Jennings and A.L. Goodhart dealt with constitutional issues; Gilbert Murray, Madariaga and Barbara Wootton with educational questions; Lord Lugard and Norman Bentwich with colonial matters.

Lothian, Joad and the veteran socialist journalist H.N. Brailsford had already contributed pamphlets which had been published by Federal Union. Now the papers produced by the discussion groups of the research institute were produced as a series of 'Federal Tracts'. These have recently been collected into a single volume and published in book form by the Lothian Trust. The phoney war was therefore a period of immense activity. During that period the press was full of discussion of War Aims. I think that we can claim to have focused that discussion as far as possible on the idea of federation.

An organisation which had grown so fast and almost spontaneously and which contained so many young people was seen by many of their experienced and academic elders as amateurish, naive, idealistic and, worst of all, enthusiastic. They had some justification, but instead of joining it and lending it stability and expertise they held aloof – most notably those in Chatham House. Here Curtis's links with Federal Union were not helpful. Not only was he actively plotting to take over the organisation, but at Chatham House he had been closely identified with the idea of imperial federation and now with Streit's proposal of an Atlantic federation. As a result he scarcely represented anyone except himself.

The Chatham House debate instead centred on European federation, and not on Streit's ideas. This was largely due to the influence of Arnold Toynbee, Leo Amery and a strange character called Count Coudenhove-Kalergi. The latter succeeded in winning very influential support all over Europe for what he called the Pan Europa Movement. In the discussions I had with him I must have misjudged him, underestimating the strength of that support. I formed the opinion that the support was more nominal than real; that he was something of a crank whose aim seemed to be to restore the Holy Roman Empire as a bulwark against Russia. However, he was also active at Chatham House and succeeded in forming a parliamentary group in support of his proposals.

The discussions at Chatham House were important because the government had voted it money to create a research institute housed at Oxford to look into possible post-war solutions to international problems, with Toynbee as Director. Soon after the outbreak of the war, in a paper to the Foreign Secretary, Lord Halifax, Toynbee proposed that the Anglo-French alliance should be converted into an Anglo-French Union under a united parliamentary control of military, foreign and economic policies thus forming a nucleus around which a European Federation could subsequently develop. The paper included the draft of 'An Act of Perpetual Association between the United Kingdom and France'. After Halifax and R.A. Butler, his Under Secretary, had seen it, an interdependent committee under the chairmanship of the former Cabinet Secretary, Lord Hankey, was appointed. Hankey was opposed to constitutional change in wartime. Instead he favoured an Anglo-French association which would lead to a post-war Anglo-French bloc of 85 million with which to confront the Germans. As a skilful civil servant he was an expert in diversionary tactics. Toynbee's research institute was instructed to investigate the problems encountered by the Austrians and Hungarians when establishing the *Ausgliech* in 1867 as a bulwark against the Slavs. In the process both Butler and Hankey showed open contempt for the 'eminent learned gentlemen' of Chatham House.

By now it was May 1940 and within the ensuing month the German army had relieved Hankey of the need of any further demonstration of Butler's 'Art of the Possible' by forcing the capitulation of France. Shortly before the war started an Anglo-French Coordinating Committee had been set up with Jean Monnet as President. As soon as the British retreated to Dunkirk and Paris fell, Monnet and Sir Arthur Salter drafted a declaration of total union. The two nations were to be one with a common citizenship, a united parliament and a common currency. A written constitution was to provide for joint organs of defence and economic policy. On June 15 both Churchill and de Gaulle were shown this proposed declaration. By the following day the French government was in Bordeaux and the British were making desperate attempts to prevent it from surrendering. At 3pm the War Cabinet met and approved a modified Declaration of Union – Churchill remarking that some dramatic gesture was clearly necessary to keep the French going. At 4.30pm de Gaulle telephoned the Declaration to Paul Reynaud, the French Prime Minister, who was overjoyed. Just after 10pm that evening as Churchill, together with Attlee and a delegation of experts, were waiting for their train to leave Victoria for France where they had arranged to meet Reynaud in Brittany, they were told that the French government had decided to surrender. They got out of the train and went back to pick up the pieces after yet another failed attempt at alliance between sovereign states.

As the British troops were being driven into isolation from the continent, Federal Union published a pamphlet entitled *How we shall win*. Taking a leaf out of the Nazi war book which had identified a party political fault in nationalist loyalties, it advocated the mobilisation of a European fifth column dedicated to the creation of a democratic European Federal Union. As an organisation it was Federal Union's last word. The war was no longer phoney. Membership and meetings inevitably fell away as members were called up. Churchill committed the country to victory and unconditional surrender as the only declared war aim, and by so doing effectively surrendered Britain's position as the spokesman for Europe.

Notes

1. The League of Nations Union held its 'Peace Ballot' in July 1935. There were just under 12 million responses. The results were:

   Question 1: Should Great Britain remain a member of the League of Nations?
   Yes: 11,090,387
   No: 353,883
   Question 2: Are you in favour of all-round reductions in armaments by international agreement?
   Yes: 10,470,489
   No: 862,775
   Question 3: Are you in favour of the all-round abolition of national military and naval aircraft by international agreement?
   Yes: 9,533,558
   No: 1,689,786
   Question 4: Should the manufacture and sale of armaments for private profit be prohibited by international agreement?
   Yes: 10,417,329
   No: 775,415
   Question 5: Do you consider that, if a nation insists on attacking another, the other nations should compel it to stop?
   a) by economic and non-military measures?
   Yes: 10,027,608
   No: 635,074
   b) if necessary, by military measures?
   Yes: 6,784,368
   No: 2,351,981

2. Lionel Curtis, *Civitas Dei*, London: Jonathan Cape, 1939.
3. Joad ceased to be a pacifist during the Second World War.
4. W.B. Curry, *The Case for Federal Union* Harmondsworth: Penguin, 1939.
5. Then Beveridge's research assistant.

8

Defending the Empire or defeating the enemy: British war aims 1938–47

Michael Dockrill

During the 1930s the sprawling and increasingly vulnerable British Empire became a major source of concern and distraction to British policy makers. Britain's prestige as a Great Power and, indeed, her very survival depended on the security of her sea communications with her Empire. In the Far East, Japan's invasion of Manchuria in 1931 and her subsequent encroachments in China threatened Britain's trade with, and investment in, that country. If Britain was driven out of China, so the argument ran, Britain's hold on Malaya and India would eventually be undermined.[1] The Japanese threat, the rise of National Socialist Germany after 1933 and Britain's alienation of Fascist Italy during the Abyssinian Crisis of 1935–6, threatened Britain with a three front war in the Atlantic, the Mediterranean and the Far East should these three powers manage to combine against her. Britain lacked the military and naval forces to defend her interests in a three front war on such widely dispersed fronts.

By 1937 British politicians were moving towards a 'General Settlement' of outstanding problems with Germany as a way out of her strategic dilemma and as a means of maintaining peace in Europe. An Anglo-German agreement would deny Italy and Japan the opportunity of taking advantage of tension and conflict between the two countries to attack Britain's extra-European possessions.

There was every indication in 1937 that Hitler might welcome a British approach, although he wanted an alliance which would allow him a free hand in Eastern Europe and not a mere settlement of outstanding German Versailles Treaty grievances. In *Mein Kampf* he had confessed his admiration for the British Empire and had expressed his desire for an Anglo-German alliance. He remained solicitous for the security and stability of that Empire after he had become Chancellor of Germany, advising Lord Halifax, the Chancellor of the Duchy of Lancaster at Berchtesgaden on 19 November 1937, on how to deal with nationalist unrest in India: 'Shoot Gandhi and if that did not suffice to reduce them to submission, shoot a dozen leading members of Congress, and if that did not suffice, shoot 200 until order is established.'[2] Halifax, a former Viceroy of India, was so impressed with Hitler that, on his return from Germany, he informed R.A. Butler, the Parliamentary Under Secretary at the Foreign Office, that 'if Hitler had worn a dhoti he [Halifax] could have mistaken his mystical approach to life for that of Mr Gandhi.'[3]

The range of global problems Britain faced in the late 1930s makes it understandable that British politicians and military leaders remained as disinterested in the problems of eastern and central Europe as they had been during the previous decade. Some resigned themselves to German primacy in that region. Lord Chatfield, the First Sea Lord, whose attention riveted on Britain's naval predicament in the Mediterranean and in far eastern waters, argued in 1937 that:

If Germany . . . tried to expand to the south east we must, in my opinion, accept it . . . If we are convinced that by German successes in Czechoslovakia, Poland, Romania and Danzig, she would eventually dominate Europe, and so threaten us at our front door or in the Near East, it would be conceivably better to fight her to prevent such an outcome, for the one thing that is clear to me is that Germany cannot remain as she is in the world.[4]

The Permanent Under Secretary at the Foreign Office, Sir Alexander Cadogan, thought that Germany might be allowed to 'find her *Lebensraum* in Eastern Europe and establish herself, if she can, as a powerful economic unit. I don't know that that necessarily worsens our commercial and economic outlook. I have never heard that Mr Gordon Selfridge ruined Harrods!'[5] Since the 1920s British politicians had convinced themselves that an economically prosperous Germany would be a peaceful Germany, and in 1937 the Prime Minister, Neville Chamberlain, 'did not think that an economically prosperous Germany would necessarily be a bad thing'.[6]

The trouble with this assumption was that, given the nature of the National Socialist party, a Germany in possession of the resources of the Balkans and Eastern Europe would have secured the economic and military capability to threaten western Europe or the Near East if she was so minded. As a Conservative M.P., Anthony Crossley, put it before the Munich Conference, 'The usual rhetorical question runs "Are you willing to fight for Czechoslovakia?" and invites the answer "No" . . . The wider question ought to be propounded in this form; "Are you prepared to contemplate a Germany which dominates Europe and its resources from the North Sea to the Black Sea?" '[7]

Naturally enough, British politicians and the public alike were reluctant to contemplate involvement in another major war so soon after the end of the Great War. The immense loss of blood and treasure during that conflict had left a deep scar on the national psyche. Furthermore, Britain was a status quo power, anxious to hang on to what she had got, and not to risk losing all in another desperate struggle. In July 1936 Anthony Eden, then Foreign Secretary, had set out the aims of foreign policy as 'first to secure peace in the world, if possible, and secondly to keep this country out of war'.[8] Chamberlain and many of his Cabinet colleagues were convinced that the end result of such a war would be to benefit the United States at the expense of British imperial and commercial interests. They distrusted the United States and despised its politicians for their woolly moralizing. Chamberlain thought that 'it is always best to count on nothing from the Americans but words',[9] while Sir Warren Fisher, the Permanent Secretary to the Treasury, complained that 'the United States cannot engage in any form of competition with us, from athletics to diplomacy without using foul play'.[10] Others feared that an Anglo-German war would result in the emergence of the Soviet Union, if it remained neutral, from the carnage as the dominant power in Europe.

Nor was it clear that the problem of Germany would go away even if the Entente Powers defeated her in a war – after all, the Great War had not settled the German question. In a memorandum on Anglo-German relations on 10 May 1938, the British Ambassador to Berlin, Sir Nevile Henderson, considered that 'even if we beat Germany again [in a war] the result, after another period of chaos, would be the same as today'.[11] After Munich, Halifax, now British Foreign Secretary, thought that a war over Czechoslovakia would have been 'a hideous choice of evils . . . it would have been at the price of immeasurable suffering imposed on the world, and the probable disruption of the British Empire, which may yet perhaps be a point of sanity for a mad civilisation'.[12]

The British Empire might well have been disrupted had war broken out in 1938. The Dominions urged the British Government to accept Hitler's Godesberg terms which even the Chamberlain Cabinet had rejected. South Africa announced that she would not go to war over Czechoslovakia, while Australia warned London that war in Europe would provide Japan with the opportunity to strike at the British Empire in South East Asia. The Secretary of State for India, Lord Zetland, informed his colleagues of the danger that war might provoke nationalist uprisings in India and in the Levant.

Given these depressing circumstances it was scarcely surprising that Chamberlain continued to crave an understanding with Germany, although after the German seizure of Bohemia in March 1939, he insisted that this must be based on genuine reciprocity. He had not ruled out colonial restitution to Germany, and Britain was prepared to offer credits to Germany to help the recovery of her trade. The Foreign Office regarded Danzig and the Polish corridor as still negotiable, since the British guarantee to Poland referred to Polish independence, not to her territorial integrity. In return for these concessions Chamberlain required Germany's return to the League of Nations, and for Hitler to reach agreement with Britain on the humanization of warfare and the abolition of the bomber as a precursor to general disarmament.

Britain entered the war on 3 September 1939 with her war aims confined to the withdrawal of German troops from Poland, the re-creation of an independent Bohemia and a general agreement on disarmament. There was no mention of the overthrow of Hitler, although it might be calculated that this would be the result if Britain's demands were accepted by Germany. However once Germany and the Soviet Union had overrun and partitioned Poland, Britain's demands were clearly unattainable. It became difficult to define precisely for what Britain was fighting. On 23 September Cadogan was hard put to think of any war aims beyond ' "abolish Hitlerism" ', which many inside and outside the War Cabinet were optimistic enough to think would occur in any case as a result of the effects of the blockade and the ensuing internal discontent inside Germany. Lady Cadogan commented that it was 'rather difficult to ask the British Empire to wage war if we don't know what we are fighting for'.[13]

By 26 September the War Council agreed that the formulation of detailed war aims was impossible and fell back on a recent speech by the Prime Minister in which he had stated that 'our general purpose..[is] to redeem Europe from the perpetual and recurring fear of German aggression and enable the people of

Europe to preserve their liberties and independence.'[14] The War Cabinet on 7 October believed that it was possible to achieve this aim if the Wehrmacht High Command replaced Hitler by the seemingly more amenable Goering, who, Halifax thought 'would be glad to secure the removal of Herr Hitler as he wished himself to live in peace and luxury'.[15]

Hitler's Reichstag peace offer of 6 October 1939 with its emphasis on colonial restitution, economic detente and a general reduction of armaments closely resembled Chamberlain's pre-war desiderate. Although this was rejected by the War Cabinet, the air was full of peace talk in Britain from October 1939 to May 1940 and beyond. A motley collection of aristocrats, communists and dissident Labour MPs were active in urging a compromise settlement with Germany, with David Lloyd George in the forefront as the potential leader of those willing to consider a German peace offer. Nor were the Dominions far behind, urging the British Government not to throw away any chance of a peaceful settlement, even if this entailed leaving central Europe to its fate. However, in January 1940, even Chamberlain did 'not believe that until Germany gives proof of a change of heart, a negotiated peace would be a lasting peace or provide us with those stable conditions which we all so earnestly desire'.[16]

With the appointment of Winston Churchill as Prime Minister in May 1940, Britain found herself with a leader who was committed to the continuation of the war à l'outrance and who was convinced that the United States would eventually come to Britain's assistance. However, when Germany's shattering offensive in the West threatened to drive France out of the war, Lord Halifax raised the question as to how Britain could now possibly hope to defeat Germany. At the end of May he and Churchill entered into a frenzied debate over a French appeal for an approach by the Entente to Mussolini to mediate a cease-fire, followed by a general settlement of European questions. Halifax, who favoured such an appeal, suggested that, in return for his mediation, Mussolini might be offered colonial possessions at the expense of Britain and France in north Africa and the Mediterranean.

In response to the Chiefs of Staff warning to the War Cabinet that if German tanks gained a foothold on mainland Britain, the country would be speedily overrun, and with the threat of massive German bomber attacks on British cities, Halifax argued that

if we get to the point of discussing the terms of a general settlement and found that we could obtain terms which did not postulate the destruction of our independence, we should be foolish if we did not accept them.[17]

While even Churchill wavered on one occasion and thought that Britain might examine a German offer, his general line was that any public revelation of peace negotiations would totally destroy British morale, that the United States would eventually join the war on the side of the Entente and that if Britain survived an initial German onslaught, she would then be in a position to obtain better terms from Germany. In the end Churchill prevailed: even Chamberlain finally agreed that no approach should be made to Mussolini and Halifax acquiesced.

Churchill's 'wait and see' policy was thus adopted by the War Cabinet. Peace feelers from a variety of sources continued to reach London. The United States military attache, Alexander Kirk, noted that it was

difficult to characterize as a peace offer a statement that although he [Hitler] professes no wish to destroy the British Empire, he will proceed to that destruction unless the British Government accepts a peace which in the Nazi mind is termed reasonable but to others tokens the ruin of that Empire as the immediate champion of democracy in the world.[18]

Churchill ordered the Foreign Office in August to inform the King of Sweden, who was active with offers of mediation, that the British Government would 'prosecute the war against Germany by every means in their power [sic] until Hitlerism is finally broken and the world relieved from the curse which a wicked man has brought upon it . . .'[19]

Nevertheless the prospect was a grim one. On 25 May 1940 the Chiefs of Staff informed the War Cabinet that without 'full economic and financial support' from the United States 'we do not think we could continue the war with any chance of success'.[20] Such support did not appear to be forthcoming during the summer of 1940. An exasperated Churchill could only resort to blackmail. When the American President, Franklin D. Roosevelt, pressed Churchill to order the British Fleet to sail to sanctuary in Canada, Churchill pointed out that the Fleet was Britain's sole remaining bargaining counter if a new British Government committed to a compromise peace came to power. The Prime Minister telegraphed the Canadian Prime Minister, Mackenzie King, on 5 June, that the United States should not 'view too complacently [the] prospect of a British collapse, out of which they could get the British Fleet and the guardianship of the British Empire, minus Great Britain'.[21]

However with Fighter Command's victory over the Luftwaffe during the Battle of Britain, Roosevelt authorised the supply of American arms and military equipment to Britain, and this was followed later by the destroyers for bases deal. British imperialists like Leo Amery resented this exchange as one-sided and as evidence that the United States was anxious to seize what she could from the British Empire in its hour of weakness, but Churchill was nevertheless desperate to accept any public token of American support for Britain.

When Roosevelt promised to persuade Congress to agree to pass a Lend-Lease Bill, and with the German assault on the Soviet Union in June 1941, Churchill's confidence in ultimate victory began to revive, although few shared his confidence – the Chiefs of Staff did not think that the Russians would be able to withstand the Wehrmacht for more than six weeks. Nor was it clear how Britain could prevail given the succession of defeats her armies suffered in Greece and north Africa in 1941. In these circumstances discussion of peace aims could hardly rise above the faintly risible, as when Churchill told Harry Hopkins, a Roosevelt intimate and the President's personal representative to London, on 25 January 1941, that

we could find nothing better than Christian Ethics on which to build and the more closely we followed the Sermon on the Mount the more likely we were to succeed in our efforts.[22]

The Prime Minister's morale was further boosted by his meeting with Roosevelt at Placentia Bay, off Newfoundland, in August 1941, when he was inveigled by the

American into accepting the Atlantic Charter declaration. This consisted of eight neo-Wilsonian generalities, proclaiming self-determination for liberated nationalities and no territorial changes without the consent of the people concerned, together with a number of clauses about freedom of trade and open access to raw materials. Subsequently Churchill insisted that the Charter referred only to those countries in Europe then under the Nazi yoke, and that it did not apply to the British Empire. His officials hoped that Imperial Preference had been safeguarded by the addition of the words 'with due respect to their existing international obligations' to the clause about free trade.

With Pearl Harbor and Hitler's subsequent declaration of war on the United States, Churchill was convinced that Allied victory was certain. However Britain was dealt further blows as a result of the disastrous defeats she suffered in 1942, when large parts of the British Empire in Asia fell to the Japanese. It also became even more difficult to formulate coherent war aims as Britain found herself caught between Stalin's demands in December 1941 that Britain accept all the gains the Soviet Union had made by agreement with Hitler in Eastern Europe and the Balkans before June 1941; and Roosevelt's insistence that all territorial questions should be postponed for consideration by a post-war peace conference. Anthony Eden, the Foreign Secretary, was the unwelcome recipient of these Soviet demands when he visited Moscow in December 1941 in order to conclude a mutual assistance pact with the Soviet Union. When Stalin agreed to postpone the question of Poland's post-war frontiers until a later date, Eden was willing to recognise Russia's absorption of the Baltic States, parts of Finland and North Bukovina and Bessarabia. The Foreign Secretary cabled London recommending acceptance of these demands. This concession earned Britain Russian goodwill, ensured that the Soviet Union would cooperate with Britain and the United States after the war and that Moscow would not sign a peace treaty with Germany during the war. He later reminded the War Cabinet that the West would be able to do nothing to dislodge Russia once she had re-occupied these territories at the end of the war.

Angered by Eden's willingness to accept Soviet demands, which were directly contrary to the Atlantic Charter, at a time when Churchill and the Chiefs of Staff were in Washington conferring with Roosevelt and the American Joint Chiefs over future strategy, the Prime Minister cabled the Foreign Secretary with the retort that the recognition of Russia's 1941 frontiers 'acquired by acts of aggression in shameful collusion with Hitler,' would 'dishonour our cause'. And further:

No one can foresee how the balance will lie [at the end of the war], or where the winning army [sic] will stand. It seems probable however that the United States and the British Empire, far from being exhausted, will be the most powerfully armed and economic block [sic] the world has ever seen, and that the Soviet Union will need our aid for reconstruction . . .[23]

A potentially embarrassing situation in the form of a resentful Roosevelt and the threat of a back-bench revolt of Tory MPs at the prospect of another Munich was averted when the Soviet Foreign Minister, Molotov, on a visit to London in May 1942, abandoned the demand for a territorial agreement and settled instead for a treaty of alliance. This was not the last the British were to hear of these Soviet demands.

The complications with the Soviet Union were highly embarrassing to Churchill who was well aware of Roosevelt's opposition to secret deals involving carving up Europe into spheres of influence. The President feared that such agreements would ignite a fresh wave of isolationism in the United States after the war. Britain could only recover those parts of the British Empire lost to Japan with American help and it would be fatal if Britain alienated Washington. The Prime Minister informed the War Cabinet as early as October 1941 that 'we ought to regard the United States as having taken charge in the Far East. It was for them to take the lead in this area and we should support them.'[24] Both Stalin's decision to postpone his territorial demands and the Anglo-American decision not to launch a second front in western Europe in 1942 were the last clear cut British diplomatic successes during the war. Churchill managed to resist American pressure for a cross-Channel invasion in that year by persuading Roosevelt to agree to an Anglo-American assault on French north Africa instead. Many American military and civilian leaders suspected that this was a diversionary tactic designed to restore British power in the Mediterranean, and while this thought was, of course, not far from Churchill's mind, there were many military arguments in favour of such a strategy. Meanwhile Roosevelt needed some American military action in Europe in that year if he was not to succumb to internal pressure to transfer the bulk of American resources to the Far East.

This was the last time Britain was able to persuade the Americans to adopt an entirely British made strategy. Although the Americans eventually agreed to an invasion of Sicily and southern Italy in 1942 and 1943, they insisted that this should not be at the expense of preparations for a cross-Channel invasion, now put off until 1944. After 1942 the balance of strength between Britain and the United States swung decisively in America's favour – militarily, economically and in terms of armaments' production – though Britain had, of course, been dependent financially on the United States since 1941. This dependence was greatly resented on the British side, especially when Roosevelt began to develop his own ideas – as confused and confusing as these often were – about a future world order in which British interests were accorded a low priority. When Eden visited Washington in March 1942 he listened incredulously to Roosevelt's ramblings about the future of western Europe, which included the setting up of a new state of Wallonia, made up of parts of Belgium, Luxemburg and northern France.

There were two main areas of disagreement between Britain and the United States concerning war aims. First, Roosevelt believed that he could achieve the United States' post-war objectives more satisfactorily by direct negotiations with Stalin from which Britain was excluded. Clearly Britain's increasingly reduced status suggested an American-Soviet combination to preserve peace after the war. At the Teheran Conference Roosevelt deprecated separate Anglo-American meetings before the main conference since these might be construed by Stalin as 'ganging up'[25] against the Soviet Union. Roosevelt adopted the same line at Yalta and his successor followed his example at Potsdam.

The United States' Treasury Secretary, Henry Morgenthau, reported after Teheran that 'the President is very much impressed with Stalin and not quite so much impressed as he has been with Churchill.'[26] Roosevelt's reluctance to give any lead on future territorial arrangements has already been noted, although in fact neither Britain nor the United States developed any consistent line about the future of Germany. Nor did Britain get much American support for her opposition to Stalin's plans for Poland – in particular the Soviet insistence that Poland accept the Curzon Line as her eastern frontier in exchange for compensation for Poland in east Prussia and Silesia. At Yalta Stalin argued 'that the Atlantic Charter principles could not be applied to the new Polish territories in East Germany' since 'no Germans were found in those areas as they had all run away'.[27] All Roosevelt appeared to require of Stalin at Teheran was that the Russians did nothing which might upset Polish American voters during the run up to the 1944 elections.

Britain finally accepted the *fait accompli* in eastern and central Europe: it was clear by 1944 that this region would be under Soviet military control and that the Western Allies would have to rely on Soviet goodwill for any concessions to democratic processes. Under these circumstances Churchill had to settle for what he could get. On 9 October 1944 Churchill and Eden visited Moscow to discuss Poland, the future of Germany and of the Balkans. During conversations with Stalin that evening Churchill insisted that 'Britain must be the leading Mediterranean Power and he hoped Marshal Stalin would let him have the first say about Greece . . . Marshal Stalin . . . agreed.'[28] In return Churchill assured Stalin of Britain's disinterestedness in Rumania and handed Stalin a list which allotted the Soviet Union 90 per cent influence in Romania, 50 per cent in both Yugoslavia and Hungary and 75 per cent in Bulgaria. The Allies' proportion in each of these respective countries was to be 10 per cent, 50 per cent, 50 per cent and 25 per cent. In Greece Britain's influence would amount to 90 per cent, with 10 per cent accruing to the Soviet Union. Stalin ticked the document with a blue pencil to signify his agreement. Churchill also indicated that the Western Allies would not object to the Soviet Union securing from Turkey the right of passage of its merchant shipping and warships through the Straits after the war. It was all rather humiliating, since, as it turned out, the Allied share in the affairs of the Balkan countries, except Greece, became meaningless once the Red Army had occupied these lands. Roosevelt was irritated when he learned of this 'percentages agreement' which was clearly a division of the Balkans into spheres of influence, a form of *realpolitik* supposedly discredited after the First World War. Moreover the Americans made the most fuss about the British Army's subsequent efforts to prop up the Greek Government against the Communist insurgency in Greece: Stalin appears to have kept to his side of the bargain, at least in the early stages of the Greek civil war.

Secondly, the Americans turned out not to be the staunch supporters of the British Empire Churchill had anticipated in 1941. Roosevelt's deep-seated anti-colonialist feelings clashed with Britain's determination to preserve her Empire come what may: Churchill told an American official in 1942 that 'we also have our traditions; so long as I am here we will hang on to them and to the Empire.'[29] Roosevelt's pressure on Churchill to offer the Indian Congress Party dominion status after the war and immediate autonomy provoked Churchill into a threat of resignation. Indeed throughout the war the Prime Minister resisted the pressure of British officials (who, unlike him, felt that things could never be the same after Britain's defeat at the hands of Japan) to issue declarations about future colonial policy in order to satisfy American sentiment that the British Empire would be a suitable post-war partner. Although the Administration's pressure over India declined somewhat after 1942, American criticisms of British rule continued, especially in the press, while Roosevelt's talk of placing French Indochina, Burma and Malaya under international trusteeship – as well as his subsequent demand that Britain hand Hong Kong over to China as a gesture of goodwill – provoked the British establishment to fury.

The British feared that the United States was seeking to expel Britain from the Far East, destroy her system of Imperial Preferences and drive British trade and commerce from the Orient. And there was no doubt that American business did perceive rich pickings for American trade and investment in the area after the war. Certainly American officials were contemptuous of an Empire which had been unable to defend its inhabitants from the Japanese. General Joseph Stilwell, General Chiang Kai Shek's Anglophobe American Chief of Staff, described Lord Mountbatten's South East Asia Command (SEAC) as 'Save England's Asiatic Colonies',[30] while General Douglas MacArthur complained that Britain was leaving the United States do all the fighting in the Far East while she sat back and waited for Japan's defeat to enable her to recover her lost empire there. At the same time, however, the Americans resented British pressure to participate in the naval and air fighting against mainland Japan.

With the end of the Second World War, Britain recovered the territories she had lost to Japan, although her trade and influence in China had been displaced in favour of the United States. However, she was bankrupt and her financial position worsened when the United States abruptly cancelled Stage II of Lend Lease in August 1945. She got little support from the United States in her resistance to Soviet demands in Eastern Europe and Germany at the Yalta and Potsdam Conferences in 1945, while the Post-Hostilities Planning Committee, on which the Foreign Office and the Chiefs of Staff were represented, issued report after report during and after 1944 which were highly critical of Soviet intentions towards British interests in the Mediterranean and the Middle East. Although Eden refused mention of the potential hostility of the Soviet Union in such documents and the British continued to pay lip-service to Anglo-American-Soviet collaboration after the war, Eden admitted in March 1945 that 'he took the gloomiest view of Russian behaviour everywhere . . . altogether our foreign policy seems a sad wreck and we will have to cast about afresh.'[31]

His successor, Ernest Bevin, who became Foreign Secretary in July 1945, soon discovered that it was difficult to formulate any new course in foreign policy, given America's unwillingness to support Britain in Europe and in the face of Soviet demands on the Straits, on Kars and Ardahan and in Tripolitania and the Soviets' refusal to withdraw from their sphere of occupation in Iran in 1946, despite the war-time pledge that they would do so. Britain was even more dependent on the United States for her economic survival – being forced to negotiate a loan with America in December 1945 – while relations were further punctuated by bitter disputes over Palestine (until Britain finally abandoned the mandate in 1947), over exchanges of nuclear information and over oil and aviation concessions. Moreover the British zone of Germany was a severe drain on Britain's depleted finances while the Americans, anxious to avoid entanglements in Europe, even appeared to be unperturbed by the prospect of a Communist Germany. Over the next three years Bevin went from one desperate expedient to another in an attempt to stave off financial and diplomatic disaster.

Nevertheless Bevin and his officials were confident that eventually Britain would be able to solve her economic and financial difficulties and then exert a more powerful role in Europe and elsewhere. On 16 May 1947, Bevin told the House of Commons that 'His Majesty's Government do not accept the view . . . that we have ceased to be a Great Power or the contention that we have ceased to play that role.'[32]

With the granting of independence to India and Ceylon in 1947 and to Burma in 1948 the British were left with only remnants of their former empire in Asia. However they were determined to hang on to the bulk of what was left, as testified by the despatch of military reinforcements to Malaya in 1947 (a crucial source of rubber and other raw materials), to deal with the Communist uprising there.

Moreover, after the First World War, the British were determined to retain their influence in the Middle East, where they were now predominant after having managed to expel the French from Syria in 1945. However, the Prime Minister, Clement Attlee, described parts of this region as 'deficit areas'[33] and, as such, likely to prove an intolerable drain on Britain's resources. He therefore suggested that Britain withdraw from the Middle East and concentrate her future defence on Africa. In a memorandum to the Cabinet Defence Committee in March 1946 the Prime Minister wrote that 'it may be that we shall have to consider the British Isles as an easterly extension of a strategic area, the centre of which is the American continent rather than as a power looking eastwards through the Mediterranean to India and the East.'[34] He was in a minority of one – the entire British establishment rose in wrath at this heresy.

Bevin argued in a counter-memorandum that the withdrawal of Britain from the Middle East would create a vacuum into which Russia would move. 'Our presence in the Mediterranean . . . is vital to our position as a Great Power.'[35] In 1949 the Foreign Secretary insisted that this position 'economically is owing to oil and cotton, vital to the United Kingdom's recovery'.[36] This being a Labour Administration, Britain's influence in the Middle East would be upheld by means of voluntary agreements with moderate Arab nationalists; Bevin argued in the spring of 1946 that 'we could not afford to be represented as defending the pashas while the communists obtained the support of the common people.'[37] The problem was that Bevin, in common with most British politicians, under-estimated the increasing strength of nationalism in the Middle East and failed to understand that 'moderate' nationalists who collaborated with Britain would be discredited in the eyes of their people.

In 1947 Bevin's efforts to revive the war-time alliance with the United States at last appeared to be bearing fruit. President's Truman's decision to take over Britain's financial responsibilities in Greece and Turkey in March 1947 was the first decisive intervention by the United States in European affairs after the Second World War and was the precursor of further American moves which culminated in the Marshall Plan and the setting up of the North Atlantic Treaty Organisation in 1949.

The collapse of the London Conference of Foreign Ministers in 1947, with the lines now firmly drawn between East and West over the future of Germany, suggested that there could be no compromise with the seemingly implacable and hostile Soviet Union. Thereafter Bevin threw in Britain's lot entirely with the United States, abandoning his 1947 search for a Western European Union which, with the Commonwealth, was intended to form a 'Third Force' capable of future independence from both the Soviet Union and the United States.

Britain had managed by 1947 to preserve a substantial world empire (with the important exception, of course, of the Indian sub-continent) and to defeat her Axis enemies. She did so, however, at the cost of increasing subservience to the United States. This was the price Churchill was prepared to pay in 1940 when he pinned his hopes for ultimate victory on eventual American entry into the war on Britain's side, rather than opting for a compromise peace with Hitler's Germany – a peace which would have been both bogus and short-lived. The British could at least comfort themselves with the thought that, as Halifax put it in a letter to the King in January 1942: 'Americans very much resemble a mass of nice children – a little crude, very warm hearted and mainly governed by emotion.'[38] In other words they could be easily led, especially by a more experienced and wise British Foreign Office. Sir William Strang, the Permanent Under Secretary at the Foreign Office, commented in January 1951, in contemplating Anglo-American relations during the Korean War:

Our problem is to deflect the Americans from unwise or dangerous courses without making a breach in the united front. This is not an easy operation, but then, whatever some people might think, diplomacy is not one of the easiest professions.[39]

A Foreign Office versifier summed up the hidden British agenda in 1945:

In Washington, Lord Halifax
Once whispered to J.M. Keynes,
'It's true they have the money bags
but *we* have all the brains!'[40]

Notes

1. Victor Rothwell, *Anthony Eden: A Political Biography 1931–1957*, Manchester: Manchester University Press, 1992, p. 142.
2. Quoted in Andrew Roberts, *'The Holy Fox': A Biography of Lord Halifax*, London: Weidenfeld and Nicolson, 1991, p. 72.
3. Ibid, p. 76.
4. Roy Douglas, *In the Year of Munich*, London: Macmillan, 1977, p. 4.
5. Roberts, p. 135.
6. Douglas, *In the Year of Munich*, p. 58.
7. Ibid, p. 45.
8. Rothwell, p. 32.
9. Christopher Thorne, *Allies of a Kind: The United States, Britain and the War Against Japan 1941–1945*, London: Hamish Hamilton, 1978, p. 38.
10. Ibid, p. 38.
11. Roberts, p. 68.
12. Ibid, p. 124.
13. Ibid, p. 179.
14. Roy Douglas, *The Advent of War 1939–1940* London: Macmillan, 1978, p. 72.

15. L.D. Freedman and M.L. Dockrill, *War Cabinet Minutes: The Microfiche Edition, An Introduction*, London: HMSO, 1989, p. 9.
16. Douglas, *Advent*, p. 147.
17. Roberts, p. 218.
18. Glen St. John Barclay, *Their Finest Hour*, London: Weidenfeld and Nicolson, 1977, p. 24.
19. Ibid, p. 24.
20. Roy Douglas, *New Alliances 1940–1941*, London: Macmillan, 1982, p. 32.
21. Martin Gilbert, *Finest Hour: Winston S. Churchill 1939–1941*, London: Heinemann, 1983, p. 473.
22. Ibid, p. 995.
23. David Carlton, *Anthony Eden: A Biography*, London: Allen Lane, 1981, pp. 192–3.
24. Thorne, p. 81.
25. Ibid, p. 81.
26. Ibid, p. 276.
27. Roy Douglas, *From War to Cold War 1942–1948*, London: Macmillan, 1981, p. 70.
28. Ibid, p. 45.
29. Thorne, p. 372.
30. Ibid, p. 406.
31. Carlton, p. 256.
32. Andrew J. Pierre, *Nuclear Politics* Oxford: Oxford University Press, 1972, p. 68.
33. William Roger Louis, *The British Empire in the Middle East 1945–1951*, Oxford: Oxford University Press, 1984, p. 28.
34. Alan Bullock, *Ernest Bevin: Foreign Secretary*, London: Heinemann, 1983, p. 242.
35. Elizabeth Barker, *The British between the Superpowers 1945–1950*, London: Macmillan, 1983, p. 50.
36. Ibid, p. 16.
37. Ibid, p. 51.
38. Roberts, p. 282.
39. M.L. Dockrill, 'The Foreign Office, Anglo-American Relations and the Korean War, June 1950–June 1951', *International Affairs*, vol. 62, no. 3, p. 468.
40. Roberts, p. 297.

9

Special in relation to what? Anglo–American relations in the Second World War

Alan Dobson

At a one day conference on Anglo–American relations at Durham University in the mid-1970s an American diplomat prefaced his talk by quipping that when people asked him about the special relationship, he always replied: 'That reminds me of when I'm asked how my wife is and I always respond – in relation to what?'

I do not propose to enter into a lengthy discussion of what might constitute a special relationship in international affairs, nor do I want to dwell too much on characteristics, divorced from the historical narrative, which might lead one to deem Anglo–American relations as special. However, it might be helpful to move from what is essentially the unique and the particular of historical narrative into generalisation in order to appreciate the character of the Anglo–American relationship before 1939 and what bearing it had on developments in the Second World War.

One might say that the relationship has been special from about 1904 because from then on Britain excluded the possibility of war with the USA from its defence planning, which was a major departure from the norms of international relations.[1] Given that the USA was growing rapidly as a naval power and that within 20 years was accorded parity with the UK, the decision by the British to exclude the possibility of hostilities with the USA from its defence plans must be quite unprecedented. In the world of *realpolitik*, not to take defensive measures against a state that has the potential to be a military threat is regarded as foolhardy irrespective of whether good or bad relations exist. During the twentieth century the USA has had the military potential seriously to challenge and later to overwhelm the United Kingdom. Furthermore, that potential has existed during a very delicate shift of power whereby the American Bald Eagle has replaced the British Lion as world leader. This is not to say that stories of twisted tails and plucked feathers cannot be told of twentieth century Anglo–American relations, but fortunately there is nothing more painful to relate than that.

Writing during the Second World War, Viscount Samuel felt that a prerequisite for achieving mutual goodwill was that the British public needed to come to an understanding of things which had created ill-will:

For them [the Americans] the history that matters begins with the Pilgrim Fathers and those that followed them, setting out to face every peril and hardship for conscience sake: seeking liberty of thought and liberty of worship across the ocean; casting off the yoke of an oppressive, tyrannous government – the government of England.[2]

Those first experiences were followed by the War of Independence; the War of 1812; the Civil War in which the British governing classes 'sympathised with the wrong side'; and British maltreatment of Ireland and mass emigration to the USA created 'in the electorate a bitter, resentful, anti-British block, enduring for generations'. This is an impressive catalogue of sources of enmity. As Samuel concludes: 'It is a painful story to tell. But it has to be told.'[3]

By the turn of the century the impact of many of these matters was diminishing with the passage of time, but there were still contentious issues: economic rivalry; ill-feeling towards Britain from some ethnic groups; a dislike of British imperialism and the class system; a continuing concern over neutral maritime rights in wartime; British disdain of American commercialism and lack of culture; and the potential for severe naval rivalry. However, as Coral Bell observed, despite the difficulties with the early Republic, the quality of the relationship between Britain and the USA already had something special about it before the close of the nineteenth century.[4]

As the twentieth century progressed unwillingness to follow the normal rules of international relations where the USA was concerned became an even more distinctive characteristic of British policy. M.P.A. Hankey, Secretary to the Committee of Imperial Defence, observed in 1928 that 'since 1904 we have not included the United States among the nations against whom we make defensive preparations.'[5] However, at the time Hankey wrote that, there were serious ructions in Anglo–American relations.

The 1920s had started auspiciously for the two countries with the success of the 1921–22 Washington Naval Conference, but things deteriorated as the decade advanced. Difficulties culminated in the failure to expand the scope of naval arms limitations in talks between themselves and Japan at the Three Power Naval Conference in the summer of 1927 in Geneva. Naval matters were not the only things to pose problems at that point in time. There was much economic friction because of American protectionism, especially of her merchant navy, and because of the British Stevenson Plan which tried to stabilise the price of rubber produced in Malaya. There was disdain in London for US President, Calvin Coolidge, and much mutual criticism across a whole range of matters from imperialism to US isolationism. These things together led to much soul-searching on both sides. Winston Churchill, then Chancellor of the Exchequer and one not normally associated with anti-Americanism, wrote in July 1927: 'No doubt it is quite right in the interests of peace to go on talking about war with the United States being "unthinkable" [but] everyone knows that this is not true.'[6]

Just over a year later Robert Craigie, Counsellor in the Foreign Office, made an assessment of Anglo–American relations. His views were similar to Churchill's. 'Except as a figure of speech, war is *not* unthinkable between the two countries. On the contrary, there are present all the factors which in the past have made for wars between states.'[7] Such statements could be taken as evidence that Anglo–American relations were not special in the 1920s and that war was not inconceivable. However, conceivable possibilities are one thing, whether they lead to changes of policy is another. Churchill was upset with the USA, partly because of the difficulties that had arisen over the Stevenson Plan, for which he was responsible, and partly because of the declining status of his beloved Royal Navy. But his anger at American actions did not lead to any discernible change in British policy. And while Craigie noted that conditions that had led to war with other states now existed between Britain and the USA, it was quite clear that he thought war was not an option. However, he advised that Anglo–American relations needed careful tending because of a natural propensity to deteriorate.[8]

There was nothing pre-ordained that dictated that relations would be smooth, but, for the most part, the tending that Craigie saw as necessary was forthcoming. Once Coolidge had sunk 'back into the obscurity from which only accident extracted him'[9], as Churchill uncharitably wrote, then there were improvements in Anglo–American relations. In 1930 a naval agreement was struck. America appeared to be taking a more moderate and subdued line about neutral rights at sea, and Ramsay MacDonald and Hoover improved the tone of relations, at least in the early part of Hoover's presidency. They deteriorated again during the Great Depression because of tariffs and preferences, war debt repayment failures and also because of Roosevelt's refusal to play a constructive role in the 1933 London World Economic Conference, which attempted to stabilise international rates of exchange.

Relations then, though improved, were never uniformly good and it is difficult to explain exactly why Anglo–American relations developed in a way that was unconventional and special. Language and culture, trade and economic interdependence, and common aspects of their respective political traditions are often sentimentally invoked to explain the development of a common sense of purpose, but that is no explanation. If it were, then one would be at a loss to explain the wars of Independence and of 1812. Craigie wrote in 1927 that among the irremovable and inherent difficulties in the relationship were:

Mutual jealousy; the clash of differing national characteristics emphasised by the existence of a common language: the growing discrepancies of speech and style within that 'common' language; intensive trade rivalry; determined competition between the two merchant marines; the uneasy relationship between debtor and creditor . . .[10]

In other words, language and economic interaction can just as easily be a source of conflict as of co-operation. Some writers have noted that differences separate more than the similarities bring together the British and American political traditions.[11]

Others have pointed to the common legal heritage and resorts to arbitration in order to settle disputes. Again one must comment that these observations often beg more questions than they answer. One wonders if relations between Britain and the USA would have emerged from the tensions of the US Civil War, and in particular from the claims relating to the Alabama, if Gladstone had not come to power in 1868 and agreed to arbitration.

Finally there are those who emphasise realist appraisals of self interest. For Britain this has involved two hostages to fortune: one strategic; the difficulty of defending Canada – and later the danger of alienating her – in a conflict with the

USA; and one economic: the massive level of British investment in the US economy and the fact that for much of the nineteenth and twentieth centuries the USA has been the first or second largest export market for British goods. For America there was the growing need for access to overseas markets and raw materials and the fear of being excluded by the European imperialists. There might have been rivalry with the British over markets, but of all the imperial powers Britain was undeniably the most liberal trader and therefore the USA had an interest in supporting her. Both countries had to contend with the thought that if there were war between them they would be able to damage each other, but how could one or the other actually win? The most likely outcome would be a mutually damaging stalemate and thus, although this is not offered as a general explanation of the growth of the tradition of arbitration, it was undoubtedly a significant factor. And finally both Japan and Germany posed considerable threats to them both. In particular the rise of German naval and military power represented a challenge to their respective interests.

But simply to say that these threats from third parties were seen in a similar way by both countries and brought them together is a kind of explanatory sleight of hand. No simple generalisation can explain why the USA and Britain have co-operated together in the great conflicts of the twentieth century, but we can establish the base line from which to start and that base line is the attitude that prevailed in Britain and was reflected, though less strongly, in the USA that war between them was practically so remote a possibility that for policy formulation it could be discounted. From that point on other factors have to be assessed in each particular situation in order to determine how and why co-operation actually arose. This involves examining the significance of linguistic, cultural and political matters; economic relations; strategic and other aspects of self-interest; personal relations between leaders and diplomats; and national public opinion.

In the course of doing this, it becomes apparent that the special relationship is not an abstract model, but an idea that emerges from the historical actors who managed relations between Britain and the USA. They perceived that there was something special, something different, something which appeared to depart from the norms of power relationships in the international sphere. Just how that operated in the Second World War and the consequences that it produced are too involved and too wide-ranging to be dealt with here, however, consideration of one particular theme, namely economic relations, may throw some light on how the relationship developed in general.

Economic rivalry between Britain and America continued during the war, but problems which had arisen or had become more acute because of increasing protectionism in the 1930s – in the guise of monetary controls and Imperial Preference in Britain and high tariffs in the USA – increasingly came under joint consideration as they tried to work out a new system for the post-war world. Many matters made the negotiations difficult. For example, they had adopted different forms of protection and the Americans thought that tariffs were far more acceptable than Imperial Preference which discriminated against non-participants. But the fundamental reason for difficulty was their traditional rivalry. In October 1943 there was a flash of refreshing candour that cut through the hypocrisy that afflicted both sides as they pursued economic national interest in the guise of altruism. A senior Foreign Economic Administration (FEA) official, Bernhard Knollenberg, commenting on the different and more favourable treatment of Lend-Lease that the USA accorded to China and the Soviet Union compared with Britain, wrote to his chief, Leo Crowley, saying that the real and 'deeper' reason for this was that neither the Soviet Union or China 'is a great traditional competitor of ours in international trade.'[12]

Ironically, that rivalry implied that Britain and the USA also had vested interests in ensuring that the world economy flourished. That meant reforming the pre-war system which had produced exchange rate chaos and a collapse of international trade. There was no fundamental difference between the prevailing political and economic forces in London and Washington. Both sides valued gains to be had from comparative trade advantages and the overall system of liberal capitalism providing it was sufficiently managed to avoid the flaws of the 1920s and 1930s. This is not to say, however, that there was not a spectrum of opinion in both countries about reforming the world economy, or that there were not serious differences about how to achieve a largely agreed upon goal, or that with regard to specific issues there were not violent arguments.

In the United Kingdom at one end of the spectrum was an unholy alliance of imperialists and left wing socialists who favoured trade preference and reliance upon a sterling currency area. They saw this as a way of both insulating Britain from the vagaries of international capitalism as suffered in the Great Depression and preventing economic domination by the USA. The imperialists also saw this kind of economic regionalism as a way of continuing Britain's imperial splendour. These two groups led the opposition to American proposals for the post-war economy.

But the anti-American group was a minority. The majority thought that co-operation with the USA was vital, though there was concern that strategically important industries such as agriculture and the airlines should be given some degree of protection.[13] There were also timetable concerns. Given the problems of war damage and reconversion to peacetime production and the need to recover lost export markets, the British wanted a long transition period which would condone economic controls and enable them to get back on their feet and into a position from which they could compete. Finally, there was concern both over striking the right balance of concessions with the USA, and whether the normally protectionist USA would be able to get laws through the US Congress in order to reciprocate with any British reforms.

On the American side there were similarly diverse views. At one extreme was the Republican Party tradition of high tariffs combined with aggressive economic penetration of overseas markets, but that kind of economic nationalism, while still strong in the Congress, was out of favour in the Roosevelt Administration. As in Britain, consensus formed round the idea of a stable international economic order that would encourage freer trade and stable exchange rates. There were strong nationalistic elements in that consensus, for many saw such an economic order to be in the interests of the USA as it enjoyed comparative trade advantages. In contrast, the British, fearing the loss of many comparative advantages by the war's end, saw international organisations to be in their interest because they would prevent America gaining overweening control of the world economy.

The Roosevelt Administration had different emphases within it. In particular Secretary of State, Cordell Hull, advocated the elimination of trade discrimination above all else. Well, almost above all else. His obsession with eliminating discrimination took second place to upholding America's economic interests as the negotiations about the post-war wheat trade with Britain in 1941–42 demonstrated.[14] In the US Treasury the preoccupation was with currency convertibility and stable exchange rates. Henry Morgenthau and his chief adviser in this area. Harry Dexter White, wanted to impose New Deal ideas about responsibly controlled capitalism on the international monetary system. On the whole they succeeded. For much of the war these different emphases caused bureaucratic tensions between the US State and Treasury Departments, but after Fred Vinson replaced Morgenthau and Will Clayton took control of the State Department economic policy-makers things improved and agreement emerged that ending monetary rather than trade discrimination was the first priority.

The American consensus on the need for a multilateral liberal economic world order was strengthened by fears that the massive expansion of US industry during the war would result in surplus production in peacetime that would trigger a depression unless overseas markets could be found. These fears were all the more potent then as it was before the post-war consumer society had been conjured up by mass advertising. However, even though the need for a multilateral liberal world economy was strongly felt, there were reservations about its benefits for certain industries and there was also a realisation that America could not go it alone. It would have to persuade other countries, and above all others the United Kingdom, that the American vision for the post-war world was one that was in other people's interests as well as their own. It was this need to persuade Britain to partner America in creating a freer world economy immediately after the war that caused friction with the UK and revealed so much about the quality of their relationship.[15]

There are a number of things about the Second World War that stand out in people's minds; the Holocaust; the carnage on the eastern front; the destruction of Hiroshima and Nagasaki; and the economic miracle that took place in the USA. A less well recognised, but no less momentous, event occurred in Britain. On 7 October 1940, Prime Minister Winston Chruchill wrote to President Roosevelt: 'The moment approaches when we shall no longer be able to pay cash for shipping and other supplies.'[16] 15 months of war reduced Britain, the world's greatest trading nation and creator of the largest ever empire, to *de facto* international bankruptcy. More than anything else, that dictated the course of Anglo–American economic relations over the following five years.

British bankruptcy was stark evidence of the shift in power in Anglo–American relations. Later in the war it was also reflected in military terms, but that did not affect policy and decision-making until late 1943 when US forces began to outnumber those of Britain and the Commonwealth.[17] The solution to Britain's economic problem came in the shape of Lend-Lease and a system of combined boards which helped to co-ordinate production. These measures allowed Britain to continue her war effort and the USA, after the State Department took over responsibility from the Treasury for working out consideration for US aid, abandoned any thought of cash payments. As a result Britain received approximately $21 billion net of aid. However, although Britain did not pay cash, costs were involved.[18]

Lend-Lease enabled Britain to concentrate on war production and abandon export markets, as making things for profit took second place to the needs of war supply. It also made the UK highly dependent upon the USA. Those three things taken together – abandonment of exports, the decimation of peacetime production and dependence upon the USA – placed Britain in a situation which made it difficult to resist US demands for non-cash payments.

In pursuing their respective economic interests, within a framework of which the Lend-Lease system was an integral part, four important matters arose for Anglo–American relations. The first involved the consideration for Lend-Lease; the second, controls over British exports to ensure that Lend-Lease was not misused; thirdly, the re-growth of Britain's gold and dollar reserves after Lend-Lease averted the danger of bankruptcy; and fourthly, a division of labour that was instituted for sound reasons, but nevertheless disadvantaged Britain in terms of post-war commercial potential, for example in the nuclear and airline industries. Of these four, the first three are of concern here.

In examining US policy, it should be borne in mind that, although the USA had a commanding negotiating position, it was not without constraints. Domestically, Roosevelt had to contend with Congress and, as the war progressed, with business elements within the Administration, both of which limited bargaining strategy. In addition, Britain was not without some leverage. It controlled or influenced a large part of the world's economy through formal and informal political ties, through the currency ties of the sterling area and Imperial Preference. Furthermore, the USA needed Britain's co-operation if a multilateral liberal world economy were to be created and Britain would not be willing to undertake such co-operation if her position were so impoverished that it would not be able to compete and gain benefit. Finally, the more avid pursuers of a tightly formulated multilateral post-war economy were restrained by Roosevelt for purely pragmatic reasons. He did not want to disrupt the alliance by quarrelling over the post-war economy: Britain was too important in the war effort and the winning of the war was the paramount goal.

Roosevelt's attitude played an important role in the talks about Lend-Lease consideration. The State Department wanted a series of British commitments: to co-operate in fashioning the post-war economy; to reduce tariffs and other barriers to trade; and to eliminate preferences – which would affect Britain much more than the USA. By the time Churchill and Roosevelt met for their first wartime conference at Placentia Bay, Newfoundland, in August 1941, the haggling over consideration was well under way.

Under Secretary of State Sumner Welles tried to get Churchill to agree to commit Britain to the elimination of imperial preference. The commitment was to be entered in the Atlantic Charter, which became the first major indication of what were likely to become Allied war aims. The Charter was duly issued, but Churchill had skilfully protected British interests. In the fourth paragraph the two leaders committed themselves to: 'endeavour, with due respect for their existing obligations [read Imperial Preference], to further enjoyment of all States, great or small, victor or vanquished of access, on equal terms, to the trade and the raw materials of the world . . .'[19]

Such mealy-mouthed commitments did not please Cordell Hull, who continued to press for something more concrete. By February 1942, after much heated debate, it looked as if he were about to get his way. State Department officials were urging Britain to accept a draft of article 7 of the Mutual Aid Agreement, which specified the consideration for Lend-Lease. The article committed both countries to early talks about substantive economic matters: to eliminate discrimination in international commerce by agreed action and to reduce tariffs and other barriers to trade.

The British Cabinet balked at these provisions.[20] There was concern that Britain would throw away its bargaining hand if it committed itself to the abolition of Imperial Preference before getting the US to reciprocate with commensurate reductions of its high tariffs. There was also a growing fear that the USA wanted to move too quickly on liberalisation, at a time when Britain would need a long transition period after the war in order to get back to normality. In the end Roosevelt gave ground in response to appeals from Churchill and in order to get this troublesome matter out of the way now that America was also in the war.

Rather disingenuously Roosevelt wrote that a trade of imperial preference for Lend-Lease was 'the furthest thing' from his mind, that America was not asking Britain for 'a commitment in advance' of negotiations to abolish Imperial Preference, and that article 7 'does not contain any such commitment'. With that assurance Churchill was content and so again, as in the Atlantic Charter, the USA was left with only vague commitments.[21]

In the operation of the mutual aid programme the Americans managed to get more of their own way. In fact their management of Lend-Lease resulted in an offensive intrusion into UK economic sovereignty. The intrusion had two complementary sides to it: controls over British exports; and a unilateral US attempt to limit the growth of British reserves to $1 billion.

In September 1941 after protracted negotiations with the USA, the British agreed not to apply

any Lend-Lease materials in such a way as to enable their exporters to enter new markets or to extend their export trade at the expense of the United States. Owing to the need to devote all available capacity and manpower to war production, the United Kingdom export trade is restricted to the irreducible minimum necessary to supply or obtain materials essential to the war effort.[22]

The British accepted these controls with reluctance and hoped that once the USA entered the war that they would be abandoned as both countries pooled their resources for the war effort. In fact the Export White Paper, as it was known, remained in force with minor modification until VE-Day under the auspices of a US policy known as the marginal theory. President of the Board of Trade, Hugh Dalton, explained to the Lord President's Committee in June 1944 that it prevented receipt of Lend-Lease items unless Britain had 'reduced the civilian population to siege levels and given up all export trade in that particular commodity'.[23]

The Americans insisted on this for several reasons: they did not want Britain to gain commercially from Lend-Lease; there was concern that Congress should not have ammunition to attack wartime aid to Britain; there was a desire to oust Britain from her export markets in Latin America; and it was also seen as a means of keeping Britain vulnerable and thus receptive to US proposals for reconstructing the post-war world economy.[24]

The Export White Paper was the first foray by the USA into Britain's commercial wartime activities. The second was more serious and intrusive into British economic sovereignty. Since the start of Lend-Lease the Americans had had discussions about limiting British gold and dollar reserves, but these talks were held almost exclusively among themselves and the matter was not raised officially with the British. The American argument was that Lend-Lease had been introduced because Britain had no gold or dollars to pay for American supplies and that its continuation could only be justified on those grounds. In reply the British believed that America's entry into the war and the notion of pooling resources – Britain gave Reciprocal Aid to the USA – changed the circumstances and justified the rebuilding of reserves that had been expended in 1939/40 in what was now a common war effort. In addition, Britain's post-war economic reconversion to peacetime production and trade would require reserves, in particular to maintain confidence in sterling in the light of rapidly accumulating debts because of war expenditure. They totalled nearly £3.5 billion in 1945 and the British argued all along that it did not make sense to limit British reserves without taking liabilities into account. The USA, with the exception of the State Department and a pro-British faction within the Office of the Lend-Lease Administration (later the FEA), remained unconvinced or at least unmoved.

In November 1942 there were simultaneous moves, by Lend-Lease officials led by Oscar Cox and by the Board of Economic Warfare under the chairmanship of Vice President Wallace, to bring in unilateral US controls over the level of British reserves. This move had dangerous implications for Britain. Nevertheless, within a few days a US Cabinet Committee was set up with a working group under Harry White. It recommended that British reserves be held between $600 and $1 billion. Roosevelt approved the recommendation on 11 January.[25]

Over the next two and a half years the USA pursued a policy which upheld the Export White Paper restrictions and actively sought to influence the level of Britain's reserves by withdrawing items from Lend-Lease and by trying to persuade Britain to give the USA more Reciprocal Aid. Throughout, the Americans tried to maintain the fiction that these policies were dictated by political and Congressional considerations alone. They denied that the USA had the aim of manipulating things in order to keep British reserves to a unilaterally established and clearly arbitrary limit. On 8 February White told Morgenthau that regarding this matter and the British: 'Our position so far has been that it involves no new policy, that the range [600 million to $1billion] is merely a guidepost for the implementation of our present policy.'[26] In spite of reducing Lend-Lease and increasing Reciprocal Aid, British reserves continued to rise mainly because of dollars brought into Britain by GIs getting ready for the invasion of Europe. Leo Crowley, head of the FEA, was unhappy about this and set in train developments that resulted in the Americans finally coming clean with the British in February 1944.

I have been wondering [wrote Roosevelt to Churchill] whether it would be feasible for you to consider so ordering your financial affairs as to reduce your gold and dollar holdings . . . to the neighborhood of about $1 billion.'[27]

This letter was sent despite State Department opposition and lack of clearance by Morgenthau, who subsequently also expressed his disagreement with its con-tent.[28] The British were outraged. Sir John Anderson, Chancellor of the Exchequer, wrote to Churchill:

If we were to accept the . . . proposal, we should have lost our financial independence, in any case precarious, as soon as lend-lease comes to an end, and would emerge from the war, victorious indeed, but quite helpless financially with reserves far inferior not only to Russia but even to France and to Holland.[29]

In the days that followed the British remonstrated with the Americans about the President's request and an apology of sorts was forthcoming, but underlying matters did not go away.[30] By late 1943 the American position on a number of economic issues as well as their announced plans for the post-war economy were causing intense concern in London. A spate of papers were prepared for the Cabinet by imperialists such as R. Hudson, Leo Amery and Lord Beaverbrook criticising American policies. Such papers received support from many in the Labour Party who thought that the economic liberalism espoused by the USA would compromise their chances of achieving both full employment after the war and the implementation of the welfare state outlined in the Beveridge Report. In the light of all this, the Cabinet decided that any further talks with the Americans on economic planning should be postponed with the exception of international monetary talks that were already too far advanced to be stopped without serious problems arising. This decision was not communicated formally to the USA, but the drift of British policy soon became apparent.[31]

Thus by the closing stages of the war there was still something of a stand-off between Britain and the USA with their respective economic aims. The USA had managed to exercise some control over the British export trade and over the accumulation of its gold and dollar reserves, but in neither case to the extent it had ideally hoped for. It had a notable success with the Bretton Woods Conference and in its creation of the IMF which besides offering more limited liability and smaller resources, controlled exchange rate alterations more rigidly than Britain wanted and offered a much shorter transition period to convertibility than Britain thought feasible. It also placed the USA and the dollar in a commanding position in the international monetary system at the expense of sterling.[32] Furthermore, the USA still had a lengthy list of conditions and policies that it wanted the UK to adhere to, but in 1944 there looked little chance of getting compliance.

The State Department, while it had adopted a sympathetic line on Britain's reserves in the belief that they had to be of an adequate size to enable Britain to resume liberal trade policies after the war, was also deeply uneasy that Britain had not given more unequivocal commitments to the American line on the post-war economy. It also worried about the failure to make progress in talks for economic co-operation in 1944 which Britain had committed itself to in the Mutual Aid Agreement. However, although Britain had evaded the more extreme US demands, its main weakness remained. It needed US help in the difficult transition back to peacetime production and trade and it was this need that the Americans were to exploit in order to get their way.

At the Second Quebec Conference in September 1944 Roosevelt nearly gave away the bait with which the State Department intended to hook Britain into both reaffirming the conditions of article 7 of the Mutual Aid Agreement and co-operating with the US in the post-war economy. In response to pleas from Churchill, Roosevelt gave commitments to a generous continuation of Lend-Lease supplies to Britain after VE-Day, which would have facilitated reconversion to peacetime production, and furthermore he conceded that conditions governing Lend-Lease should not be such as to hamper the growth of Britain's exports, though of course Lend-Lease items could not be used in the export trade. Unfortunately for Britain the Americans blatantly reneged on these commitments. Britain's situation was then made even worse, in an economic sense, by the abrupt, and in relation to previous calculations, the premature end of the war with the atomic assaults on Japan. British reconversion to civilian production was still in its early days and the export trade was still a shadow of its pre-war self.[33]

The abrupt ending of the war and the cut-off of Lend-Lease left Britain economically prostrate. According to assessments made by John Maynard Keynes, British reserves stood at $1.9 billion and the 1945 balance of payments was $5 billion in the red. The prospective deficit for 1946 was $2.5–3.5 billion. Sterling debts stood at $12–14 billion. Much of Britain's capital equipment needed replacing and there was a massive task ahead in reconverting the economy to peacetime production and in expanding British exports – now a third of their pre-war volume. Faced with these problems, the British believed that they needed much assistance from the USA and a long transition period before adopting fixed exchange rates and abandoning controls in favour of a freer international economic policy. The Americans, however, determined that things should be otherwise.[34]

William Clayton and Fred Vinson, representing the State and Treasury Departments respectively, took the line that financial help had to be linked with overall British economic policy and the fulfilment of commitments that Britain had made in the Mutual Aid Agreement and at Bretton Woods. The Americans were poised to dictate economic policy to their ally.

In the autumn of 1945 Keynes led a British negotiating team to Washington to seek help. The progress of the talks was excruciatingly painful for the British. Under intense US pressure they shifted from one untenable position to another. At first they asked for a $5 billion gift; then they sought a part gift part loan arrangement; and then an interest free loan. In the end Britain was offered and, after crisis meetings of the Cabinet, accepted a loan of $3.75 billion and a further $650 million for Lend-Lease pipeline supplies at 2%. In return for this American largess Britain committed itself to co-operating with the USA in establishing an International Trade Organisation (ITO) that embodied free trade and non-discrimination policies, and which brought Imperial Preference directly under threat. Britain would have to enter the IMF, but also make currently earned sterling freely convertible within 12 months of the loan agreement coming into force, which was much more onerous on Britain than the transitional clauses of the IMF would have been. It had to abandon quantitative import controls that discriminated against the USA by the end of 1946, except where non-convertible currencies acquired prior to then were involved. It was to undertake negotiations to write off or fund sterling debts and then release them in stages as convertible currency. It was not to use the loan to discharge other debts or accept subsequent loans on more favourable terms. A waiver of interest would be permitted on balance of payments grounds, but it was not to result in Britain's liabilities to other countries being treated more favourably than those to the USA.[35]

The Financial Agreement was signed on 6 December 1945, but it was not ratified by the US Congress for several months. During that time the danger of non-ratification was used to pressurise the British, in particular to get them to accept the US point of view on the Anglo-American Bermuda Air Services Agreement of 1946.[36] Taking all these things together has resulted in some scholars claiming that the USA dominated the relationship by 1945, that there was thus nothing special in it in the way that most think of a special relationship, and that in a wider context the dominant economic position that the USA had attained by 1945 amounted to hegemony over the free world.[37]

By 1945 the relative decline of Britain and the relative and absolute growth of the USA was self-evident, though one should not overestimate Britain's decline nor discount entirely the widespread expectation that it would recover ground in the post-war period. For Britain and the USA, there seemed less need than ever for defence plans vis-a-vis each other, but at the end of the war the significance of that tended to be discounted anyway. The achievements of their economic co-operation during the war – Lend-Lease and Reciprocal Aid and the division of labour in order to maximise wherever possible production for the war effort – tended to be regarded as past history. And so for a while, instead of valuing the things that had created and enhanced the special relationship between them, the things that divided them seemed to take precedence and the tending of the relationship that Craigie had identified as being so important was neglected.

The British certainly felt aggrieved by the conditions of the American loan and resented the way the USA used its economic leverage in other negotiations. At the same time there was a feeling in Clement Attlee's Labour Government that the Americans had overplayed their hand and that some conditions could simply not be fulfilled. In the meantime, Anglo-American relations deteriorated. Economic matters underpinned much of this, but as time passed a catalogue of non-economic matters appeared as well. There was the abrupt ending of nuclear co-operation contrary to understandings between Churchill and Roosevelt; there were differences between Secretary of State Byrnes and Foreign Secretary Bevin on policy in Europe and toward the Soviets; Truman and Attlee did not get on well; there were political differences between the two because of Labour's socialism; and there was disagreement about the future of Palestine and a Jewish homeland, which eventually became the bitterest dispute between the two in the early post-war years.

From this turmoil two important threads of development emerged which impacted on Anglo-American relations in a decisive way: one was the perception of the growing threat from the Soviet Union; the other was the modification of US international economic policy, in particular its attitude towards the UK, which came about for a variety of reasons.

At first, the Americans pressed on with their plans for a multilateral trade system within ITO to oversee things. However, its own negotiating position was undermined by congressional elections in 1946, which returned a Republican majority sceptical of reform and inclined to protectionism. In addition other countries, including Britain, continued to try to moderate American demands and to lengthen the transition to the dispensation of freer trade.

In the summer of 1947 British determination to maintain economic controls was strengthened by the abortive attempt to make currently earned sterling convertible in accordance with the US Financial Agreement. Convertibility could not be sustained. The Americans acknowledged, and even conceded, that British discrimination against the USA was permissible if it were necessary to obtain essential goods.[38] In currency terms, it was recognised that the kind of disequilibria that the IMF was designed to cope with were of a much smaller order of magnitude than the deeply unbalanced world economy that existed in 1947. Instead of international convertibility of currencies under the auspices of the IMF, the USA now concentrated on regional convertibility in Europe and also reluctantly came to the conclusion that it would have to tolerate the sterling area. In fact by 1947 the USA had become more tolerant altogether of regional economic controls and discrimination on the part of its allies. The main priority now was to strengthen Western economies at almost any cost in order to prevent them from becoming weak and vulnerable to communism. The USA's liberal multilateral international economic order would have to wait a while before being realised. It was still there, but as a long-term goal to be achieved only after a period of economic regionalism had strengthened western economies. Thus the transition period that the British had striven for was, in a way, achieved.

In the trade field in the 1940s the USA itself was unable to get the ITO, which was negotiated in Geneva, accepted by Congress. Truman withdrew it from Congress in 1950 and the General Agreement on Tariffs and Trade (GATT) was used instead to try to reduce economic protectionism. However, so far as the abolition of imperial preference was concerned the GATT was unsuccessful. After the Torquay GATT Conference of 1951 an American official wrote:

Negotiations were terminated because the Dominions were not willing to give up the preferential advantage they enjoy in the United Kingdom market and the United Kingdom, with its very narrow Government majority, was unwilling to do anything which could be pointed to as weakening the Empire Preference system.[39]

Even after the USA changed direction and realised that it would have to tolerate economic controls, protectionism and discrimination from its western allies and try to build up regional western economic blocs, it still found its allies recalcitrant. In the Marshall Plan the USA wanted Britain to lead the movement for European reconstruction. The USA envisaged a regional economic system emerging in Europe that would prosper through intra-European trade and a European system of currency convertibility. To underpin all this, and to provide a political pay-off for the economic discrimination that the USA would have to suffer in the short-and medium-term, there was to be European integration, which would result in a strong western political bloc that would be able to help contain communism. Again the British were not as co-operative as the Americans hoped.

The British refused to integrate and lead Europe from within. The ERP Administrator, Paul Hoffman, was angered by this and in late 1949 attempted to brow-beat the British with threats of suspending further Marshall Aid funds unless they involved themselves in European integration. It was left to Secretary of State Acheson and his deputy James Webb to point out to Hoffman that Britain was too important to be antagonised in this way and that Truman would not endanger the Marshall Plan.[40]

By 1950 it was clear that for one reason or another America's ideal economic world order had been compromised. Imperial Preference remained and sterling was only partially convertible. The Bretton Woods system was in limbo and the GATT was very much a second best alternative to the ITO and in any case had only meagre successes until the 1960s. Partly because of domestic political developments, partly because of economic realities, and partly because of resistance from Britain, the USA's attempts to create a multilateral liberal international economic order immediately after the war were frustrated. The USA was pushed into tolerating British economic practices and policies which it would have condemned in an ideal world or if it had been the hegemon that some have claimed it was. Above all, the need for British support in the war against communism moderated the pressures that the USA could bring to bear on Britain in the field of economic policy.

In early 1950 there took place a debate among US ambassadors in Europe about the character of the Anglo-American relationship and this is what the US Ambassador to London had to say:

. . .there is no country on earth whose interests are so wrapped around the world as the UK. Among her crown colonies she is in more vitally strategic areas than any other nation among the community of Western nations. She is the center of a great Commonwealth. The US enjoys the benefits of being a neighbor to the most important member of this Commonwealth whose relationships with the UK can no more be disguised or eliminated at the moment, or in the future, than can the relationship between the Hawaiian Islands and the US. She is the center of the sterling area. . .This area is held together not alone by the circulation of an identical currency or other currencies easily convertible into it. It is held together also by an intricate and complicated system of commercial and financial arrangements built up tediously by the British. . . . There is no substitute for the sterling area and none can be erected in any short period of time. But beyond all these considerations the UK is the only power, in addition to ourselves, west of the Iron Curtain capable of wielding substantial military strength. This assembly of facts, though some may disagree with a few of them, make a special relationship between the US and the UK as inescapable as the facts themselves. And no amount of dialectical argument can erase either the facts or the conclusion.[41]

A few months later Truman and his Secretary of State Dean Acheson made comments which illustrated that they too basically subscribed to this view. In December 1950 there was a very difficult conference with Attlee in Washington prompted by indiscreet remarks by Truman at a press conference, which seemed to suggest that atomic weapons might be used in Korea. The Anglo-American talks were very difficult ones and there was little rapport between the two sides on the personal level. Nevertheless, in a National Security Council meeting on 12 December Acheson commented that the conference had shown how important 'a close relationship with the UK is, since we can bring US power into play only with the co-operation of the British. The President said that this was true both in the Atlantic and the Pacific'.[42]

Thus, while the Second World War witnessed unprecedented close co-operation between the USA and Britain, it also saw a massive change in their relative power, and serious incursions into the economic sovereignty of the latter. In December 1945 that intrusiveness extended its farthest with the Anglo-American Financial Agreement's provisions and the subsequent pressure on Britain to accept conditions in other negotiations as a price of ratification. There is a certain irony in that neither conditions like those of the British Loan nor wartime intrusions into economic sovereignty would have been, or indeed were, accepted by other states. That says something about Anglo-American relations. In a rather perverse way, the intrusions into British economic sovereignty were tolerated because the overall relationship was so close and because both had vested interests in working together to create a better and more liberal post-war economy.

When the two states continued to try to achieve those goals in the realities of the post-war world they were confronted with two major problems: one was that economic disruption was far greater and more intractable than the Americans had initially imagined it would be; and secondly the main priority became resistance to communism. Working within these dynamics and that of their ongoing, if now troubled relationship, both Britain and the USA, but especially the USA, realised that policies would have to be modified and more recognition given to British requirements.

Relations between America and Britain were therefore much more complex than can be explained in terms of US economic hegemony. Testimony to that is provided by the continuation of Imperial Preference and sterling controls, the failure to get European integration through the Marshall Plan, and US resignation to making do with regionalism for a considerable period of time before a multilateral liberal economic world order could come into existence. The specialness of their relationship continued into the post-war world though some of its characteristics changed. However, as this chapter has tried to demonstrate, the term special relationship is not to be taken as a means of giving a simplistic general explanation of Anglo-American relations. Like the diplomat said, we need to know what was special and when and in relation to what. In some small way by concentrating on the economic side of the relationship it is hoped that the forcefulness of that anecdote has been demonstrated and a better understanding of Anglo-American relations and its significance in world affairs has been imparted.

Notes

1. Public Record Office, Kew, London, hereafter PRO, CAB 24/199, 27 November 1928, 'Three Questions of Imperial Defence Related to Anglo American Relations', note by Hankey, circulated on the authority of the Prime Minister.
2. P. Gibbs (ed.), *Bridging the Atlantic: Anglo-American fellowship as way to world peace*, London: Hutchinson, 1944, p. 35.
3. Ibid, p. 35.
4. C. Bell, *The Debateable Alliance*, London: Oxford University Press, 1964, pp. 11–12.
5. PRO, CAB 24/199.
6. Martin Gilbert, *Winston S. Churchill, vol. 5, Companion part 1*, London: Heinemann, 1979, p. 1033.
7. PRO, CAB 24/128, CP 344, memorandum by Craigie, 13 November 1928.
8. Ibid.
9. PRO, CAB 24/199, CP 359, memorandum by Churchill, 'Anglo-American Relations', 19 November 1928.

10. PRO, CAB 24/128, CP 344.
11. For example, Max Beloff, 'Is there an Anglo-American political tradition?', *History*, 36, 1951, pp. 73–91. For different views of Anglo-American relations see Alan Dobson, *The politics of the Anglo-American economic special relationship*, Brighton and New York: Wheatsheaf/St Martin's Press, 1988, and 'The Years of Transition: Anglo-American relations 1961–67'; *Review of International Studies*, 16, 1990, pp. 239–58; D.C. Watt, *Succeeding John Bull: America in Britain's place 1900–75*, Cambridge: Cambridge University Press, 1984; David Reynolds, 'Re-thinking Anglo-American relations', *International Affairs*, 65, 1988/89, pp. 89–111; R.B. Woods, *A changing of the guard: Anglo-American relations 1941–46*, Chapel Hill: University of North Carolina Press, 1990. For further reading see D.A. Lincove and G.R. Treadway, *The Anglo-American relationship: an annotated bibliography of scholarship*, Westport: Greenwood Press, 1988.
12. US National Archives (hereafter NA), RG 169, box 163, folder: British Capital Goods, Knollenberg to Crowley, 15 October 1943.
13. Alan Dobson, 'A mess of pottage for your economic birthright: the 1941–42 wheat negotiations and Anglo-American economic diplomacy', *Historical Journal*, 28, 1985, pp. 739–50 and Alan Dobson, *Peaceful air warfare: the United States, Britain and the politics of international aviation*, Oxford: Clarendon Press, 1991, chapters 5 and 6.
14. Dobson, 'A mess of pottage', op cit.
15. For more, if rather differing analyses see Dobson, *Anglo-American economic special relationship*; R.N. Gardner, *Sterling-Dollar diplomacy in current perspective*, New York: Columbia University Press, 1980; G. Kolko, *The politics of war*, London: Weidenfeld and Nicolson, 1969; Woods, op cit; L.S. Pressnell, *External economic policy since the war* vol. 1, London: HMSO, 1986.
16. W.F. Kimball, *Churchill and Roosevelt: the complete correspondence*, vol. 1, Princeton: Princeton University Press, 1984, pp. 49–51.
17. M.A. Stoler, *The politics of the second front: American military planning and diplomacy in coalition warfare 1941–43*, Westport: Greenwood Press, 1977; K. Sainsbury, 'Second front in 1942: a strategic controversy re-visited', *British Journal of International Studies*, 4, 1978, pp. 47–58; Kimball, vol. 1, pp. 2–23.
18. R.G.D. Allen, 'Mutual aid between the United States and the British Empire', *Journal of the Royal Statistical Society*, 109, 1946, pp. 243–7; Alan Dobson, *US wartime aid to Britain*, London: Croom Helm, 1986.
19. PRO, CAB 66, WP (41) 202 and 203; H.V. Morton, *Atlantic meeting*, London: Methuen, 1943; T.A. Wilson, *The first summit: Roosevelt and Churchill at Placentia Bay*, Boston: Houghton Mifflin, 1969; Dobson *Anglo-American economic special relationship*, Chapter 2.
20. Ibid; see also in particular PRO, CAB 66, WP (42) 21, 5 January 1942 and PRO, CAB 65, WM (14) 42, 2 February 1942.
21. Kimball, vol. 1, pp. 357–8 and 360–1.
22. Text in NA, State Department 841.24/720, Admiral Winant to Secretary of State, 3 September 1941; Cmnd 6311, 'The Export White Paper', 10 September 1941; for more detail see Alan Dobson, 'The export white paper of 1941', *Economic History Review*, 39, 1986, pp. 59–76.
23. PRO, FO 371/40883, memorandum by Dalton, 'Supersession of the Export White Paper', 28 June 1944.
24. Dobson, 'The export white paper of 1941', op cit.
25. Roosevelt Library, Morgenthau Diary, 592, p. 292. Stettinius to Morgenthau, 3 December 1942, in which he quotes Cox's memorandum to him of 23 November 1942; Ibid, pp. 110 and 150–78, 17 and 18 December 1942 respectively; NA, RG 169, box 163, minutes of Dollar Position committee, 29 December 1942; Ibid, box 721, BEW Board Meeting, 29 December 1942.

26. Roosevelt Library, Morgenthau Diary, 607, p. 99, White to Morgenthau, 8 February 1943.
27. Roosevelt Library, PSF, box 49, folder; GB 1944–45, Roosevelt to Churchill, 22 February 1944.
28. NA, 841.24/2197A draft letter and memorandum by Acheson, 21 February 1944; Roosevelt Library, Morgenthau Diary, 709, p. 109, 13 March 1944.
29. PRO, FO 371/40881, Anderson to Churchill, 24 February 1944.
30. Kimball, vol. 3, pp. 35–6 and 65–6.
31. PRO, CAB 66 WP (43) 566, Hudson memorandum, 14 December 1943 and WP (43) 576, Amery memorandum, 20 December 1943; Kenneth Young, *Churchill and Beaverbrook: a study in friendship and politics*, London: Eyre and Spottiswoode, 1966, p. 261; Lionel Robbins, *Autobiography of an economist*, London: Macmillan, 1971, p. 203.
32. A Van Dormael, *Bretton Woods: birth of a monetary system*, London: Macmillan, 1978; F. Block, *The origins of international economic disorder*, California: California University Press, 1977; Dobson, *Anglo-American economic special relationship*.
33. Ibid, pp. 65–74.
34. PRO, FO 371/45699, Keynes, 'Overseas Assets and Liabilities of the UK', 12 September 1945.
35. PRO, CAB 128/4, CM (45) 59, 5 December 1945, Cmnd 6708, 'Financial Agreement Between the Government of the United States and the United Kingdom', 6 December, 1945.
36. Dobson, *Peaceful air warfare*, chapter 6.
37. See Kolko, op cit; Block, op cit; Woods, op cit; W.H. Becker and S.F. Wells (eds.), *Economic and world power: American diplomacy*, New York: Columbia University Press, 1984. Figures quoted in the last of these show US GNP in 1945 at $220 billion compared with $91 billion in 1939. In 1947 US trade amounted to 33 per cent of the world total. In 1948 it produced approximately 41 per cent of the world's goods and services.
38. PRO, CAB 129, CP (49) 114, 10 May 1949, where the President of the Board of Trade refers to a 'private understanding' with the USA concerning discrimination.
39. Truman Library, PSF, box 165, folder; Conferences, Tariff Conference, Torquay, England, memorandum by J.R. Steelman.
40. Ibid, Acheson Papers, box 64, folder; memorandum of conversation, August–September 1947, minutes by Webb of a luncheon meeting, 25 October (dated 3 November), minutes of conversation between Acheson and Truman, 17 November 1949; Dobson, *Anglo-American economic special relationship*, pp. 113–25.
41. Library of Congress, Harriman Papers, box 271, folder; Marshall Plan, Country File, UK 20, Douglas to Secretary of State Acheson, Bruce, Harriman, Perkins and Bohlen, 7 May 1950.
42. Truman Library, box 220, folder; NSC meetings, memorandum for the President, 74th meeting, 12 December 1950; Dean Acheson, *Present at the Creation*, New York: W.W. Norton, 1969.

10

The Battle of Britain

John Ray

The first time I saw a man die in war was on Sunday 15 September 1940, at about twenty to three in the afternoon. I was watching a broken formation of German bombers returning from a raid on London, when they were set upon by RAF fighters. One bomber came blazing down through the sky and a man jumped out, his parachute snaking behind him like a string. It didn't open and I watched him fall and fall. Whenever I think of the Battle of Britain that vivid memory always comes back to me.

What I did not realise then was that I was seeing not one, but three battles going on overhead. The first was the main Battle of Britain, that struggle for aerial supremacy between the Luftwaffe and the RAF. Secondly, there was something of a contest within the Luftwaffe over strategy and tactics. Should London have been chosen as a target? To what extent should German fighters stick closely by their bombers during raids? That afternoon the fighters were noticeably distant. There was a third battle. It occurred almost exclusively among the top echelons of RAF commanders, concerned tactics, and is generally known as the Big Wing Controversy. How large should RAF fighter formations be when meeting the Germans? Should they be in single squadrons, or pairs? Or should there be Wings of three, four or five squadrons? And did it matter whether the Germans were tackled before or after they had bombed?

What do we mean by the Battle of Britain? Here, British and German perceptions often differ. The British see it as a separate battle, standing in its own right and refer to the daylight struggle which occurred between 10 July and 31 October 1940. Those were the dates given by Dowding in his Despatch on the battle, written in the following year.[1] Already I sense the iconoclasts taking their axes, like Gladstone to the upas tree, hoping to destroy a myth. However, they should be warned. There are a number of myths concerning the battle, but not always those recently suggested. In fact, there is now a place for a book or lecture entitled 'The Myth of the Myth'.

The Germans see the contest in a different light. For them it was only one phase in the general Western Campaign which opened with the invasion of Denmark and Norway in April 1940 and did not finish until the attack on Russia in June 1941.[2] Why the difference? Is it that German historians have a more panoramic view of history than their British counterparts? I think not. More probably, each side likes to stress that part of the period in which it did best – and say less of the other parts.

In my view, any study of the Battle of Britain must take into account the subsequent night Blitz. Without that it is not possible to see in perspective what happened to Dowding or to explain his dismissal as Commander-in-Chief of Fighter Command. Thus we have a battle of five main phases. First came attacks on convoys in the Channel, from early July. Second, by early August, attacks moved to targets in southern Britain – airfields, factories and radar stations. Third, and this was a phase in which the Germans did well, heavy raids were made on Fighter Command airfields near London. Then came a short period of daylight bombing of London, followed lastly by the long haul of the night Blitz, which started in September and lasted until May 1941.

What were the aims of each side? For the Germans there was an element of surprise and disappointment when Britain did not surrender at the same time as France. Most Germans believed that she would, as did many Europeans, especially French leaders. So did some Americans, for example, Joseph Kennedy, the ambassador in London. So, apparently did various other ambassadors. All believed that Britain had little to fight on for, or with.

However, when the Germans realised that there was to be a battle, they decided to win in one, or both, of two ways. First, the Luftwaffe would overcome the RAF, especially Fighter Command, preparatory to a seaborne invasion. The Germans reckoned, with some good reason, that if they could put their army ashore the British Army would be defeated. Or, second, the Luftwaffe would overcome the RAF, especially Fighter Command, and then would follow a period of sustained bombing of military, economic and political targets until not only heavy damage was done, but also morale was broken. This would force the British Government to the conference table.

On the British side the aims were more modest. In essence, Britain merely wanted to stay in the war. It was believed that if Fighter Command and the Royal Navy could hold off the Germans till the autumn, worsening weather would preclude a seaborne invasion, and Britain would last into 1941. Then, help would arrive from the Empire and, more especially, from the USA. This hope was not so Micawberish as might at first appear. There had been a belief held for some years by British political and Service chiefs that Germany did not possess the economic power to sustain a long war. In boxing terms, if Germany did not win by a quick knock-out in the first or second round she would lose a long contest on points. And there was another factor which is often overlooked. This was that during 1941 and 1942 the new generation of RAF heavy bombers would be coming into service – the Stirling, the Halifax and the Manchester (from which the Lancaster was developed). With these it was hoped to hit back at Germany in an aerial offensive, the policy subscribed to by most senior RAF staff since pre-war days. Here was the Trenchard Doctrine of aggressive strategic bombing, which was to come into effect with such devastating power over the succeeding years.

Therefore, increasingly, I view the Battle of Britain as a kind of holding operation, intended to keep the Germans at arm's length until Britain was ready to hit back.

Next it is important to appreciate that the battle fought was not the battle anticipated and this was to have a strong bearing on the subsequent struggle. The campaign anticipated from pre-war days was that the Germans would despatch large formations of bombers – up to one thousand a day – flying directly from Germany, unescorted because of the distance, crossing the North Sea and attacking Britain from a mainly north-easterly or easterly direction. They would make a landfall somewhere about the coast of East Anglia and would go on either to bomb the industrial midlands or north, or come south to attack London. It was for this anticipated battle that Dowding disposed his forces, with No. 12 Group, under Air Vice-Marshal Leigh-Mallory guarding the midlands and north, and No.11 Group, in those days under Air Vice-Marshal Gossage, protecting London and the south. It was assumed that the brunt of attack would be shared by both Groups.

The reality of battle was quite different. When, to their surprise, the Germans so quickly overran France in 1940, they found laid out before them a veritable Aladdin's cave of aerodromes and air-strips which they were able to develop, from which they could attack Britain from a mainly southerly, or south-easterly direction. And, being so close, these attacks were made by escorted bombers. There is, I think, a valid criticism to be made of Dowding's strategy that he did not alter the balance of his forces sufficiently quickly to meet the battle as it was rather than the battle as he had presumed it would be. In doing so he allowed too great a burden to fall on the pilots of No.11 Group here in the south-east, under their commander, Air Vice-Marshal Park.

What of the various strengths of the two sides? The impression is still generally held, and it was certainly given at the time, that a Luftwaffe of Juggernaut strength was faced by a mere handful of RAF fighters. This was Goliath versus David, and the origin of 'The Few'. In reality, however, the RAF entered the battle with a number of advantages, and the Luftwaffe with a number of disadvantages, which went some way to redressing the balance.

The main advantage for Fighter Command was that it was fighting the battle for which it had been created in 1936, namely the defence of the Home Base. It was not a strategic Command and that was one strong reason why Dowding was so adamant that no more of his fighters should be sent to France.

In 1940 the RAF possessed the World's best aerial defensive system. No other country – neither Germany nor Russia, not France or the USA – had a scheme of air protection to equal that set up in Britain. It was a system of which Dowding was more the builder than the architect and depended particularly on the rapid transfer of information. Incoming planes were detected by radar, known in those days as RDF (Radio Direction Finding), then messages were transmitted by radio, telegraph and telephone so that single-seater fighters, Hurricanes and Spitfires could meet intruders at or beyond the coast.

It must also be remembered that the British defensive system consisted not only of Fighter Command. There was Anti-Aircraft Command, whose accuracy and intensity of fire increased throughout the battle, a fact acknowledged by a number of German pilots.[3] Also there was Balloon Command. It is undoubtedly true that not many aircraft were brought down by balloons. Nevertheless, the fact that they were placed in certain vital positions, and about 1,400 of them were flown, dissuaded the Germans from attacking some vulnerable targets.[4]

Another factor in the RAF's favour was the slowness of the start of the German campaign. Hitler waited for some weeks after the fall of France, with a blend of hope and anticipation, expecting that Britain would surrender, and this gave Fighter Command an invaluable period in which to reform, reorganise and retrain squadrons. The Germans' best opportunity of launching a seaborne invasion, following straight on from Dunkirk, was missed, much to British relief. Consequently, as so often occurs in history, a small, well-prepared force was given the opportunity of overcoming a larger enemy. More recently there were similar circumstances during the Falklands Campaign.

What were the German disadvantages? At root, the Luftwaffe alone was being asked to defeat Britain without help from the other two Services. The German military engine was being required to fire on one cylinder out of three. Soon after the defeat of France the German Army was ready to launch an invasion of Britain and looked, naturally, to the German Navy for escort. This the navy was unable to provide. Here I must digress and look back to the Norwegian Campaign, which is often painted as an unmitigated disaster for Britain and France. It did, however, have one sovereign benefit for Britain in that during the campaign the German Navy suffered more heavily relative to the Royal Navy. Three cruisers and ten destroyers were sunk, with a number of other ships, including two battle cruisers damaged and out of commission.[5] Therefore, although the German Army wanted landings on a wide front to give more options of attack when ashore, the navy could offer to protect only a narrow passage at the Dover Straits. This, claimed some German generals, would be like putting their men through a sausage machine. Each Service blamed the other. The Army High Command believed that the navy's heart was not in 'Sealion', the plan for invasion. I am always amused by Admiral Ruge's later comment when he claimed that the German Army would never have crossed the Channel because the German soldier is sick if he crosses the Rhine.[6]

While those two Services were arguing, each looked, naturally, to the Luftwaffe, the only Service with the power to make immediate and direct contact with Britain. Both realised, of course, that the success of any seaborne attack depended first on aerial supremacy being obtained. At that stage the Luftwaffe's services were offered by its commander, Hermann Goering – an ardent Nazi, friend of Hitler and a man whose light seldom saw the cover of a bushel – who was not displeased that the limelight was falling on his air force. In fact, in Goering's belief, if the Luftwaffe did its job properly there would be no need for seaborne landings, as Britain would be defeated by the power of aerial bombing alone.

But at that stage there was no plan for attacking Britain by air. War with Britain had not been considered before 1938 and not until the following year were plans drawn up for a campaign. Then, strategic attacks were prepared, particularly on British industry and seaborne supplies.[7]

The Luftwaffe, however, was a tactical, not a strategic air force. It had been ever since the Spanish Civil War, when its value was realised as a form of flying artillery, or flame thrower, running ahead of ground forces. The air force was developed for this role – and how well it met the task in Poland, Norway, the Low Countries and France. At the Channel coast, however, the system came to a halt. A great drawback was the lack of a heavy bomber. The largest was the He. 111, which looked big, but was no more than a medium bomber, with a bomb-load of just over 4,000 lb. and a range of some 1,000 miles. Compare that with the real strategic heavy bombers used by the Allies later in the war. Stirlings and Lancasters, Liberators and Flying Fortresses could carry ten, twelve or eighteen thousand pounds of bombs over ranges of more than 2,000 miles. Without a heavy bomber, from the outset the Luftwaffe would be hard pressed to achieve success.[8]

Also, the German Air Force was constrained by the very narrow timescale offered. Hitler's Directive No. 17, finally ordering the Luftwaffe to destroy the RAF was not issued until 1st August and the great 'Eagle' attacks intended to achieve that end did not come until the middle of the month.[9] When it is remembered that the weather in the Channel would probably deteriorate from the end of September, the Luftwaffe was being asked to succeed within a period of some six or seven weeks. Such a success was just not on.

What of the numbers game? Here again there is the perception of a German Air Force of overwhelming numbers being opposed by a few hundred aircraft of the RAF. In reality, 'The Few' were not so few as many people imagine. Those brave pilots who served in action with Fighter Command between 10 July and 31 October, and who consequently were entitled to wear the Battle of Britain clasp, numbered 2,927. 'The Few' were, in the main, the pilots of No. 11 Group, under Air Vice-Marshal Park, Dowding's protege, on whom the Commander-in-Chief's planning allowed the main burden of battle to fall. Some 400 of them were opposed by the might of Luftflotten II and III, stationed opposite and comprising about 1,800 aircraft.[10]

Dr Horst Boog, historian of the Luftwaffe, has said that the Battle of Britain was essentially a fighter battle.[11] I would dare to go further. The struggle hinged round the result of a contest between two sets of single-seater fighters – on the German side, the Me. 109; and for the RAF, Hurricanes and Spitfires. These were the lords of the air and nothing could live in the sky with them. Therefore it is instructive to note the balance here. In the early stages of battle the Luftwaffe had about 760 Me. 109s; Fighter Command had about 710 Hurricanes and Spitfires.[12]

During the battle, British production outstripped that of Germany, and there was excellent work from fighter repair units. Overall in 1940 British fighter production exceeded German by a ratio of 3:2. Udet, responsible for much German production, believed at the end of the French Campaign that more aircraft would not be needed as the war was virtually over. On the British side much credit has been given to Beaverbrook, the Minister of Aircraft Production, and not enough to the man who had done so much from pre-war days, namely Sir Wilfrid Freeman. Nevertheless, it is easy to dismiss the part played by Beaverbrook as myth, yet he was a driving force at a time when so much was required of factories.

Much is made of British losses during the Western Campaign. Some 467 Hurricanes (mainly) and Spitfires were destroyed even before the Battle of Britain began, pearls without price in Dowding's eyes. What is less commonly appreciated is that the Germans, too, suffered heavily at that stage. In May and June the Luftwaffe lost some 247 Me. 109s and Me. 110s, together with about 15 per cent of their fighter pilot force. This was another factor that evened the balance a little more.[13]

What of the men, their machines and the tactics employed? In general, German pilots were more experienced in war than those in the RAF. Many had gained experience in Spain, Poland and Norway even before coming to the West. RAF pilots had gathered long flying hours, but not in action. There is no substitute in war for the experience of actually flying in combat. German pilots believed sincerely in what they were doing for their nation and had the confidence bred from success. It has been said that Germany had a Prussian Army, an Imperial Navy and a National Socialist Air Force. They had Goering as their commander and, through his position in the State, he was able to gain many benefits for them.

RAF pilots were of three categories and they too believed in what they were doing, appreciating how far Britain's fate depended on their efforts. Some, nonetheless, have made the point that they were so busy trying to stay alive there was not much time to dwell on such matters. There were the Regulars, many of whom had held commissions or appointments since the mid–1930s. Also there were pilots of the Auxiliary Air Force, often regarded as well-to-do flyers, with their own squadrons. Pilots of the Volunteer Reserve, founded in 1937, were fed into squadrons as they were needed. Humour had it that the Regulars were airmen trying to become gentlemen, the Auxiliaries gentlemen trying to become airmen and the Volunteer Reserve trying to become neither.

On both sides the pilots were young. One of the youngest was Squadron-Leader Bruce Ogilvie, who flew as a pilot-officer, aged 18, with No. 601 Squadron. Air Marshal Sir Denis Crowley-Milling, who flew as Bader's wingman with No. 242 Squadron was then a pilot-officer aged 19. If you were 21 you were becoming an old man; at the age of 25 you certainly were.

Concerning fighters, my research has shown that pilots who tended to fly one type throughout the battle generally came to regard it as the best machine. German pilots had great faith in the 109. It was fast, particularly in the dive and climb and better than the Spitfire and Hurricane over 20,000 feet. There was good vision, although the cockpit was rather restricting for a big man. The centralised armament, in the opinion of some, made for better shooting and the cannon had good destructive hitting power.

Those who flew Spitfires believed, as I do, that this was the most beautiful of aircraft. It was as fast as the Me.109 and more manoeuvrable. The eight guns gave a terrific rate of fire. I remember one evening watching a He.111 have its tailplane almost sawn off by a long burst from a Spitfire. Spitfire pilots had great confidence in their machines.

But so did Hurricane pilots. The Hurricanes were the most underestimated planes and it should be remembered that they were more numerous than Spitfires in the battle. It was a larger aircraft and could soak up more punishment. The cockpit gave good vision and one Hurricane pilot told me that in his machine he would cheerfully have taken on a Spitfire, having the ability to turn inside it.

In tactics, the Germans were superior both before and during much of the battle. The RAF had trained on vic-threes, where two wingmen were looking inwards, giving close attention to holding position close by the leader's tail. Some pilots later commented that such a formation was good for air displays, but of little use in combat.[14] Perhaps this was a little unfair because the vic-three was designed to meet formations of unescorted bombers and against those would have been very effective. A vic of three fighters firing 24 machine-guns against bombers would have caused great damage.

The Germans, from the Spanish Civil War, had developed the finger-four formation. Imagine, with the fingers of one hand stretched wide, a plane at the tip of each finger. They flew about 150–200 yards apart, with each pilot looking inwards and outwards, up and down, guarding the rear and flanks of his comrades.

In action the four broke into two pairs, the Rotte (each having a leader) and a wingman whose task was to guard the leader's tail. So often in the battle one sees reports of British fighters getting on to the tail of a 109, only to find themselves attacked from behind, obviously by the wingman.

During the Battle, some RAF squadrons changed tactics, using three fours, or pairs, or even line abreast. Often the fortunes of a squadron depended upon the ability of the squadron-leader in adapting and, sadly, this was sometimes reflected in the casualty rate. Someone like Group-Captain George Darley, Commanding Officer of No. 609 Squadron, adapted tactics and his men suffered fewer casualties. Compare this with the experience of the pilot of No. 145 Squadron who commented that they stayed in vics over Dunkirk and throughout the Battle. By August they had lost heavily and had to be sent to Scotland to reform.

Concerning military intelligence, which is knowledge of the enemy in battle, it may be said in general that the RAF tended to overestimate the numbers and power of the Germans while the Luftwaffe underestimated the RAF, especially in regard to the value of radar. There is, however, one belief on intelligence that must be put right. A number of books, some by most competent historians, have stated that throughout the Battle Dowding had the benefit of knowledge from Ultra, the Enigma machine and that he knew where and when German attacks would be made. This was not so.[15] Martin Gilbert has shown that not until 16 October did Churchill agree that Dowding should be made privy to Ultra information. Until then he had to rely on other sources.[16]

What of leadership in the Battle? I never fail to be amazed how little interest Hitler appeared to take. So often in war German campaigns succeeded when the Fuhrer took a personal interest and command. At that stage, nevertheless, he was more involved in preparing his campaign against Russia, in spite of the traditional fear of a war on two fronts. Responsibility for the battle was passed over to Goering. Never was faith more misplaced. At this stage the Commander-in-Chief of the Luftwaffe was more concerned with luxurious living, adding to his art treasures and hunting on his country estates. He should have been at the Channel coast, leading and inspiring, but it is noticeable that some of his conferences were held hundreds of miles away at his mansion in East Prussia.

On the British side there was keen interest in the battle, especially from Churchill. Not only did he visit fighter headquarters and aerodromes, but also several times entertained Dowding, and once, Park, at Chequers. His was a more inspiring form of leadership. Dowding's leadership was of a reserved nature, which was respected by his men, although he failed signally to settle the quarrel over tactics between his two subordinates, Park and Leigh-Mallory.

By September the Germans had not won the daylight battle and turned increasingly to night bombing. Here was a change in strategy that was to cause Fighter Command and Dowding far greater problems than they had previously encountered. Within two months, Dowding was replaced.[17]

How does one summarise the battle? In my view the Battle of Britain was, for Britain and several other countries, the most important of the war. It was what I would call an 'either/or' battle. Either Britain did not lose and could stay in the war; or she did lose and was forced out. What were the results of this? First, by not losing, Britain gave hope to many nations of Europe which were occupied during the war years. She was regarded as a beacon of light amid the darkness of oppression.

Had Britain been defeated, Germany would have invaded Russia earlier and would, in all probability, have won. Moscow and Leningrad would have been taken and Bolshevism overthrown fifty years before it was. In the Far East Japan would earlier have launched attacks on the old European empires of France, Holland and Britain. Japanese forces might well have got not only to the gates of, but into, India. Probably Australia would have been invaded, a thought that still occupies minds there.

The United States, I believe, would have become more isolationist, if only for the reason that there would have been no European springboard from which to hit back at Germany; later in the war Britain acted as a type of floating aircraft carrier with naval base and military barracks. The Americans would, through force of circumstances, have turned their eyes elsewhere.

In Britain an enemy victory would have led to a severe regime. I do not doubt that some people would have collaborated, but it would have been under harsh German military law. For example, a German Army Order of 9 September 1940, signed by General Halder, ordered the removal of all men aged 17 to 45 to the Continent as soon as possible, obviously for slave labour.[18]

The greatest fear is for what would have happened to European Jewry. Five or six million Jews were put to death and I believe that some 13 million lived in Europe at the time. What would have been the fate of the others? Their chances would have been slender in a holocaust twice as large as the one that happened. Little did I think on that distant day, 52 years ago, as I watched a young man fall to his death, that the battle above would have such an effect on my life, or, I dare to suggest, on those of the readers of this book.

Notes

1. Sir Hugh Dowding, Battle of Britain despatch, Public Record Office, Kew, London, AIR 8/863, 1941, paragraphs 13 and 210.
2. Field Marshal Kesselring, *The memoirs of Field Marshal Kesselring*, translated by L. Hudson, London: William Kimber, 1974, pp. 75–84.
3. Sir Frederick Pile, *Ack-ack*, London: Harrap, 1949, pp. 142–3.
4. D.J. Smith, 'Balloon barrages', in W.C. Ramsay (ed.), *The Blitz: then and now*, vol. 1, London: After the Battle, 1987, pp. 86–95.
5. E. van der Porten, *The German navy in World War Two*, London: Pan, 1972, p. 92.
6. H. Probert and S. Cox (eds), *The battle re-thought*, London: Airlife, 1991, p. 84.
7. H. Schliephake, *The birth of the Luftwaffe*, London: Ian Allan, 1971, pp. 48–50.
8. B. Cooper, *The story of the bomber 1914–1945*, London: Cathay Books, 1974, pp. 64–121.
9. H.R. Trevor-Roper (ed.), *Hitler's war directives*, London: Sidgwick and Jackson, 1964, pp. 37–8.
10. D. Wood and D. Dempster, *The narrow margin*, London: Hutchinson, 1961, appendix 19.
11. Probert and Cox, p. 32.
12. R. Suchewirth, *Historical turning points in the German war effort*, New York: Arno Press, 1968, pp. 64–7.
13. W. Murray, *Luftwaffe*, London: Allen and Unwin, 1985, pp. 44–5.

14. H.R. Allen, *Who won the Battle of Britain?*, London: Arthur Barker, 1974, pp. 34–5.
15. See, for example, John Terraine, *The right of the line*, London: Macmillan, 1985, pp. 178–9.
16. Martin Gilbert, *Finest Hour, Winston S Churchill, Vol. 6, 1939–41*, London: Heinemann, 1983, p. 849.
17. E.B. Haslam, 'How Lord Dowding came to leave fighter command', *Journal of Strategic Studies*, vol. 4, no. 2, 1981, pp. 175–86.
18. Milch Papers, 1940. The secret dossier on the military administration of England, HQ Army Command, 9 Sept. 1940, microfiche 565, iv/58/5, Department of Aviation Records, RAF Museum, London.

11
Britain and the Resistance in Europe 1939–45

Ralph White

This is a problematic subject, not least when we consider Britain's involvement in European resistance movements against German occupation, as we do here, as an expression of British identity with Europe during the Second World War. I say this for several reasons. First, Britain's role, like European resistance itself, had three dimensions: there is the aspect of rationale and motivation; there is the aspect of organisation and operation; and there is the aspect of achievement and result. Each of these provides its own evidence of Britain's identity with Europe, which was often out of kilter with evidence from the others. Further, British participation in resistance movements developed such that Britain's relationship with Europe changed dramatically during the course of the war. Finally, a point so obvious as to be blinding: resistance was clandestine activity, and Britain's role was especially secret, unknown to all but a tiny handful of politicians and military and civilian staff. One consequence of this secrecy is that many of the records of the relevant organisations are either non-existent or still inaccessible. It is, nevertheless, the case that notable scholarly literature has been produced in recent years dealing with such secret activities as intelligence and subversion – including studies of Britain's role in the resistance;[1] yet I still find that this remains a subject which one studies through a glass rather darkly.

This elusiveness has led to a diversity of interpretations. Evidence has been cited to justify an optimistic, perhaps idealistic view: that British support for European resistance was inspired by the conviction that Britain shared with the states and peoples of Europe a great common interest in the achievement of national and liberal democratic freedom from Fascist control; that to this end, a remarkable organisation, the Special Operations Executive (SOE), was created to sponsor a volunteer Anglo-European secret force which played a crucial role in fomenting resistance, which in turn made, at the least, a noteworthy contribution to the defeat of the Axis powers and the liberation of Europe. On this view, Britain's involvement therefore expressed the most direct and intimate identity with Europe, not just strategically, but politically, ideologically and even morally, as part of a crusade for an anti-Axis, post-Fascist Europe. Further, the working and the effectiveness of SOE cemented this identity in practice and contributed to the enhanced status and prestige of Britain as a European power at the end of the war.[2]

Against this, evidence has been produced to justify a more pessimistic analysis. It has been argued that the essential motive for British support for resistance was strategic and therefore contingent, and was intended to serve specifically British interests rather than contributing to the emergence of a new Europe. Further, the assumption that subversion could have been a major war-winning strategy has been seriously questioned, as has the performance of SOE itself, and the overall contribution of resistance to allied victory. On this view Britain's role was not a significant expression of an identity with Europe, except in a limited strategic sense; rather it was a means for the often ineffective prosecution of British military and political self-interest, which did as much harm as it did good to Britain's standing in Europe in 1945.[3] Obviously these two overviews are oversimplified; one result being that they are not as mutually exclusive as they might seem. In order to explore this further I want to distinguish between the theory and the practice of Britain's part in the resistance at different times during the war.

1

The primary context for British involvement was indeed strategic, and turned on the events of 1940. It is true that British interest in the possibilities of subversive activity predated not only 1940 but the outbreak of war in 1939. This activity was, however, both limited and largely unsuccessful and the organisations concerned operated on the margins of British policy and strategy with only minimal resources.

The situation was transformed in 1940 with the German victories in northern and western Europe, culminating in the defeat of France in June. This knocked a hole in the bottom of British strategy, which had assumed the capacity of the Maginot Line and the French army, assisted by the British Expeditionary Force, to hold any German onslaught in the west. Britain stood almost alone, its principal European ally defeated: in these dire circumstances the Chiefs of Staff and the War Cabinet reshaped a war strategy by elevating subversion to stand alongside the two other key elements: naval blockade and bombing offensive. This tripartite strategy involved continuity as well as novelty: continuity because the principle was sustained that the most effective way of defeating Germany was indirect, by exposing Germany's supposed weakness to fight a longer war through the lethal variations of economic warfare; and novelty because of the promotion of subversion – but how can we explain this?

Negative and circumstantial factors were important: the summer of 1940 was a perilous time for the British war effort, when the German military cause seemed invincible to many contemporaries, and Britain lacked substantial land strength of her own or anyone else's to match the triumphant Axis forces. The elevation of subversion in these circumstances has often been seen as an unrealistic, improbable gesture, a snatching at straws by ministers and chiefs of staff finding their strategic cupboard all but bare.

Yet the ministers and chiefs of staff were genuine in their commitment to subversion at this time, for what they believed were four positive reasons. First, they continued to believe in the vulnerability, even the fragility, of the Nazi system in both political and economic terms. Subversion made sense as a means of sustaining pressure alongside naval blockade and bombing offensives, which would expose fundamental weaknesses in the regime, which was now even more stretched by virtue of its recent expansion in northern and western Europe. Second, it was assumed that the circumstances of the defeated and occupied peoples of Europe were favourable to widespread subversion, which if appropriately organised and harnessed could play a major part in the eventual defeat of the Axis powers. Thirdly, it was within the scope of Britain as the great undefeated ally – with its international traditions and its proximity to, and historic links with, Europe and especially its links with the cause of European freedom, independent nationalism and democracy – to fulfil the role of leader of European resistance. Finally, British ministers and Chiefs of Staff were also convinced that the record of German victory so far had been made possible in part by Fifth Column activity, a formidable weapon which should be turned against the Axis powers.

How was this role to be played? As early as May 25 1940, when the Chiefs of Staff considered 'a certain eventuality', namely the fall of France, they agreed that if this happened 'The creation of widespread revolt in Germany's conquered territories would become a major British strategic objective. For this a special organisation would be needed and in their view ought to be set up promptly.'[4] It was, and on July 22 the War Cabinet approved a document drafted by Neville Chamberlain which became regarded as SOE's charter, which asserted that 'a new organisation shall be established forthwith to coordinate all action, by way of subversion and sabotage, against the enemy overseas.'[5] So SOE's writ was not limited to Europe and it was organised to function on a world wide basis; yet it was at this time that Churchill is reputed to have declared to Dalton, the first ministerial chairman of SOE, the words 'now set Europe ablaze.'

So the stage was set: despite the minuscule experience of the bodies hitherto responsible for clandestine warfare, now being subsumed in the new, single organisation, SOE as it was set up in July 1940 embodied a remarkably high doctrine of British-led European subversion as a key part of a war-winning strategy. Thus the British government initially committed itself to the cause of European resistance in a way that fused national self-interest with that of occupied Europe's desire for freedom, and that implied an intimate strategic, political and ideological identity. This was something on which the conservative, imperialist Churchill and the socialist, internationalist Dalton agreed; that Britain's interest and her destiny lay in mobilizing the enormous reservoir of anti-fascist nationalist and democratic discontent in occupied Europe. But to what extent this could be achieved, in the sense of a clear definition of the shape of a post war, post Fascist Europe, remained unclear.

Indeed, the problem with this high doctrine of resistance was not that it was not genuine but that it was aspirational and vague. Both the theory and practice of Britain's involvement had to be defined in and by wartime reality; rhetoric had to be translated into policy. In this process it became clear that much of the original vision of the scope of British-led European resistance had to be scaled-down. I want to concentrate on some of the main aspects of this scaling-down process, chiefly because of their implications for Britain's European identity, especially those aspects which suggest a more limited view of British interest. And the dimension I shall focus on primarily is that of rationale, because this provides the evidence of identity of the chief policy makers: the War Cabinet, the Chiefs of Staff and SOE's senior staff. Their perceptions I take to be more historically significant, but no more interesting, than those of the SOE agents themselves.

2

The central, and in 1940 unanswered, questions were: What was meant by subversion? How would it work? and; How could Britain promote it? Dalton started with a left wing, almost revolutionary vision of an occupied Europe consumed by permanent, open unrest, in which the working classes, and especially socialists and trade unionists, would play a central part. The role of SOE was to promote subversion in the widest sense, through the use of 'many different methods, including industrial and military sabotage, labour agitation and strikes, continuous propaganda, terrorist acts against traitors and German leaders, boy-cotts and riots'.[6]

As Dalton and his senior colleagues in SOE thought through the problem of translating this conception into a practicable strategy, it had to be redefined in the light of a whole series of powerfully limiting factors. First, the domestic con-straints: SOE's resources were initially minimal and indeed never developed throughout the war to the level required to fulfil the 1940 prescription of clandes-tine activity as a major strategy. A particular reason for this was that access to occupied Europe for agents and equipment proved more difficult than imagined, and in the main possible only by air. The scale of SOE's activity turned primarily therefore on the availability of aircraft, in short supply especially early in the war, and with rival claimants for their use. Throughout the war SOE found itself competing with Bomber Command and the priorities of the strategic air offensive, as well as with the Secret Intelligence Service (SIS) and the priorities of intelli-gence, because SIS also wanted air transport for its own work in Europe. Dalton had proposed that 'subversion should be clearly recognised by all three Fighting Services as another and independent Service'[7] and that SOE should be accepted as that fourth service. In practice the traditional bias of the Chiefs of Staff toward regular warfare meant that SOE's priorities generally came second, whilst the Foreign Office's concern for diplomacy, and SIS intelligence, meant that through-out the war SOE was ranged against powerful Whitehall institutions, whose interests predominated over those of clandestine warfare.

There were two major external constraints. Many of the governments-in-exile were recognised by the British government as legitimate and could not easily be ignored by SOE in planning operations in their countries. In general these governments resented any SOE tendencies to operate without consultation with them, and wanted to retain as much control over what happened – including resistance – in their own countries as possible. Usually they opposed plans for the more radical and independent forms of subversive activity that increased, through reprisals, the suffering of their peoples and exposed divisions between different resistance groups and between those groups and themselves. The assassination of Heydrich was the exception rather than the rule.[8] Thus, throughout the war, SOE's relations with governments-in-exile, although sometimes cordial, were more often fraught with difficulty.

The second external constraint was provided by the potential for revolt and resistance in occupied Europe. This quickly proved to be much less substantial than was originally imagined and, in contrast, the Axis capacity to maintain effective control emerged as altogether more formidable. An important military intelligence report of September 1940 concluded that:

none of the countries at present under enemy domination, with the possible exception of Poland and Czechoslovakia is likely from its own resources to be in a position to initiate risings on any considerable scale. Such risings are only likely to be brought about as an outcome of careful plans and detailed organisations controlled and assisted from this country.[9]

Spontaneous and premature uprisings were to be discouraged as militarily ineffective and dangerously provocative.

We see here the germ of what eventually displaced the Daltonian doctrine between 1940 and 1942 to become the predominant SOE strategy of subversion: the theory of secret armies and what David Stafford calls 'the detonator concept'.[10] Much impressed by the clandestine forces that had emerged in Poland and Czechoslovakia, SOE Chiefs evolved the view that secret armies should be built up and supported by SOE in occupied Europe and then mobilized and detonated in conjunction, and only in conjunction, with allied invasion. Guerrilla warfare and premature uprisings were not part of this doctrine, though sabotage, used sparingly, was.

This rationale reflected a more military or paramilitary sense of subversion than Dalton's grandiose and more political project; it conceived resistance in Europe as very much the handmaiden of British policy and strategy and was ostensibly more compatible with the priorities of both the Chiefs of Staff and the governments-in-exile. Nevertheless it sustained the 1940 vision of subversion as a key element in the defeat of the Axis powers and in this way compensated for the delay now implied in the execution of resistance activity. And when in the summer of 1941 SOE demanded the number of planes and sorties it required to equip a series of secret armies in occupied Europe to mobilize the following year, the Chiefs of Staff recorded their scepticism about secret armies and conceded only a minimum of SOE's requests.[11] The need to encourage subversion and sabotage was accepted but resources on the scale that SOE had asked would have been possible only at the expense of Bomber Command and SIS. A further important decision was taken that on logistical grounds it would henceforth be impossible to supply the secret armies of Poland and Czechoslovakia in preparation for national uprisings, and assistance should be concentrated in those regions, namely in western Europe, where British regular forces would be in action – such was the logic of the detonator concept. This did not mean that Polish and Czech resistance were no longer to be supported, but that SOE now assumed limits to the scale and scope of their activities, in contrast to the priority henceforth attached to resistance in western Europe.

This detonator logic was undermined by two further external developments in 1941: the participation of the Soviet Union and the United States as allies in the war. These two great powers had the resources in regular land forces to take on the Axis forces directly; and from the moment in late 1941 that the possibility of a Second Front was raised, the defeat of the Axis powers without dependence on subversion as a major strategy was possible. Formal armies of the necessary size could henceforth be provided as the basis for Allied victory in Europe; the Americans were initially sceptical of subversive strategy anyway, and thus, for the last two or three years of the war European resistance became treated as an auxiliary factor, whatever its form, no more than a bonus to the strategies that became dependent on regular forces and conventional warfare.

The paradox is that from 1943 to 1945, as the course of the war in Europe shifted in the Allies' favour and the defeat of the Axis became more probable, so the resistance movements in Europe and the operational capacity of SOE reached their maximum strength. This coincided with the time when the scaling-down of the scope of British-led European resistance had come to its climax in that subversive activity was no longer treated as a major war-winning weapon.

3

In this final period there were nevertheless three significant roles defined for SOE to fulfil: in the Mediterranean, in western Europe and in the post-liberation phase; and between them they highlight an aspect of SOE's rationale we have not yet looked at: its politics.

In a sense the detonator concept de-politicized Dalton's original conception of an ideologically inspired European revolt, backed but not controlled by Britain, which would lead to a radical reshaping of a post-war European order. This had given way to the belief in politically-neutered secret armies operating under closer British control. This was confirmed by the way SOE trained its agents to see themselves as above politics, not to become involved in the political conflicts of the countries in which they worked, and, indeed, to profit from this neutrality in being able to appeal equally in the name of a common anti-Axis cause to local resistance groups. SOE was certainly political in its assumption that the motivation to resistance to Axis domination was indeed political and ideological, and part of the 1940 vision was that SOE should be responsible for propaganda to this end. In fact, propaganda was hived off to be the work of the separate Political Warfare Executive in 1941. In any case British policy-makers were ill-prepared for the extent to which the experience of defeat and occupation exposed and intensified the divisions within European societies – divisions which expressed themselves in the conflict within many of the resistance movements of occupied Europe. This was especially so after Barbarossa, in June 1941, when the communists threw their formidable capacity for clandestine activity into the European resistance effort. In this sense SOE agents were political innocents abroad; and when it was realized that certain European resisters appeared as willing to fight each other as the Axis powers, the initial reaction of both SOE and the Foreign Office was to try to reconcile their differences in single national resistance movements and secret armies. The dream of nationally united resistance died hard; if the divisions within European movements could not be healed, their subversive effectiveness was compromised and the whole question of the kind of post-war order that would emerge was thrown into question – much to the concern and even alarm of both governments-in-exile and Allied governments.

This political dimension came to the fore in the final phase of the war from 1943 to 1945 when resistance movements became stronger, Axis defeat closer and as Soviet influence in Eastern Europe increased and the problems of the post-war European order became more central. SOE's role vis-à-vis European resistance henceforth reflected an interplay between short-term strategic and longer-term political factors, as the reality of divided resistance in occupied Europe, and of a Europe between Soviet and western spheres of influence was absorbed and choices made. These choices further illuminate Britain's conception of her self-interest and her European identity.

First, the Mediterranean and the Balkans. In 1943 with the postponement of Operation Overlord, together with the development of a Mediterranean strategy and the decision not to land regular Allied forces in the Balkans, an alternative policy was adopted of further support for guerrilla activities in Yugoslavia, Greece and Albania. The object was to tie down and weaken Axis forces and create the impression that Allied landings in the eastern Mediterranean were imminent. In the Chiefs of Staff directive to SOE of March 1943 priority was given to sabotage and guerrilla warfare in the Mediterranean and the Balkan countries, ahead of the build-up of secret armies and sabotage in areas of projected allied operations in north-western Europe.[12]

The new and serious British commitment to Balkan guerrilla activity was dictated by military criteria, but it pitched SOE and the British government into the political dimensions of resistance activity of the first magnitude. For, by 1943, in both Greece and Yugoslavia substantial resistance movements had emerged that were in conflict with each other as well as the Axis powers. In both cases groups loyal to the monarchical governments-in-exile found themselves embroiled in conflict with left wing and communist forces. In Greece, SOE supported the republican communist groups EAM/ELAS, a policy which alarmed Churchill and the Foreign Office, who were committed to the survival of the monarchy as the basis of post-war Greece. This conflict in British policy between shorter-term military and longer-term political interests was also exposed in Yugoslavia. Initially SOE had backed Mihaelovic's royalist Chetnik forces, but as evidence mounted of first the existence and then the effectiveness of Tito's communist partisans, together with that of the questionable resistance record of the Chetniks, the dilemmas for British policy intensified. In both cases the British tried to get the warring factions to work together, but failed. British reaction was remarkably different: in the case of Greece political priorities overruled strategic ones, and British support was given to the monarchical side in what became a civil war. In Yugoslavia, support was switched from Mihaelovic to Tito on the grounds of the greater credibility of his guerrilla activity. And in Albania SOE opposed support for right wing resistance groups on the grounds that this would foment conflict with the predominant communist groups, which the Chiefs of Staff thought more militarily effective anyway. In all these cases there was serious conflict between British policy makers, reflecting differing perceptions of the relative merits of political and strategic priorities in each country. These differing perceptions also reflected the problem of deciding how to satisfy the different British priorities that developed at this time. These were:

1. the need to defeat the Axis powers;
2. the need to defeat communism in countries which were to remain in the British and western orbit after the war, such as Greece;
3. the need to maintain British influence in countries which were to remain within a predominantly Soviet sphere;
4. the need to remain on good terms with the Soviet Union, if possible.[13]

In the last phase of the war British policy reflected these cross pressures more acutely in the Balkans than in western and northern Europe, where the alignment of military and political priorities proved less difficult. Here SOE strategy was closely integrated with overall allied strategy, with emphasis mainly on preparations for Operation Overlord in 1944. SOE was encouraged to continue sabotage and to build up resistance groups: in 1943 these were not, however, supplied on the scale SOE demanded, rather, with the exception of Denmark, they were held back (with mixed effects on morale) until the landing of Allied forces. Support for sabotage in Poland and Czechoslovakia also continued but for both practical and policy reasons not for the strengthening of their secret armies.

In 1944 France, as the focus of Overlord, became SOE's top priority in the west. With the support of both Churchill and the Foreign Office, SOE managed to prise more aircraft from an ever recalcitrant Bomber Command, but still never as much as demanded. Thus the SOE station in Cairo complained that resources were being diverted from the Balkans. Churchill had visions of guerrilla warfare enveloping south-east France and demanded substantial support for the maquis in the south; but more sober counsels prevailed and SOE gave priority to supporting resistance in north-west France, to aid Overlord directly – via the deception plan Bodyguard. But the key point here is that although SOE's capacity, and that of French resistance, were increasing, no integral place was found for resistance in the Overlord plans prepared by COSSAC and SHAEF. This reflected the judgement of military planners of the reliability and efficacy of resistance activity, which in turn reflected the degree of support SOE was able to provide. This marked a final stage in the scaling-down process we have been considering. However, it was not assumed that resistance could make no contribution: simply that it was too uncertain to be relied upon and therefore built into plans. Instead resistance was treated as a bonus, and the support given to resistance was intended to make the most of this bonus. But the bonus was itself planned, in that the SHAEF directives set out objectives for SOE working in conjunction with the American OSS, with regard to both resistance activity before and after D-Day. This activity consisted principally of the sabotage of German strategic goods and communications, deception, and guerrilla warfare in the south of France to preoccupy German forces. Elsewhere in Europe SOE agents were directed to remain quiet and concentrate on counter sabotage, although sabotage was encouraged to hamper German withdrawals and maintain morale.

American involvement in this phase of European resistance was a major logistical factor, substantially increasing the supply of aircraft and materials. Cooperation with SOE worked well, both in strategic terms and on the ground – not least in the ninety three inter allied Jedburgh teams dropped behind enemy lines into France between June and August 1944. There was little or none of the conflict in Europe between OSS and SOE that disfigured their relationship elsewhere, in the Far East for example.

So we come to the post-liberation phase where military and political priorities went largely hand-in-hand in north western Europe. SOE was charged with counter sabotage, mopping-up operations and helping to maintain law and order in the newly liberated lands. In this, SOE was working on behalf of the British policy of restoring democratic-capitalist regimes, based on the governments-in-exile, with whom SOE now cooperated more closely. This included helping to neutralise and disarm the more radical and communist elements in the local resistance groups which might have challenged the democratic-capitalist order post-war: in this sense SOE's role reflected a more specifically conservative set of

British priorities. As these priorities were shared by large sections of interest and opinion in north western European society in 1945, the question of identity remains an open one.

Elsewhere in Europe, the conflict between political and strategic priorities remained sharp, with SOE often caught between the Foreign Office and Chiefs of Staff. In eastern Europe the practical difficulties of providing the most substantial supplies were compounded by the Foreign Office's wish not to alienate the Soviet Union in those countries accepted as predominantly within the Soviet sphere of influence. These included the so-called satellite states (Bulgaria, Rumania and Hungary) as well as Poland and Czechoslovakia. British policy toward the Italian partisan movement also exhibited cross-pressures between the aims of supporting them, controlling them, and neutralizing the communist elements within the overall policy of establishing a pro-western, democratic-capitalist Italian regime.

So the conclusion to this survey of the extensive changes in the rationale of the British involvement with resistance is that the radical scaling-down of its military role was accompanied by a transformation of its political role as the predominant anti-Fascism of the early war years which was partnered and even replaced by the anti-communism of the 1943–1945 period. This change was confirmed in the continuation of clandestine warfare after 1945, despite the formal disbanding of SOE in 1945, as part of Britain's cold war policy.[14] The implication must be that British identification with Europe developed during the course of the war from a comprehensive and radical but ill-defined military and political commitment to the cause of European resistance in 1940 to a far more limited and conservative conception of the overlap of British and European interests in 1945.

4

The evidence found in the changing rationale of resistance is one thing; that provided by the organisation and activity of SOE is quite another. Here we are considering the several thousand individual men and women who volunteered to risk, and often to give their lives, as part of a British campaign in the cause of European freedom, usually and more especially, the freedom of a particular European country. Agents were recruited for their ability to undertake clandestine activity in particular countries or regions of Europe and whatever the mix of their individual motives their identification with their European cause was unquestioned. Indeed, most agents – possibly two thirds – were natives of the countries in which they served; the cooperation between them and their British-born colleagues, and between these agents and the local resisters who worked with them testified to an identity at its most intimate and intense. The problem is to evaluate the significance of identity of this informal and personal kind shared by a few thousand people engaged in highly secret activity, against the kinds of identity implied in strategic policy, the details of which were unknown to the SOE agents themselves.

This problem exists because there is a sense in which the activity of resistance and the rationale of resistance were worlds apart, with only the senior management of SOE acting as a point of intersection. The identification with Europe felt by the ministers, officials and Chiefs of Staff who ultimately determined the role of SOE became, after 1940, far more nuanced and pragmatic than that of the men and women engaged in clandestine operations. This point is sharpened when we remember again that the scaling-down of the theory of resistance was in fact accompanied by a scaling-up of resources and operations, so that in its support of guerrilla warfare in Yugoslavia and for Operation Overlord in France, SOE made two of its most ambitious contributions to winning the war. Experienced from within, Britain's participation appeared to reach a climax.

This raises a final point: to what extent did British identity turn not just on rationale and activity, but on effect, on achievement? One could say that it was the presence, rather than the performance, of the SOE agents and missions that was decisive as an expression of British commitment. The actual results served to establish – or diminish – the credibility of resistance activity in the minds of British policy makers, governments-in-exile, and the resistance groups and societies of occupied Europe. On the credit side one can cite the progressive increase in agents and supplies going to occupied Europe during the war, all sorts of individual operations that were successful, plus the moral and psychological support provided to resistance and opposition in occupied Europe generally. On the debit side however must be noted the minimal backing provided earlier in the war and the unevenness of support thereafter, the failures and even disasters, especially those associated with enemy penetration, and the fact that there remains a question mark over whether resistance activity played more than a marginal role, certainly in strategic and economic terms, in the Allied victory.

In conclusion, one has to say the evidence of Britain's identity with Europe provided by Britain's role in European resistance is double edged. For that role exhibited, in some aspects, a commitment to Europe of a remarkable and perhaps unparalleled kind, whilst in others it revealed the pursuit of a far more limited and limiting sense of national self-interest.

Notes

1. Two of the best overall studies are M.R.D. Foot, *SOE. An outline history of the Special Operations Executive 1940–46*, London: British Broadcasting Corporation, 1984; and David Stafford, *Britain and European Resistance, 1940–1945*, Basingstoke: Macmillan Press, 1983 (repr). For the problem of sources see Foot, op. cit. 'Notes on Sources', p. 251 and the preface to Stafford's work.

2. A hopeful view of the British contribution to European resistance can be found in e.g., M.R.D. Foot, *SOE. An outline history of the Special Operations Executive 1940–46*, London: British Broadcasting Corporation, 1984; *SOE in France*, London: HMSO, 1968 (2nd impr. with amendments); Sir Colin Gubbins, 'Resistance movements in the war', *Journal of the Royal United Services Institute*, 93, 1948; Henri Michel, *The Shadow War*, London: Andre Deutsch, 1972; and Bickam Sweet-Escott, *Baker Street Irregular*, London: Methuen, 1965.

3. Critical appraisals are variously offered in, e.g., Basil Davidson, *Partisan Picture*, Bedford Books Ltd, 1946; *Special Operations Europe*, London: Gollancz 1980; Richard Deacon, *A history of the British Secret Service*, London: Panther 1968; and Alan Milward, 'The economic and strategic effectiveness of resistance', in S. Hawes and R. White, *Resistance in Europe 1939–1945*, London: Allen Lane, 1975.

4. Public Record Office (hereafter PRO), London, CAB 66/7 WP(40) 168.

5. This document is still (1993) classified: it is quoted by Foot, op. cit., p. 21, and Stafford, op. cit., p. 26. Stafford cites it as PRO WP(40) 271.

6. Hugh Dalton, *The Fateful Years*, London: Muller, 1957, p. 368.
7. 'The fourth arm'; secret paper from Dalton to Chiefs of Staff, 19th August 1940: cited by M.R.D. Foot, *SOE in France*, op. cit. p. 9.
8. See C. MacDonald, *The Killing of SS Obergruppenfuhrer Reinhard Heydrich*, London: Papermac. 1990.
9. Quoted by Stafford, op. cit. p. 43 as from MI (R) report on 'Probable state of readiness and ability of certain countries to rise against the Nazi regime', 4 September 1940, COS (40) 683 in PRO CAB 80/17.
10. Ibid., Ch. 2 'Secret armies and the detonator concept'.
11. Ibid., Ch.3 and Documentary Appendix 5. Report by the Joint Planning Staff, 9 August 1941, JP (41) 649 in PRO CAB 79/13.
12. Ibid., Documentary Appendix 7, Chiefs of Staff memorandum, 20 March 1943, COS 142 (o) in PRO CAB 80/68.
13. The complications of Balkan resistance, and of Britain's role, have provoked considerable literature e.g., P. Auty and R. Clegg (eds), *British Policy Towards Wartime Resistance in Yugoslavia*, Basingstoke: Macmillan 1975; E. Barker, *British Policy in South-East Europe in the Second World War*, Basingstoke: Macmillan 1976; N. Beloff, *Tito's Flawed Legacy: Yugoslavia and the West 1939–1984*, London: Gollancz 1985; F.W. Deakin, *The Embattled Mountain*, London: Oxford UP 1973; J. Rootham, *Missfire: The Chronicle of a British Mission to Mihailovic 1943–1944*, London: Chatto and Windus, 1946.
14. See Richard Aldrich, 'Unquiet in death: the post war survival of the "Special Operations Executive" 1945–51' in A. Gorst, Lewis Johnman and W. Scott Lucas (eds), *British Contemporary History 1931–1961: politics and the limits of policy*, London: Pinter, 1991.

12

Britain and Eastern Europe during the Second World War

Anita J. Prazmowska

The end of the war caught the British policy makers, notably the Foreign Office and sundry committees established to grapple with problems of post-war reconstruction, entirely unprepared to cope with the implications of the growth of Soviet influence in the liberated areas of Poland and Czechoslovakia. The flavour of debates taking place within the governmental bodies can be reconstructed by looking at a few, and undeniably representative, communications which originated within these circles. Thus on 14 March 1945 Philip Nichols, the British Ambassador in Prague, summarised what he felt were British objectives in relation to Czechoslovakia:

a) to ensure that she does not fall completely within the Russian orbit but that;
b) she continues to be dependent upon the Western Powers as well as upon the USSR.[1]

A search for a definition of British interests in Poland is more difficult. Indeed in the spring of 1945 the Foreign Office seemed to be advocating that the Lublin authority's aim of establishing a totalitarian regime should not be opposed. As Sargent, the Deputy Under Secretary at the Foreign Office, minuted on 13 March

It is out of all proportion that we should endanger our fundamental policy of post-war co-operation with the Soviet Union for the sake of an issue which, even if it is not entirely academic or quixotic, is at any rate not vital to British interests in Europe.[2]

The matter of acquiescing or not to the expansion of Soviet political influence into central Europe was not entirely an academic point. For at stake were complex economic issues; coal was but one of these. The European Economic Committee, into which the Soviet Union was being invited for the purpose of sharing coal supplies from the eastern zone of Germany, Poland and Czechoslovakia, was very keen to coax the Soviet authorities into co-operation.[3] While the full extent of Britain's economic collapse in 1945 was not fully recognised, it was appreciated that there would be a need to expand foreign trade. Moreover, the Balkans, Poland and Czechoslovakia appeared to be areas where there existed a potential for the development of such trade.[4]

The vague and uncoordinated picture which emerges from deliberations that took place within the Foreign Office was that as the war was drawing to a close British aims were only hazily defined in relation to the Soviet Union. As a consequence those aims were also unclear towards Poland and Czechoslovakia. That the Soviet Union was likely to try and assert a degree of military and economic (and thus inevitably political) control appeared to be accepted as a foregone conclusion. Whether these developments would be advantageous to Britain was not clear.

Indeed, perhaps the key question of this chapter should instead be whether this lack of policy, evident in 1945, was relevant to Britain's European role in the long term. Perhaps one should assume that since central Europe had never previously occupied a position of notable importance in Britain's political and economic evaluation of her European policy, that such neglect was logical. But on the other hand it is worth noting that logical though British disinterest might have been, the war had drawn Britain directly into the affairs of the governments in exile of both states. In the case of Poland this had meant that an army of more than 100,000 Poles had been placed under direct British military control. Polish troops under British command had been used entirely in fighting in north Africa and on the western front. More importantly, no plans had been developed by the British Chiefs of Staff for assisting or facilitating the Poles in the prime objective of liberating Poland. During the course of the war, Britain came to exercise a key role in debates relating to the internal affairs of the Polish and Czech governments. It also had the ability to limit and facilitate their foreign policies and to control their contacts with their respective territories. In all these matters British interests remained a key factor. Thus the questions which I propose to ask are:
1) What were the British objectives towards central Europe during the war?
2) To what extent did the need to establish and maintain an alliance with the Soviet Union stand in the way of the British government establishing better relations with the exile authorities and thus in the way of Britain creating areas of potential political influence after the war?

Until the fall of France the official policy towards Czechoslovak and Polish issues was that they were essentially a French concern. Halifax, the Foreign Secretary, allowed Benes to reside in Britain on the strictest understanding that he would not abuse British hospitality by pursuing political activities.[5] Since Daladier refused to accept Benes' claim that he was heading a government in exile, the British government also took that view. Not until July 1940 was the Czech National Committee recognised as a provisional government.[6]

The Chamberlain government had made a commitment to the defence of Polish territory in March 1939; this was confirmed by an alliance signed in August 1939. The defeat of the Polish army, in any case a foregone conclusion, and the departure of the Polish government from Poland seemed to have, according to the British Foreign Office, closed that chapter. The creation in September of a new government in Paris headed by General Sikorski – an acrimonious process – was viewed by the Foreign Office without any appreciation in particular that this was presently, or could in the future become, a British matter. Indeed Cadogan conceded that the French, on whose territory this authority would reside, should be allowed to influence the political profile of the new Polish government.[7]

Chamberlain refused to discuss war aims and when pressed repeatedly to commit Britain to the restoration of Czechoslovakia to its pre-Munich Conference status, and Poland to her pre-September borders, refused to do so. His explanation was that the matter required serious consideration and in any event it was difficult to do so while it was impossible to see who would be the victors and who the vanquished.[8] Halifax confirmed this point emphatically in a memorandum handed to the French Government in December 1939. In it Halifax endeavoured to obtain an assurance from the French that they would not make commitments in excess of those made by the British government.[9] Thus Halifax stated: 'It is only in the light of the circumstances prevailing at the time when their object is achieved that the lines of any territorial settlement can be profitably achieved.' The recovery of their liberties by the Polish, Czech and Slovak people was the only general commitment which the British government was prepared to make.

Such evident lack of generosity towards the defeated nations can nevertheless be explained. The British were well aware of the difficulties which could be caused by prematurely and imprudently uttered promises. The First World War offered ample warning against such haste. The need to retain the good will of the neutral states was not a matter which could be easily overlooked. Unfortunately, British inactivity in the face of German aggression undermined the pro-British elements in allied neutral states. Fear of Germany and anxiety about the extent of German–Soviet co-operation played an important role in the considerations of most neutral European states, notably in Rumania, a country rich in oil resources.[10]

The British Foreign Office was not entirely disinterested in the question of post-war territorial settlements. From the onset of the war, anxiety was expressed about the restoration of the borders of the inter-war period. Their instability had been a matter of some concern to the British government during the whole of the inter-war period. Successive British governments disapproved of French involvement in volatile politics of central and south eastern Europe. Halifax's memorandum to the French government dated 15 December 1939 suggests that some thought had been given to the question of the small states which had never been viable. Thus Halifax revealed that the British government hoped to encourage co-operation between the Balkan states and Poland, Czechoslovakia and Austria.[11]

British disinterest in the Polish government in exile and the Czechoslovak National Committee was to a certain extent overcome when military considerations were taken into account. The fall of France forced politicians and military leaders to plan for a war in which Britain was going to play a key role in the liberation of Europe. Since both the Polish and Czechoslovak authorities placed all manpower available to them at the disposal of the British, it was obviously advantageous to make full use of these. Nevertheless it is very important to stress that irrespective of this cooperation no commitments were made by the British government to either the Polish government in exile or the Czechoslovak government. The contribution of Polish and Czechoslovak soldiers, sailors and pilots to the joint war effort was welcomed and encouraged by the British. The British authorities nevertheless did not participate in talks taking place between the Poles and Czechs which were aimed at establishing the basis for political and economic cooperation after the war. Some form of economic cooperation between these states, was considered useful as it offered a prospect of stability in a hitherto unstable region. Until Soviet disapproval for the Polish-Czechoslovak federation was made known the British government welcomed discussions aimed at bringing the two together. The Foreign Office comment on Benes' scheme for 'The Reconstruction of central Europe' dated October 1940 had suggested disinterest and at the same time, approval.[12]

Soviet entry into the war and the fact that neither Britain nor the United States were able to define the date when they proposed to open the Western Front affected Britain's relations with the exiled authorities of Poland and Czechoslovakia. But the question which needs to be asked is whether British policies towards central Europe became no more than a game in allied diplomacy? In other words did Britain betray her Polish and Czechoslovak allies and acquiesce or signal acquiescence to Soviet expansion into Central Europe?

Although it could be argued that the entry of the Soviet Union into the war at one stroke negated for Britain the need to have friendly relations with representative organizations of the occupied European states, this development also strengthened the Polish and Czech need to retain British and American interest in their affairs. This was most notable in the case of the Polish government in exile headed by Sikorski. The signing of the Polish-Soviet agreement enabled the creation of a Polish army on Soviet territory. The Poles entertained extensive hopes that a great army in exile would thus be created in the West and in the Soviet Union, enhancing the political position of the exile government. The British military authorities were not indifferent to these developments. In the circumstances of acute manpower shortage and because of political differences between the Churchill government and the Commonwealth governments, notably the Australian one, Polish manpower in the Soviet Union and the promised expansion of the Polish units in north Africa and on the British Isles, was a valuable contribution to the British war effort. At the end of 1942 Polish units that formed in the Soviet Union were moved to Iran and placed at the disposal of the British. This action had not been authorised by Sikorski and he was unable to extract political commitments to the defence of Polish interests from Churchill. But the Poles did not want the British to fight for them; more than anything else they wanted to have the opportunity to liberate Polish territories themselves. Thus at the end of 1942 Sikorski presented an extensive plan for the opening of the Balkan front and a military thrust through the Balkans into the heartland of Germany.[13] This bold plan would have enabled the Polish units to liberate Poland but also, in the wake of their military progress, to establish political influence in south eastern and central Europe. Unfortunately for the Poles, the idea of opening a Balkan front was a controversial issue within the British political and military leadership and thus not one to which the British could be easily committed. Polish manpower was instead prepared to go into action in Italy.

Prior to the German attack on the Soviet Union the British government thought it inappropriate to make any long-term plans for future territorial settlements. After the Soviet entry into the war this stance could no longer be maintained since the question of Soviet territorial acquisitions made during the period between September 1939 and June 1941 was bound to crop up in British-Soviet talks. Nevertheless the British Foreign Office went to great lengths to ensure that it was never seen directly championing the Polish or Czechoslovak causes. British politicians were deeply concerned about the course of Polish-Soviet relations. They were nevertheless not prepared to see these either obstruct or constrain their considerations on the subject of the Soviet Union. At key moments, ranging from

Beaverbrook's mission to Moscow in the autumn of 1941, to Eden and Churchill's subsequent visits to Moscow, discussion of the Polish case was always meticulously avoided. The course of British-Soviet relations was in no way affected by the apparent, but in reality illusory, closeness existing between the British and Polish governments. At the beginning of 1943 even that illusion was not allowed to prevail.

On the whole the question of central and Eastern Europe was a constant subject in British-Soviet relations. But one should not overlook the extent to which Churchill felt compelled to bow to American pressures. During the course of British-Soviet negotiations in spring 1942 American interference became particularly strong and obstructive. The Foreign Office was willing to accept Soviet demands for recognition of the incorporation of the Baltic States and the eastern regions of Poland into the USSR. Eden's pragmatic analysis that neither at present nor after the war would Britain want to incur the distrust or hostility of the Russian ally, was rejected by the American politicians. Not trusting the British to be firm enough with the Russians, Roosevelt endeavoured to prevent the agreement from being concluded. Pressure was put upon Churchill and Molotov was invited to Washington, all with the purpose of breaking up the British-Soviet understanding. Churchill felt compelled to bow to American opinions and as a result when the treaty was signed with the Soviet Union in May 1942 it contained no commitment to the June 1941 borders.[14]

The military realities of the war nevertheless forced both Britain and the United States to accept that it was they who needed continued Soviet participation in the war. Thus by the spring of 1943 when the Russians were able to show that the hitherto relentless German progress had been halted, never to regain its momentum, Churchill and Roosevelt were willing to accept Soviet claims to the Curzon Line and the occupation of the Baltic States.[15] Henceforth, in spite of Sikorski's appeals to Roosevelt and attempts to elicit feelings of obligation from the British military leadership, it was determined that Poland would not be a divisive issue in allied negotiations. This is not to say that it ceased to be a problem for the remainder of the war, but it was not one which could split the unity of the Big Three.

One of the most painful episodes in the history of the Polish government in exile was the moment when Germany revealed the existence of the Katyn graves on 15 April 1943. Churchill's suspicion was that the responsibility for the atrocities lay with the Soviet Union. He nevertheless could not and would not allow this tragic discovery to affect Britain's relations with the Soviet Union. Indeed, though from Tunis came much needed news of victories against Rommel, the indefinite postponement of the Second Front meant that the British government studiously avoided becoming entangled in Polish-Soviet difficulties. Churchill rebuked Sikorski and Stalin for allowing the matter to get as far as a public diplomatic breach, he insisted that the spectre of the dead should not obscure the needs of the living.[16] A certain amount of sympathy for the Poles, felt by Churchill, was translated into no more than a willingness by the British to offer their good offices to mediate between the Soviet and the Polish government in exile.[17]

In August 1944 the British response to the Warsaw Uprising gave further proof of a determination to accept that Poland was in the Soviet sphere of influence. The uprising had been planned by the Poles on the assumption that allied assistance would be not merely forthcoming, but would be vital to its success.[18] Indeed, both the government in exile and the underground leadership in Poland had hoped that the planned national uprising would be coordinated with the allies and would form part of a final western offensive against Germany. Unfortunately for them the British miliary and political chiefs had made a decision at the beginning of the war not to concede Polish requests for representation on major military committees. Thus all attempts to open discussions of war plans and hopes that military action in Poland and outside could be co-ordinated, were unsuccessful. In October 1943, as a result of Sikorski's insistence that the Special Operations Executive should coordinate its plans with the Polish Home Army, the Chiefs of Staff briefly discussed the subject only to defer the matter.[19] The Home Army started the uprising at the beginning of August 1944. The decision, nearly entirely political in its motives, was badly thought out. The capture of Warsaw by the Home Army in the wake of the German withdrawal was essentially an attempt to prevent the Red Army from entering Warsaw as liberators.[20] Lack of Anglo-American support and Soviet hostility to the uprising doomed the effort to becoming one of the most futile, albeit tragic, episodes in Polish history. Churchill, who was at the time at a particularly delicate stage of negotiating with Stalin, was unwilling to authorise action which would provoke Soviet distrust. Thus the initiative for deciding whether to send supplies to Warsaw was handed over to the Soviet leadership.[21] On 4 August the Chiefs of Staff considered the request of the Polish government for supplies to Poland. It was decided not to run the risk of high casualties and not to fly planes with supplies from British occupied territories in Italy. On political and military grounds the decision could not have been different. Poland lay in the Soviet sphere of military operations and that fact more than anything else imposed limits on British involvement in any undertakings planned by the government in exile.

Benes created an entirely different problem for the British leadership. Unlike Sikorski's team who distrusted the Soviet Union, Benes was willing to enter into discussions with the Soviet Union in the hope of actually drawing it into central European politics. In June 1943 Benes enquired whether the Soviet Union would be willing to sign a tripartite agreement with Poland and Czechoslovakia. The British Foreign Office which had desperately tried to keep out of the Polish-Soviet conflict caused by the Katyn revelations, discouraged this idea on grounds that it would open up floodgates 'to demands from the other Allies for similar treaties not only with Soviet Russia but also with ourselves'.[22] This shows that the British government was as unhappy about the anti-Soviet policies of the Polish govern- ment in exile as it was about Benes' pro-Soviet conciliatory gestures. The sugges- tion is that for British politicians neither policy was convenient. The fear was that either approach could create circumstances in which Britain would be forced to interfere, affecting British-Soviet relations in turn. Both exiled authorities, through their initiatives, created a threat to Britain's freedom. Their long-term plans might not have necessarily conflicted with any defined objectives of the British government towards central Europe, but then that was not the issue.

Soviet military victories more than anything else determined the distribution of political power in central Europe. At the end of 1942 British politicians presumed that the Red Army would liberate those areas. Although it could be argued that at the Teheran conference the British politicians signalled to the Soviet Union Britain's unwillingness to support the Polish government in exile, in reality that was a foregone conclusion even before the end of 1943. Soviet disapproval for schemes for the Polish-Czechoslovak federation effectively marked the end of serious talks on that subject. But if it could be suggested that the British bowed to the Soviet pressure to cease supporting the idea, it should also be recognised that the British government always viewed the proposals in academic terms. No plans were made for direct British involvement in central Europe. In early 1943 Eden accepted that no proposals for east and central Europe could be pursued without Soviet approval.[23] In February Eden asked Clark Kerr, the British Ambassador in Moscow, to broach the subject of allied co-operation in maintaining stability in east and central Europe.[24] Molotov's response was to raise doubts about the legitimacy of the exiled governments' authority to speak on behalf of the people in the occupied territories. In view of this the Foreign Office abandoned any attempts to pursue the matter.[25]

Both the Polish and Czechoslovak governments in exile tried to ensure British representation in their territories. This in particular became an urgent matter, when it became clear that the liberation of central Europe was going to take place in the wake of the Soviet military thrust east. The request of the Czechoslovak government that a British Liaison Officer or a Military Mission should accompany the government when it returned to Czechoslovakia was rejected by Eden in April 1944, as was a request for British troops to be stationed there.[26]

The Poles faced the implications of the Soviet entry into Poland earlier. At the beginning of 1943 they had had to contend with the possibility of Red Polish units being formed in the Soviet Union. In March it was announced in Moscow that a new Polish authority had been created there. By the autumn of 1943 it was the government in exile which sought to re-establish a dialogue with the Soviet Union. Belatedly it was realised that the Red Army was free to enter Poland without any constraints on it. Thus Mikolajczyk, who had replaced Sikorski, sought to persuade the British government to assume responsibility for the liberated Polish territories.[27] A desperate bid for British or American troops to be stationed in Poland was simply not an idea which was going to be entertained by either of the allies.

It is interesting to note that in July 1944 Eden believed that it was possible to balance two objectives. He does not seem to have recognised the incompatibility of these hopes. Thus he wrote in a memorandum intended for discussion by the Cabinet:

The foundation of our post-war European policy must be the Anglo-Soviet alliance, the basis of which will remain a joint interest in preventing any recurrence of German aggression. Within this framework our policy throughout Europe must be to consolidate our position in those countries with which our relations have been traditionally close and intimate: France, Low Countries, while at the same time avoiding any direct challenge to Russian influence in Central European countries adjacent to the Soviet Union. In those countries we should, however, avail ourselves of every opportunity to spread British influence, profiting for this purpose from the new relationship we have established during this war with Poland and Czechoslovakia.[28]

With hindsight, we can see in this statement so many seeds of Britain's failure successfully to achieve the stated objective. One is the degree of British closeness with the Soviet Union, which is clearly overstated. Soviet disillusionment with the failure of the other allies to open a Western front cannot be ignored. British inconsistency towards the Polish issue created a vast pool of possible recriminations. Notwithstanding the fact that Churchill personally pressurised Mikolajczyk to yield to Soviet territorial demands, the presence of virulently anti-Soviet Poles in London would and did heighten Soviet distrust. The British use of Polish troops and the continuation of plans for their expansion right into 1945 must have been carefully considered by the Soviet authorities. The possibility of their being used in any future confrontation with the Soviet Union could not have been entirely discounted.

The relevance of developments taking place in the occupied territories could be suggested as another weak point of Eden's analysis. Lewis Namier warned the Foreign Office in 1939 of the inevitable alienation of exiled groups and their overestimation of their power.[29] In addition to these developments there was another source of British weakness. It could be suggested that the stock of goodwill towards Britain had been severely tested during the war. Both governments in exile had learned not to depend on their hosts. Britain's preoccupation with her own military effort and her relations with the Soviet Union did signal neglect, an impression which would be difficult to contradict in 1945.

Finally, and probably most importantly, the realities of the post-war period would have to be approached largely from the perspective of reconstruction. While British politicians spoke of mediation and retention of British influence, they were unwilling to admit that there were no funds earmarked by them for economic assistance for central Europe and the Soviet Union. Perhaps Eden should have admitted that British interest in central Europe had been scant and would so remain.

Notes

1. Public Record Office [PRO], Kew, London, FO 371 47107 N2839/365/12, 14 March 1945.
2. PRO FO 371 48192 R5063/5063/67, 13 March 1945.
3. PRO FO 371 45668 UE1397/17/53, 29 March 1945.
4. PRO FO 371 45694 XC/A/4037, March 1945.
5. E. Taborsky, *President Edvard Benes, Between East and West 1938–1948*, Stanford CA: Hoover Institute Press, 1981, pp. 36–37.
6. E. Taborsky, *Edvard Benes*, p. 39.
7. PRO FO 371 23152 C15148/8526/55, 27 September 1939.
8. PRO FO 371 22947, 26 November 1939.
9. PRO FO 371 22947 C20438/3669/62, 15 December 1939.
10. D.B. Lungu, *Romania and the Great Powers, 1933–1940*, Durham NC: Duke University Press, 1989, pp. 211–226.
11. PRO FO 371 22947 C20438/3669/62, 15 December 1939.
12. PRO FO 24289 C10776/2/12, 7 October 1940.
13. Polish Institute and Sikorski Musuem A XII 3/80 11 December 1942.
14. E. Bennett, *Franklin D. Roosevelt and the Search for Victory. American-Soviet Relations 1939–1945*, Wilmington: A Scholarly Resources Inc. Imprint, 1990, pp. 49–52.
15. M. Kitchen, *British Policy Towards the Soviet Union during the Second World War*,

London: Macmillan, 1986, pp. 152–153.
16. M. Gilbert, *Road to Victory. Winston S. Churchill 1941–1945*, London: Heinemann, 1986, pp. 389–390.
17. Ibid. p. 243.
18. J. Ciechanowski, *The Warsaw Rising of 1944*, Cambridge: Cambridge University Press, 1975, pp. 158–159.
19. PRO CAB 79/66 COS(43) 255 Mtg(0), 20 October 1943.
20. Ciechanowski, p. 243.
21. M. Gilbert, *Road to Victory*, pp. 871–873.
22. PRO FO 371 37037 3835/3835/38, 16 June 1943.
23. PRO FO 371 35338 U321/67/G70, 4 February 1943.
24. Ibid.
25. PRO FO 371 35388 U897/67/G70, 26 February 1943.
26. PRO FO 38945 C5716/1347/12, 28 April 1944.
27. PRO FO 371 34562 C13615/231/G55, 16 November 1943.
28. PRO FO 371 39041 C8983/8983/G62 7 July 1944.
29. PRO FO 371 23153 C19384/8526/55, 29 November 1939.

Index